Leading to Change

Susan Moore Johnson

Leading to Change

The Challenge of the New
Superintendency

Jossey-Bass Publishers
San Francisco

Substantial discounts on bulk quantities of Jossey-Bass books are available to corporations, professional associations, and other organizations. For details and discount information, contact the special sales department at Jossey-Bass Inc., Publishers (415) 433-1740; Fax (800) 605-2665.

For sales outside the United States, please contact your local Simon & Schuster International Office.

 Manufactured in the United States of America on Lyons Falls Pathfinder Tradebook. This paper is acid-free and 100 percent totally chlorine-free.

Library of Congress Cataloging-in-Publication Data
Johnson, Susan Moore.
    Leading to change : the challenge of the new superintendency /
Susan Moore Johnson. — 1st ed.
    Includes bibliographical references and index.
    ISBN 0-7879-0214-4 (acid-free paper)
        p.   cm. — (The Jossey-Bass education series)
    1. School superintendents — United States.   2. Educational
leadership—United States.   3. School management and organization—
United States—Case studies.   4. Education and state—United
States—Case studies.   I. Title.   II. Series.
LB2831.72.J65   1996
371.2'011—dc20   96-4460
                                                                    CIP

FIRST EDITION
HB Printing   10 9 8 7 6 5 4 3 2 1

The Jossey-Bass
Education Series

Contents

Preface

High dropout rates, low test scores, and increasing social disorder in the schools leave little doubt that American public education must change. Initial reports on school reform have shown that the work is slow and hard, succeeding in a few schools but floundering in many more. In the face of such uneven progress, many believe that a strong superintendent can be a champion of reform, assessing a district's needs, devising solutions to its problems, taking charge of its policies and practices, providing support to principals intent on improving their schools, inspiring confidence among teachers, and ensuring compliance by the reluctant and the recalcitrant. The dismissal of an ineffective superintendent is thought to mark the end of bad times; the appointment of a new superintendent is heralded as the beginning of a new age.

Leadership is often invoked as the solution to any and all problems. However, those who do so seldom define what leadership is, and superintendents who aspire to lead rarely find clear explanations of what they can expect from constituents or what they should do. Our culture's models for leadership emerge from the military, social movements, religious groups, and politics—not from school districts. The lessons those models offer are only partially relevant to superintendents, who must devise strategies for leading hundreds of educational professionals who work in public bureaucracies that are embedded within political systems.

The Study of New Superintendents

How do superintendents conceive of leadership? What do they do to promote leadership? How do others respond? Six years ago I began to explore those questions in a study sponsored by the National Center for Educational Leadership at Harvard's Graduate School of Education. There was no recent empirical study of the superintendency, and I assumed that a better understanding of school district leadership would be useful in the context of school reform. Between 1989 and 1992 I followed the work of twelve newly appointed superintendents through the first two years of their tenure. By exploring the interactions of superintendents and their constituents, I hoped to understand how leadership is exercised in the superintendency.

The model of effective school leadership that emerged from this study is a collaborative one, in which superintendents work together with their constituents to improve public education. The superintendents studied here exercised three kinds of leadership. As educational leaders, they brought to bear their knowledge and experience in diagnosing local educational needs, discerning possibilities for educational improvement, and recommending strategies for improving teaching and learning in their districts. As political leaders, superintendents interacted with city officials, school board members, and union leaders in an effort to secure the funds, decision-making authority, and public regard needed to improve their schools. As managerial leaders, superintendents used the structures of their district organizations to connect school leaders and influence the schools' practices. Effective superintendents were versatile in combining these three approaches to leadership.

The experiences of these superintendents demonstrate that all leadership is shaped by the overlapping contexts—historical, community, and organizational—in which it occurs. Effective superintendents adjust deftly to changes in context, thus augmenting their chance to influence others.

The Audience

This book is intended mainly for superintendents, central office administrators, principals, school board members, and teachers. With its focus on newly appointed superintendents, it should be of particular interest to individuals aspiring to that role and seeking examples of what works. But it should also be of considerable interest to experienced superintendents. Although this book focuses on superintendents, its case examples and lessons are relevant to leaders in other public-sector organizations who have similar responsibilities and challenges. Finally, students of leadership will find in this research one of the very few available longitudinal studies of leadership. It joins biographical studies of leadership in other contexts to enlarge our understanding of what leadership looks like in practice.

Overview of the Contents

Chapter One lays out the challenge of leadership for the superintendency, examining how changes in the context of public education have altered the demands on school leaders. It considers how popular notions about heroic leadership fall short in providing guidance for superintendents, whose authority and influence are constrained by the structures in which they work.

Chapter Two focuses on the search and selection process. Long before a district chooses a superintendent, it decides what sort of leadership it seeks—leadership for change, stability, or continuity. Much of the search centers on making the right match between a particular candidate and a district's needs. The understandings reached at that time between candidates and communities define much about the kind of leadership that will follow.

The following three chapters center on issues of educational leadership. Chapter Three is about the superintendent's role in crafting a vision or plan for improving the schools. The case studies presented here demonstrate that the process by which a vision or plan is developed is as important as its content in determining how constituents will receive it. Superintendents who offer clear, worthwhile ideas as they collaborate with constituents about their district's vision win the greatest respect and attention.

Chapter Four presents the cases of three superintendents who introduced reforms that followed from their visions. These reforms included school-based management, increased teacher profession-alism, and the elimination of tracking and academic departments in elementary schools. Three factors seemed to determine how responsive teachers and principals were to these superintendents' initiatives—whether the reform was seen to address the important educational needs of the district; whether, given the local context, the strategy for introducing the change was appropriate; and whether teachers and principals respected and trusted the superin-tendent who asked for their help in implementing the reform.

Chapter Five explores what superintendents can do to counter teachers' skepticism about their intentions and capabilities. Those superintendents in the districts studied who won teachers' confi-dence and subsequent investment in districtwide initiatives first worked hard to secure the funding, autonomy, and educational resources needed for teachers and principals to do their work. These superintendents then spent time in classrooms and earned reputations as credible educators, listening responsively to teach-ers' ideas and convincing teachers that they deserved their trust and support.

The next two chapters deal with the superintendent as a politi-cal leader. Chapter Six examines the types of politics—partisan, participatory, and patronage—that new superintendents encounter and illustrates how different contexts make different demands on superintendents. Using short case studies, the chapter goes on to examine the superintendent's political leadership with three groups—the school board, local government, and teachers unions.

Chapter Seven closely examines the political leadership of one superintendent, Andrew Cronin from suburban Clayton, who simultaneously dealt with three political issues, each having implications for his promise to ensure equity and excellence in the schools.

The following two chapters consider the managerial leadership of the superintendent. Chapter Eight explores the question of whether managers can be leaders, concluding that school superintendents who hope to lead must also manage well. Three case studies illustrate different approaches to managerial leadership.

Chapter Nine considers how the new superintendents studied used the structures of their organizations to advance shared understandings and consonant actions among constituents. In deciding how much centralization and standardization to seek in their systems, how their central office staff would be organized, and how their district's principals would be selected and supervised, superintendents controlled key levers of leadership in their organizations.

Chapter Ten begins by explaining why school improvement depends on new approaches to school organization and school leadership. It describes the teaching mission of the superintendency, which pervades effective superintendents' leadership as educators, managers, and politicians. It offers six broad lessons for collaborative leadership, as well as suggestions about how best to prepare superintendents for this challenge.

Susan Moore Johnson   Newton Highlands, Mass.
                                                            January 1996

To my children, Krister and Erika,
who have emerged as leaders in their own right

The Superintendents and School Districts

· ·

The school districts described in this book are located in four dif-ferent states in the Northeast. All names are fictitious, and some details have been changed slightly to preserve anonymity.

Ashmont, a small working-class city, has one of the state's lowest per-pupil expenditures. Approximately half of Ashmont's 4,300 students live in poverty, and only about 40 percent of Ashmont's high school graduates attend postsecondary education. Louis Antonellis, who grew up and attended school in Ashmont, was promoted to the super-intendency from another administrative position within the district.

Clayton, an inner-ring, upper-middle-class suburban district, has become increasingly diverse during the last decade. The district, noted for its academic excellence, serves nearly six thousand stu-dents speaking thirty-five different languages. Superintendent Andrew Cronin, who had never before headed a district, was ap-pointed from an administrative post in a nearby urban district.

Fernwood is a small summer resort town with approximately three thousand public school students. The population is ethnically di-verse and mostly working-class. The school budget is relatively small, although the district is building a new high school. Dick Fitzgerald came to the district with experience as a superintendent in another working-class district.

Glendale, the third-largest city in the state, is predominantly white and middle-class. Approximately 70 percent of Glendale's 12,500 students go on to postsecondary education. Ray Garcetti was appointed superintendent from within the district, where he has long been employed.

Highboro, a predominantly white, suburban city of ninety thousand middle-class and upper-middle-class residents, funds education generously, and Highboro's ten thousand students excel academically. Newly appointed Arthur Holzman is an experienced superintendent from another upper-middle-class, suburban district.

Millsburg, with a population of one-hundred sixty thousand, is a largely poor and working-class city. Almost two-thirds of the twenty-four thousand students are either African American or Latino. The per-pupil expenditure in 1988 was the lowest in the state. Ben Moreno, an experienced superintendent, was selected from outside the district.

Newbridge, a densely populated town of thirty-three thousand working-class and middle-class residents, is white and multiethnic. Approximately 70 percent of Newbridge's graduates attend postsecondary education. Anna Niles, newly appointed from a suburban district, is an experienced superintendent.

Oakville, a predominantly white, middle-class town of forty thousand, takes great pride in its schools. Although by no means the wealthiest district in the area, Oakville has one of the highest per-pupil expenditures in the state and sends over 80 percent of its graduates on to postsecondary education. Before being appointed superintendent, Mike Ogden was a central office administrator in a nearby district.

Riverton, a city of ninety-eight thousand, is diverse racially, ethnically, and economically. Per-pupil expenditures for Riverton's eight thousand students are among the highest in the state. Maureen Reilly, a longtime teacher and administrator in the district, was promoted to the superintendency from another position in the central office.

Summit, one of the largest cities in the state, is largely working-class, though a strong group of middle-class citizens participate actively in school politics. The student population of eight thousand is largely white. Wayne Saunders, experienced as a central office administrator, was appointed superintendent from outside the state.

Union, a poor, inner-city school district with twenty-eight thousand students, is almost entirely African American and has many recent immigrants. Students' performance on standardized tests is weak, and very few graduates pursue postsecondary education. When Clara Underwood was appointed superintendent from her position as assistant superintendent in a nearby district, Union had just emerged from receivership.

Westford, a densely populated, multiethnic city, has a large number of immigrants in its student population of 6,500. The new superintendent, Thomas Wells, was appointed from outside the district, having previously held the superintendency in a comparable city district.

Leading to Change

Part One

Great Expectations

1

The Promise and Prospect of Leadership

Frank E. Spaulding recalls that he was in a "confident state of mind" when, in 1895, he assumed the superintendency of schools in Ware, Massachusetts: "I had already learned much which I knew would serve me well" (Spaulding, 1955, p. 13). His self-assurance and sense of purpose never flagged during the next twenty-five years, as Spaulding won renown for successfully redesigning instructional and administrative practices in five school districts across the United States.[1] Spaulding said that he was committed to one objective in his work—achieving "the fullest practicable development of the potentialities of every child and youth of the community" (Spaulding, 1955, p. 115)—an objective he sought to accomplish through the efficient and pragmatic management of human and financial resources.

In reading Spaulding's account, one is inevitably impressed by his determination, resourcefulness, and achievements. Also striking, however, is the context in which he worked. The few central players in his realm—board members, businessmen, mayors—were white men whose shared values remained largely unexplored and uncontested.[2] During Spaulding's time, superintendents who presented themselves as "efficiency experts" could expect school boards to defer to their judgment.[3]

The America of Spaulding's day was, as Raymond E. Callahan (1962) reports, a "business-dominated, efficiency-conscious society" fueled by the forces of industrialism (p. 178). According to David Tyack and Elisabeth Hansot (1982), "no other lay group had as much an impact on public schools as did businessmen" (p. 110), and "in school districts, the individual leaders who exerted the most influence on the public schools were local superintendents" (p. 113). As Larry Cuban (1976) explains, businessmen and school district superintendents concurred about the expertise of "schoolmen": "If superintendents could convince lay boards of their expertise, professionalism, and the rational approach to decision-making, then few boards could challenge them. In an era of almost unanimous agreement that organizations should be run scientifically and efficiently, schoolmen became experts" (p. 127).

Through the first half of this century, superintendents remained in charge of their districts. Although "organized teachers protested the undemocratic and hierarchical quality of the 'reforms' [the local superintendents] advocated," individual teachers rarely challenged their managers' authority to run the schools (Tyack and Hansot, 1982, p. 114). Moreover, school districts during Spaulding's time were comparatively simple organizations, subject to top-down control and close supervision by the superintendent. Successful leadership, as it was understood in that context, depended primarily on the careful and just exercise of formal authority within a relatively predictable and orderly environment.

Spaulding recalls, perhaps with some exaggeration, that during his entire twenty-five years as superintendent, "every one of the thousands of recommendations that I made was adopted, with only one trifling change by the Board of Education, almost always by unanimous vote" (p. 690). While head of the schools in Newton, Massachusetts, he introduced an astonishing array of changes in ten years, ranging from a plan for continuous promotion of pupils to a national exchange program for teachers. And despite complaints from citizens in his five school districts about the excessive size of their budgets, he repeatedly gained approval for new expenditures. When he petitioned the Ware school committee to buy new books,

Spaulding recalls that the chairman urged, "You just go ahead and order whatever you want, whatever you find the schools need, and I'll get the money" (p. 36). When he went before Ware's advisory committee to ask that they approve substantial increases in his budget, Spaulding won unanimous approval. In Cleveland, the board granted Spaulding a "free hand" in determining policies and practices, declaring that "educational policies should not be imposed on the new superintendent by the board of education" (p. 529).

Teachers deferred to Spaulding's authority, reportedly attending without challenge the regular meetings he called. In Newton, where he introduced merit pay for teachers, Spaulding personally assessed the financial worth of every individual, reportedly generating no public challenges or professional complaints: "Not a single word of criticism of the merit plan, not a single expression of dissatisfaction with the results of its application, reached me either directly or indirectly" (p. 319).

Spaulding implies that his success was due to his own superior administrative skills, but one can only wonder how his approach to administration and leadership would fare in today's school districts. Much has happened in this society since Spaulding retired—the McCarthy hearings, the *Brown* decision, the Vietnam War, the Civil Rights Movement, the Women's Movement, Watergate, Iran-Contra—to undermine citizens' confidence in public officials and increase the determination of individuals and interest groups to be heard. Some hint of the problems Spaulding might encounter today can be found in his account of how he personally wrote Ware's elementary school curriculum and then handily won the board's approval in just one meeting. Reflecting on his unilateral approach almost sixty years later, Spaulding still judged it "wise, practical, and fully justified," but he acknowledged wryly that current standards would have required a "modern" process with "a committee (probably several committees), in which would have been represented teachers, parents, and possibly pupils, not to mention other groups, whose members would have worked together 'democratically'"

(p. 32). Spaulding reckoned that if he had proceeded in the "modern" way, by the time he left his job at Ware, the "democratic" committee would only have just begun its work, while his more efficient approach produced "courses of study ready before the end of August to guide the work of the Ware Schools" (p. 32).

How would Spaulding, with all his confidence and expertise, deal with the constituents of today's school districts, who expect to contribute their knowledge and state their priorities before decisions are made, who can overtly or covertly thwart any superintendent's plans to control classroom teaching, and whose active support the superintendent needs if school improvement efforts are to succeed? And how would Spaulding, accustomed to exercising his political skills with a small group of like-minded men, respond to the criticisms and demands of organized teachers or parents? Would the formal authority of the superintendency and the informal authority of Spaulding's reputation provide him with the same opportunity today to single-handedly institute change?

Although some experts, like Jeffrey Pfeffer (1978), question whether leaders really make any important difference in organizations, many people still believe in the promise of leaders like Spaulding—shrewd, well-informed, take-charge leaders who seem to know what schools need and stride into troubled systems ready to fix them. As educational challenges become increasingly complicated, many districts search urgently for individual leaders who will stand above others, command respect, provide answers, and get results. As Larry Cuban (1988) observes, "one only has to read the brochures sent out by school boards advertising superintendent vacancies to see that only heroes need apply" (p. 147).

But today's school administrators work in far more complex environments than Spaulding did, environments that make great demands on them as leaders while granting them far less deference as formal authorities. If superintendents are to promote leadership for better schools, they cannot simply make good decisions and issue sound orders (see Cohen, 1990; Elmore & Associates, 1990; Sarason, 1982; David, Purkey, & White, 1989; Sizer, 1992; Weiss & Cambone, 1991). They must persuade teachers, administrators, parents, and community leaders to join them in improving schools. New approaches to teaching and learning will find their way into teachers' lesson plans only if they are promoted collaboratively by the district's educators leading in concert.

The Limits of Heroic Leadership

Our conventional expectations of leaders are drawn from the lives of extraordinary individuals whose success in politics, the military, social movements, and industry is legendary. Great leaders like Mahatma Gandhi, General George Patton, Alfred P. Sloan, Jr., and Martin Luther King, Jr., are celebrated and analyzed repeatedly in film and literature. (See, for example, Howard Gardner [1995] and Garry Wills [1994b].) These leaders, as we have come to know them, clarify problems, create order, inspire confidence, and make things right. It is no surprise, then, that we expect leaders—even leaders who hold ordinary jobs in conventional organizations such as school districts—to be heroic, executing great feats, uttering memorable words, motivating many followers. Though perhaps reassuring, such beliefs about leadership are unrealistic for several reasons.

Diminished Positional Power

First, in most organizations today, and certainly in school districts, positional power is seriously constrained. At some times, in some organizations, and in some cultures, formal authority commands absolute respect and ensures full compliance from constituents.[4] Few organizations in the United States today confer on their leaders such absolute authority. Even when those in positions of authority have substantial formal powers, members of their organizations rarely follow with heartfelt allegiance. People learn quickly to feign deference in hierarchical settings while holding close their own values and views. As John Gardner (1990) observes, "Leaders are

almost never as much in charge as they are pictured to be, followers almost never as submissive as one might imagine" (p. 23).

President Eisenhower, accustomed to exercising the authority of
a military general, found his administrative powers as president
insufficient. " 'The President still feels,' an Eisenhower aide remarked
to [Richard Neustadt] in 1958, 'that when he's decided something,
that *ought* to be the end of it. . . . And when it bounces back undone
or done wrong, he tends to react with shocked surprise' " (Neustadt,
1990, p. 10). In that regard, school superintendents are like U.S.
presidents. In 1982, Edwin M. Bridges found that although superintendents lack the formal authority to veto teacher appointments,
transfer unacceptable subordinates, set salaries, dismiss incompe-
tent teachers, or make work assignments and schedules, they were
still surprised to discover the limits of what they could do: "On the
one hand, the leader finds it difficult to abandon the power fantasies
that have been nurtured and reinforced during the preparatory
phase of his career. On the other hand, the leader has little sense of
how he can effectively expand the scope of his influence in a setting that is not conducive to leadership" (p. 206). Thus, the formal
powers of the position are often far weaker than they might seem,
and although people may expect their presidents, CEOs, and school
superintendents to act like heroic leaders, they are often ambivalent about supporting those authorities if they actually do (Kellerman, 1984b).

Notably, though, assigning greater authority to the superintendency probably would not meet education's needs for leadership,
since this would simply concentrate power at the top of the organization. If a school district aims to successfully educate children,
many different people must diagnose problems, devise plans, and
make decisions without direction from above; they must exercise
interdependent leadership. This collaborative approach to leadership is quite different from the top-down approach that Thomas
Sergiovanni (1992a) calls "follow me" leadership, a strategy that
"often gets people to cooperate" but "cannot inspire the kind of

commitment that will make schools work and work well, because it tends to induce a state of subordination among teachers" (p. 31). Rather, Sergiovanni asserts, "the true leader is one who builds in substitutes for 'follow me' leadership, which enable people to respond from within" (p. 31).

Complexity's Constraints

A second difficulty confronting leaders who intend to rely on formal authority as a lever of change is that organizations have become so complex that no individual, not even the one who is paid the most and sits atop the hierarchy, can understand and direct everything that happens. This is particularly true in decentralized organizations like school districts, where the real work of the enterprise takes place in many different schools and programs located in widely dispersed classrooms and buildings. Robert Crowson and Van Cleve Morris (1991) observe that "just how much leadership the higher level of the superintendent's office can (or should) provide vis-à-vis individual schools and classrooms, remains unanswered. Understandably, the many difficulties accompanying inquiry at any time into that ambiguous construct *leadership* are compounded mightily when one seeks to identify the impact of a top executive officer upon 'production-level' behaviors" (p. 192).

Before the 1960s, school districts were far simpler than they are today. There were no categorical programs such as Chapter 1 or PL 94–142 and therefore no central office staff to monitor them. Schools in the same district offered generic rather than distinctive programs. By contrast, school districts today incorporate many specialized roles (special education tutors, paraprofessionals, media specialists, social workers) and programs (culinary arts, sports writing, health education). No superintendent can closely supervise teaching and learning throughout such a school district as Spaulding did in his day. Moreover, when work strategies cannot be prescribed at the start but instead require continuous adaptation and independent judgment, the head of the organization cannot hope to regulate what happens, even by remote control. When state legislators and resolute school district administrators tried during the 1980s to mandate curriculum and control pedagogy, they failed badly (McNeil, 1986).

In fact, teachers, principals, and district officials are increasingly interdependent; each needs the others to do a good job, and therefore each has leverage over the others (Johnson, 1990). These relationships are not unique to schools. John Kotter (1985), exploring issues of interdependence in private corporations, concluded "there is no way that one can perform well in a leadership job today without a deep understanding of the diverse and interdependent milieu surrounding the job. This means knowing who *all* the relevant parties are, even though there may be thousands of them" (p. 39). This interdependence necessarily limits the authority that the head of any organization, including a school district, can exercise; but it is also the factor that makes organizationwide change possible and collaborative leadership necessary.

Advocates at the Door

Further constraining the power of formal authorities are the individuals and interest groups that actively petition leaders in an effort to influence their priorities. Mayors must answer to environmental advocates, bank presidents must acknowledge the concerns of community representatives, and superintendents must heed the concerns of business leaders, the clergy, and booster clubs. The formal rules of the organization and the conventions of today's society entitle advocates to have their say, and those in positions of authority are often obliged to respond.

Unquestionably, the influence of interest groups on public education has expanded over time. Tyack and Hansot (1982) report that when researchers asked superintendents of the 1950s about the pressures of outside interest groups, "over half the school chiefs replied that they had experienced none" (p. 178). It may be, as these authors suggest, that these superintendents had come to "internalize the values of the communities they served" (p. 178) and thus were unaware of the pressures. Given the conflicting values and interests that exist today in most communities, however, it seems likely that a superintendent responding to such a survey would need a separate page to list all the groups that claim his or her time and attention.

What's Left for Leaders?

Therefore, except in some nostalgic yearnings for simpler, more certain times, conventional notions of heroic leadership in schools are of little use. Jerome T. Murphy (1991) concludes that "the image of the steely-eyed, top-down manager who has all the vision and all the answers" is increasingly outdated as "power and knowledge become more dispersed, as multiple constituencies demand attention, as schooling becomes more decentralized and professionalized, and as mistrust of government grows" (p. 512).

Notably, the fact that positional authority is limited does not mean that it is unimportant or useless, for while people may be ambivalent about formal leaders, they do not ignore them. Though perhaps only temporarily and conditionally, constituents grant formal authorities respect simply by virtue of their position; they listen to their plans and proposals; they respond to their questions; they try new approaches and accept new responsibilities.[5] Thus, while a position of authority surely does not by itself ensure leadership—"'powers' are no guarantee of power; clerkship is no guarantee of leadership" (Neustadt, 1990, p. 10)—it does provide the occasion and the opportunity to lead. Today's school leaders must understand both the limits and the potential of their position, carefully balancing their use of positional authority with their reliance on others, gradually building both a capacity and widespread support for shared leadership and collaborative change.

Leadership as a Collaborative Process

In school districts, leadership involves much more than superiors pronouncing expectations that subordinates dutifully satisfy.

Although the acts of such "leaders" may deliver immediate results
from the "followers"—a report delivered or a meeting held—the
influence of such leadership goes no further than one simple trans-
action. Top-down leadership does not generate creative and cooperative initiative in others, which is what must happen if change is
to permeate the school system.

Current and emerging conceptions of leadership depict a more
collaborative process. At a 1991 conference, "Looking for Leadership," sponsored by the National Center for Educational Leadership, panelists emphasized the interdependent character of
leadership. Elsa Porter, a private sector consultant, characterized
good leadership as an "elegant conversation" (Bolman and Deal,
1994, p. 90). According to Wilfred Drath and Charles Palus (1994),
shared leadership is a process of "meaning making" through which
members of an organization develop and endorse approaches to
action that are consonant with their organization's culture. Similarly, Rodney T. Ogawa and Steven T. Bossert (1995) explain that
"leadership flows through the networks of roles that comprise organizations. The medium of leadership and the currency of leadership
lie in the personal resources of people. And, leadership shapes the
systems that produce patterns of interaction and the meanings that
other participants attach to organizational events" (p. 225). This
perspective on leadership, which diminishes the importance of roles
and positional authority while augmenting the importance of
process and organizational culture, places greater emphasis on
shared responsibility and less emphasis on the dramatic acts and
inducements of key individuals. Interdependence becomes an organizational advantage rather than a liability.

Implicit in all discussions of leadership is the notion of transformation. Theorists and practitioners agree that leadership is not
about stasis but about change. Joseph C. Rost (1991) asserts that
"change is the most distinguishing element of leadership, and if the
integrity of that word is not preserved, people cannot possibly distinguish leadership from other social processes" (p. 115).

Therefore, the emerging conception of leadership in school districts is one of reciprocal influence, through which individuals holding different roles collaborate to improve education. Position remains important, but it is never enough. The interaction of leadership is not simply top-down but runs in several directions, creating opportunities for influence and constraints for action that affect all participants.

Studying Leaders: Traits and Context

Early studies of leadership began with efforts to identify the personality traits of seemingly effective leaders. What, researchers asked, distinguished these individuals from the rest? The lists of characteristics that emerged from such research were long and exhaustive. Gouldner (1965, p. 22) reports that Charles Bird studied twenty different analyses of leadership and found seventy-nine traits mentioned among them. Long lists of unrelated characteristics, such as "energetic," "forceful," "attentive," and "confident," provide little assistance to those wanting to select or become leaders. It is not clear from such studies how these traits developed in identified leaders (Gouldner, 1965) or which traits are essential for leadership. It seems likely, as R. M. Stogdill (1948) contends, that particular constellations of traits, not random collections, enable individuals to lead, but we do not know what those constellations are.

Moreover, these analysts approached leadership traits as if they were static and context-free. The circumstances of leadership also matter, for it seems that behaviors that work in one setting may have little impact or even fail in others (Bossert, Dwyer, Rowan, and Lee, 1982) and that different situations present different demands and possibilities for leaders. Garry Wills (1994a) concludes, "So much for the idea that a leader's skills can be applied to all occasions, that they can be taught outside a historical context or learned as a 'secret' of the control of every situation. A leader whose qualities do not match those of potential followers is simply irrelevant; the world is not playing his or her game" (p. 67).

Leadership in Context

Recent discussions of leadership emphasize the role that context plays in the activities of leaders (Wills, 1994a, 1994b; Heifitz, 1994). Leadership looks different—and is different—depending on whether it is exercised in a legislature, on a battlefield, at a rally, on a factory floor, or in a school district. Superintendents head large bureaucratic organizations composed primarily of teaching professionals who prize their autonomy and resent bureaucratic control. Moreover, school districts are not autonomous but depend for their support on a surrounding political entity—a town, city, or county—headed by elected officials. Each of these features limits the superintendent's use of top-down leadership and increases the district's need for collaborative leadership.

Superintendents work within a set of embedded contexts. Each of these contributes to demands and opportunities for leadership by defining not only what changes are possible or likely but also how change may be accomplished. First, the context of the *times* matters. Certain educational goals and strategies are developed and favored during one historical period, only to be discounted and abandoned in another. Current times present superintendents not only with particular challenges—how to do more with less, how to ensure equal opportunity in an increasingly stratified society, how to incorporate technology into teaching—but also with an array of attractive models for fixing education, including small schools, smart schools, caring schools, accelerated schools, essential schools, and charter schools. The availability of these solutions often increases the public's expectations for quick, certain results.

Whereas the period in which Spaulding worked was marked by stability, predictability, and steady growth in enrollment and funding, today's superintendent serves during times that are dynamic and often volatile, creating unprecedented demands for superintendents to be versatile, responsive, and resilient. The times in which one lives and works not only create possibilities for action, they also shape leaders as individuals by encouraging certain approaches and discouraging others. Spaulding was reinforced for being an authoritative and authoritarian manager in part because he became superintendent during the first rather than the second half of the twentieth century. In his day respect for authority was certain, and thus top-down management was easy.

Second, there is the context of *locale*. The school superintendent, like every municipal official, businessperson, and agency head, works in a particular community with distinct demographic characteristics, social customs, political practices, and financial conditions. As one school principal in this study observed, "The textbook doesn't apply equally well in every town." Whereas school districts once functioned as virtually independent entities, their interests and practices are now entwined with those of their city or county government, business community, and social and religious organizations. School budgets are increasingly tied to the financial condition of the district's city, county, or state, and superintendents seeking to institute reforms must attend to the people who control educational funding.

Also, differences in social class lead to sharp contrasts between and within school districts. Some communities have well-educated and well-to-do parents and teachers, whose knowledge and prosperity make them attentive and responsive to possibilities for school improvement; less-educated and less-affluent parents and teachers in other communities may be unprepared for reformers' initiatives.

Nancy Pitner and Rodney Ogawa (1981) found that the superintendents they studied commonly believed that they had to align decisions about schooling with their communities' values: "They must see to it that their schools' programs and methods of operation were consistent with their communities' values. This responsibility would be easily met if societal consensus existed regarding educational outcomes and processes. Such a consensus, however, does not always exist in school districts" (p. 50). Superintendents sometimes find themselves at odds with local values and, instead of conforming, endeavor to change the local context. Stories of conflict between determined school leaders and resistant community members abound. While superintendent of the New York City schools, Joseph Fernandez's support for *Children of the Rainbow*, a new teachers' resource guide that addressed the importance of tolerance in a multicultural society, drew opposition from certain communities, and the dispute cost him his job. The local context, then, provides both opportunities and constraints for those who lead.

Third, for all leaders, there is the context of the *organization* in which they act. One business or school district may be hierarchical and unionized while another is flat, decentralized, and union-free. The particular organizational context influences what a leader can do, whether that individual is a shop steward or a company president. Organizations have distinct cultures with associated norms, symbols, and traditions.[6] A school district may be well funded or in debt; it may be highly regulated or informally governed; it may have a legacy of good management or shoddy neglect; it may advance norms of acceptance and inclusion or endorse stratification by academic ability, race, gender, or social class.

If school districts were truly centralized and hierarchical, superintendents might rely on edicts to effect change. But school districts are in fact decentralized and relatively flat organizations, with differences across schools and classrooms in even the most tightly administered system. Control is further attenuated by the fact that schools are staffed by professionals who reject prescriptive practices. Because teachers reinterpret the curriculum every time it is taught and because improvising to meet students' individual needs is at the heart of instruction, superintendents must rely far more on collaboration than control in their efforts to influence teaching practice.

Each school district also has its own particular history, which influences what a superintendent can do there. Some districts have experienced turmoil and turnover, others stability or stagnancy. Newly appointed superintendents may be obliged to cope with the legacy of past adversity—disappointment over failed referendums for additional funding, lingering animosity from teacher strikes, or divisions created by desegregation orders. Alternatively, superintendents may enter districts that, after years of untroubled and undistinguished performance, are optimistic about the future and poised for progress. Thus new superintendents must not only understand the times in which they live and work but also the particular history of the district they enter.

Seldom considered in research and theory about the context of leadership are constituents, those participants in the organization with whom leadership is exercised. As Erik Erikson observed, who constituents are often determines who their leaders will be: "The answer to 'Who leads?' depends on the answers to 'What is the setting?' and 'Who are the followers?'" (quoted in Kellerman 1984b, p. 74). Once we recognize that leadership is a multidirectional relationship, it becomes clear that it is also a negotiated, consensual one. Constituents, whether they are followers or collaborators, grant others the authority to lead. And sometimes they withhold that authorization, even from those sitting in positions of power (Smith and Berg, 1987). Heifitz (1994) concludes that "people in authority influence constituents, but constituents also influence them. We forget this at our peril" (p. 19).

Superintendents' constituents are many and varied, ranging from those inside the district, such as the budget director and paraprofessionals, to those outside the formal system, such as the mayor and parents. One particular group, the school board, hires the superintendent and then expects him or her to lead both them and those in the schools—a curious relationship and a challenging responsibility. Other groups, such as veteran teachers and principals, often believe that they rather than some itinerant superintendent know what is best for the district, and they grant the superintendent authority to lead only after a period of critical review and informal negotiation. In building support for their initiatives and protecting their programs from attack, superintendents must discover their political allies and adversaries. A prospective leader must repeatedly consider what sorts of relationships to build with various constituents, some of whom expect to be told what to do while others expect to be asked what should happen.

Constituents bring diverse expectations, strengths, and skills. Would-be leaders must take all these into account, for together these individuals construct the character of their relationship with the superintendent and the patterns of leadership in the district. Rost, citing the seminal work of Berger and Luckmann (1966), reminds us that "leadership like other social phenomena is socially constructed through interaction, emerging as a result of the constructions and actions of both leaders and led" (Rost, 1991, p. 258). If, as Garry Wills (1994a) notes, an aspiring leader does not respond to reality as constituents understand it, he or she will fail: "To sound a certain trumpet does not mean just trumpeting one's own certitudes. It means sounding a specific call to a specific people capable of response" (p. 67).

Moving Forward in Context

School leaders must therefore attend simultaneously to several embedded contexts—those of the times, the locale, and the organization—contexts that themselves often interact. For example, the constituents' expectations of their leaders are shaped by the period in which those constituents live, while the structure and norms of the organization are influenced by local conventions and values. The complexity of this environment illustrates why a lengthy list of leadership traits, however derived, cannot explain what makes for good leadership. It is important, however, to be clear that effective leaders are not simply organizational chameleons, conforming to the demands of the contexts wherever they land. Rather, influential leaders are persons with strong values and sophisticated skills, persons who understand the needs of their organization and discover how to use their position, whatever it may be, to work with others in moving their organization forward.

We return, therefore, to the potential for the individual to achieve constructive change in an organization. For finally it is individuals leading in context whose work we must understand if research is to constructively inform practice. The challenge of leadership study today is to conduct research that reveals how designated leaders and their constituents work together within this complicated set of contexts to achieve their goals.

Studies of leadership have rarely looked systematically at the interaction of individual leaders and their contexts. McCall and Lombardo (1978) contend that studying leaders apart from the contexts in which they work strips away much of the meaning of such research: "The reductionist view of leadership fragments reality. Leaders and their groups are embedded in complex, often contradictory organizational systems, and to examine them outside this context ignores the richness of reality" (p. 7). Nancy Pitner and Rodney Ogawa (1981) note that ignoring the context of superintendents' work has "greatly inhibited the description of important dimensions of organizational leadership" (p. 61). Moreover, as Immegart (1988) observes, little research has centered on current, real-life people and events: "Investigating real situations has not been a high priority for very many researchers. Some kinds of research cannot be done using real-world situations, but if the goal is to get at behavior or to gain knowledge about what leaders do and how they do it, then more studies of actual situations are needed" (p. 268). Karl Weick (1978), too, cites the need to "watch leaders on line" (p. 60).

Although superintendents hold a prominent position and are considered important educational leaders, research about them and their work is scant. Notable exceptions include Blumberg (1985), Carlson (1972), Cuban (1976), and Tyack and Hansot (1982). In his review of research on the school administrator, Bridges (1982) notes that study of the superintendency is one of "the most important gaps" in research on educational administration: "The superintendent stands at the apex of the organizational pyramid in education and manages a multi-million dollar enterprise charged with the moral and technical socialization of youth, aged 6–18. Despite the importance of this administrative role to education and society, less than a handful of studies analyzed in this review investigated the impact of the chief executive officer. This topic merits both reflection and empirical examination since nothing of consequence is known about the impact of the occupants of this role" (p. 26). More than a decade after Bridge's review, little has changed.[7]

The Purpose and Design of This Study

This study undertakes a close look at the work of school superintendents in context, first in an effort to understand how superintendents seek to exercise leadership from their position of authority and second to see how constituents respond to superintendents' initiatives. It considers not only a variety of individuals whose leadership traits and styles differ but also a variety of local and organizational contexts, each of which presents a different set of opportunities and constraints for the prospective leader.

By looking intensively at the experiences of twelve individuals in twelve different settings, I set out to advance an understanding of leadership not only for school superintendents but also for others in positions of authority in complex organizations. In order to isolate the influence of the individual, I decided to study the work of newly appointed superintendents, following their leadership initiatives through the first two years of their administration. I could investigate what a school board and community sought in a new superintendent—leadership for change, continuity, or restoration— and consider the extent to which they got what they wanted. By examining the period following entry, contrasts between new superintendents and their predecessors would be revealed, contrasts that illuminate the differences that the individual makes.

In order to understand superintendents' role as leaders, it was critical to explore their interactions with constituents, for it is in these interactions that leadership occurs. This presented a substantial methodological challenge; superintendents have numerous constituents both inside and outside their organization, and identifying and tracking such patterns of influence was therefore extremely complicated.

In selecting the sample for this study, I chose twelve districts that would ensure variety in size, location, wealth, history, racial and ethnic composition, and political climate. The twelve superintendents in this study varied in important ways as well. Five had gained experience in the superintendency in other districts, while seven were taking on their first assignments in the role. There were nine men and three women. Two were members of minority groups, an African-American woman and a Latino man. Of the twelve, eight were hired from outside their districts, four from inside. And beyond the demographic differences, there were individual differences in style and preferences.

From February 1989 through June 1992, a group of advanced doctoral students and I conducted 312 interviews with respondents in these twelve districts. Data collection involved two long interviews with each superintendent, one approximately six months into his or her first term and a second a year later. Over the next two years, we also interviewed approximately twenty-five constituents in each district, asking how their new superintendent was hired, what they expected from him or her, what they thought of the superintendent's early actions and approaches, and what difference, if any, this superintendent had made in their schools and work. The methodology is explained in detail in the appendix.

Although many attach the term "leader" to anyone in a position of formal authority, I regarded the superintendents in this study only as *potential* leaders, whose new positions provided the opportunity to lead and to spawn leadership among others. My goal was to discover how the new superintendents used their position to influence the attitudes and work of others and to discern whether something that respondents called "leadership" emerged in these interactions.

Throughout, I was attentive to the ways in which the contexts of a superintendent's work determined his or her options and shaped constituents' expectations. I wanted to know how becoming a superintendent at a particular time in history affected an individual's efforts to lead—did the society's preoccupation with accountability affect constituents' expectations of their new superintendent? I wondered whether the prevailing values of a community limited what was possible—how did local politics influence leadership opportunities? I considered how a particular district's organization affected what could or would happen—what difference, if any, did the district's size or administrative structure make? How did teachers' and administrators' attitudes toward the central office affect their interactions with the superintendent? I explored how an individual's personal characteristics—his or her capacity to reflect on practice, envision the future, negotiate compromises, or stand firm—played out in particular settings. This analysis of leadership in context is meant to enable prospective and current superintendents, as well as aspiring leaders in other contexts, to reflect constructively on their own circumstances, successes, and failures. Further, this work can help constituents seeking to exercise influence collaboratively to better understand the interactional character of leadership and their own capacity to lead.

The Complexity of Current-Day Leadership

This work demonstrates again and again the challenges superintendents face in exercising and promoting leadership in school districts today. The complex worlds they enter are far removed from the seemingly orderly, respectful communities Frank Spaulding headed a century ago. Louis Antonellis, one superintendent in this study (all names used in this work are fictional), was appointed during a raucous meeting of the Ashmont school board, held at the height of a teachers' strike that delayed the opening of school. Clara Underwood assumed the superintendency in Union, an urban district languishing in receivership, while local officials faced indictments for mismanagement of funds. Wayne Saunders was the seventh person in six years to hold the superintendency of the Summit city schools.

Not surprisingly, teachers and principals were disturbed by the disruption and distrust in such districts, and consequently they were skeptical about the promises, intentions, and skills of their new superintendent. They withheld their support until they were convinced that these new administrators deserved it; in the end, they judged some to be worthy, others not.

Despite this reserve and caution, constituents still held real hopes for their superintendents as leaders and collaborators in leadership. Constituents granted superintendents time to demonstrate their wisdom as educators, to mobilize political support for action, and to use their managerial authority in ways that would promote collaboration and constructive change.

Today's Superintendent: Educator, Politician, and Manager

There were three types of leadership—educational, political, and managerial—apparent in the work of all the influential superintendents studied.[8]

When teachers, principals, and community members look to superintendents for *educational* leadership, they seek to understand their vision, values, and purposes as educators. Were these superintendents committed to high standards? Did they intend to see that all students would be educated? Did they advocate a particular approach to pedagogy? Could they help local educators further the instructional gains that the district had already made? Were they likely to invest in teachers' learning? Principals sought evidence that their new superintendents understood schools and teaching. Teachers wanted to be assured that these aspiring leaders respected them as professional colleagues.

Constituents also relied on their superintendents for *political* leadership in securing funds, building coalitions in support of school improvement, and fairly distributing resources among competing priorities. The belief that politics should be kept beyond the boundaries of responsible school leadership found no support in this study. Superintendents were expected to be adept at negotiating, lobbying, and securing backing for worthy endeavors. Though the politics at play varied widely, from patronage politics to participatory decision making, no superintendent could hope to lead without acting politically.

Finally, superintendents were expected by their constituents to exercise *managerial* leadership. School districts are fundamentally bureaucratic organizations, some more formal and elaborate than others but all requiring thoughtful and thorough management. These superintendents had to be creative in using the structures of their organization to encourage communication and participation, allocate resources efficiently, provide supervision and support, make plans for moving forward, and ensure accountability and consistent understanding of standards.

Constituents looked to superintendents for leadership in these three dimensions, and they often withheld support if it was lacking. When educational leadership was weak, teachers and principals often discredited the superintendent as being misguided and preoccupied with the wrong things. When political leadership was weak, the schools suffered undue financial cuts, became the captives of special interests on the school board, or became the battleground for citizens with competing priorities. When managerial leadership was weak, people became preoccupied with bureaucratic errors, communication among educators faltered, and potential school leaders could not act constructively.

The Need for Balance and Proportion

Not only were all three approaches to leadership essential, they had to be connected and balanced in order for effective organizational change to occur. That is, the educational priorities of a superintendent often determined his or her political strategies and managerial approach. While these superintendents all had their preferred "long and short sides"—feeling more comfortable and skilled either as educators, politicians, or managers—the complex, changing settings in which they worked meant they could not rely exclusively on their most familiar and comfortable approaches to leadership. Different districts required different approaches in different proportions. Constituents who said that their superintendent was "all politics" or "just a bureaucrat" implied that these aspects of leadership were being pursued for their own sake rather than in support of improving the schools; the necessary triangle of educational, managerial, and political expertise was unconnected or incomplete.

The search process served to create a match between a community's image of itself and a candidate's presentation of his or her strengths. Having assumed their new positions, superintendents who hoped to effect change had to exercise all three facets of leadership: in negotiating budgets with city officials, for example, they exercised political leadership but defended their positions with educational values and data about managerial realities. Different situations necessarily changed the shape of the leadership triangle from moment to moment and from day to day.

The stories that emerge from this study are unique and complicated; they demonstrate that it is the successful interaction of a particular individual and a particular context that makes leadership work. Some superintendents ably interpreted the character of their new district and acted in ways that constituents perceived to be consonant with their culture and responsive to their needs. Other superintendents deliberately challenged local beliefs and practices, unsettling those in the district but moving them beyond the status quo. Still other superintendents paid little attention to the local context and applied old solutions to new situations, only to generate doubts or distrust.

Constituents wanted to trust their new superintendent and count on him or her as an advocate within and outside their district. Such trust depended on their confidence in the superintendent's values and personal integrity; it rested on evidence that their new superintendent understood teaching and respected them as professionals and colleagues, and it was secured by the new superintendent's commitment to remain with them for enough time to make a difference. Only when constituents felt such assurances did they venture beyond the conventional relationship of authorities and subordinates to the new working relationships of collaborative leadership.

Changing Contexts

Not only did the districts' contexts differ from one another, each differed over the course of an individual's tenure, often as a result of the superintendent's own action. Heraclitus, the Greek philosopher, wrote, "You could not step twice in the same rivers; for other and yet other waters are ever flowing on" (Nahm, 1964, p. 70). Superintendents and many other leaders of the day soon find that the context for leadership, like the river, is ever-changing. Thus a prospective leader must continuously reinterpret that context and diagnose its needs. Moreover, any superintendent—effective leader or no—who steps into the river changes its course and must adapt to the new currents thus created. Aspiring leaders must assess the effects of their own action or inaction and then consider how best to proceed. Because the superintendent is also changed by the context, its demands, and its responses, he or she must be self-aware, reflective, and open to new insights in the process of learning to lead.

The next chapter considers the search process by which the new superintendents in this study were appointed to their positions. It is during this process, well before a superintendent is granted formal authority to head a district, that the accommodation between the individual and the context begins. Those looking for leadership ask, "Who are we as a school district? What do we need? What does each candidate offer?" Simultaneously, candidates ask, "What is this district and community like? What do the people need and what will they expect? Is this the place for me?" How the participants in the search process answer those questions and adapt to one another determines much about the prospects for leadership from the superintendency.

Notes

1. At one time Spaulding was the highest-paid superintendent in the United States. He became a professor of educational administration at Yale University and was honored at his retirement in a symposium sponsored by former associates (Hill, 1936).

2. David Tyack (1976) writes that, at that time, "the notion that successful men were disinterested found nearly universal expression in the early textbooks on school management. . . . Rare indeed was the school man who would argue that businessmen did not necessarily represent the good of the party at large" (p. 140).

3. Such experts, conversant in the techniques of "scientific management," used "time and motion studies" to determine the most efficient method of completing any job. Close management of workers and an incentive-based pay system were combined to ensure high levels of productivity. Efficiency experts applied the general principles of scientific management to public education through the 1930s. Raymond E. Callahan (1962) writes a compelling account of the harm this system brought to public education, including a discussion of Spaulding's role in this period. For further discussion of the relationship between school boards and superintendents between 1850 and 1950, see Tyack and Hansot (1982, pp. 114–121); Blumberg (1985, pp. 14–27); Tyack and Cummings (1977, pp. 46–66); and Cuban (1976, pp. 111–139).

4. For example, Freud found that in both the Catholic Church and in armies, "all decisions [come] down from the top, and [are] followed because of the love and faith that the institutions induce in the

believers and the men. Decision making in these organizations remains a virtual monopoly of the one on top, modified at best by the need for information from below" (Hill, 1984, p. 34). Similarly, Ann Ruth Willner (1984) explored the forces at work with the political charismatic, a leader who causes "a group of people or an entire nation to fall under the binding spell . . . so that his word becomes their only law and his command their almost sacred duty to obey" (p. 2).

5. Heifitz (1994, pp. 102–124) provides an extensive discussion of the resources for leadership available to those in positions of authority.

6. Edgar Schein (1992) argues not only that different organizations have distinct cultures, but also that the role of leadership is to manage and change culture. Deal and Kennedy (1982) analyze various business cultures and their CEOs' successful efforts to create and sustain them.

7. One exception is a recent survey conducted by the American Association of School Administrators, *The 1992 Study of the American School Superintendency*, which provides comparative data on the characteristics and experiences of a random sample of 1,724 superintendents, stratified by district size (Glass, 1992).

8. Larry Cuban (1988) described "three dominant images of what a superintendent should be: instructional supervisor, administrative chief, and negotiator-statesman"(p. 113). The data from this study, initially examined without the benefit of Cuban's conceptual framework, support this characterization of the superintendency.

2

Looking for Leaders

With a flourish, a January 1989 headline in the Newbridge *Gazette*—"Super Search Begins"—heralded the start of the town's efforts to hire a successor to its superintendent of eighteen years. Intent on acquiring the best, the Newbridge school board asked an educational consultant, Elizabeth James, to run the search. Over the next six weeks James met with twenty-six community groups to learn what kind of person they wanted for the job. She drew up a job description and advertised the position in major newspapers, and she personally pursued prospective applicants. Thirty-seven men and eight women applied. James prepared summaries of the candidates' qualifications and rated each on a three-point scale— very strong, less strong, least strong. With James's assistance, the school board selected and publicly interviewed eight semifinalists.

The *Gazette* quoted James as saying, "In selecting the semi-finalists, the board was looking for individuals with proven leadership ability, with experience working with a diverse population, with budgetary and personnel management skills, and particularly for goodness of fit with the Newbridge schools and the community." The quest, which began by reviewing candidates' skills and experience, soon moved to considering the potential match between individual applicants and the district—its needs, history, locale, and organization. Expectations were high that Newbridge, a small, multiethnic, working-class town, would attract and select not only an individual of great talent and experience, but also someone who was particularly drawn to the specific opportunities and challenges of educational leadership the town offered.

In broad outline, the search processes of the twelve districts discussed in this book looked much like that of Newbridge. More than half of them hired consultants to manage the process. Most conducted formal or informal needs assessments to guide their selections. Almost all their search committees included members of interest groups—unions, community agencies, parents of special education students—either as advisors to the consultant or as full-fledged members. All but one district spent over six weeks on the process—advertising widely, attracting an array of candidates, winnowing a large group of applicants down to a small group of finalists, and interviewing them publicly and privately before making a choice. With the exception of Ashmont, a small city district with a history of patronage, where the school board accepted the superintendent's resignation and appointed an insider to succeed him within the first thirty minutes of a regularly scheduled meeting, the processes were as deliberate and measured as one might expect for the important task of selecting a superintendent.

In each case, public deliberation and media coverage highlighted the paper credentials and prior experience of the candidates, but the search committees were actually far more curious about less objective criteria—appearance, sense of humor, ability to listen. Notably, much of this interest was not publicly discussed. Had it been possible to simply determine the exact skills required for the job, assess the candidates according to objective criteria, and then select the individual with the highest cumulative rating, identifying the "best" candidate might have been possible. But in each district the search and selection process proved to be far more intuitive than rational—and far more unpredictable than press accounts revealed. Everyone was looking for leadership, but few could agree on what leadership is or how to appraise a candidate's promise as a leader within their particular setting.

In part the search process is complex because no single candidate can possibly embody all the skills, strengths, and traits sought by school districts. The superintendents' job description reflects the combined wish lists of an array of constituents with varied preferences and priorities. Therefore when school boards consider applicants' qualifications, they must judge how those qualifications will play out in practice and make hard choices about what they value most.

Also, the search and selection process is less than rational because it is embedded within the context of a particular district. Each school district has a unique history of successes and failures that has shaped school officials' beliefs about who can best head their schools. Each community has its own social, economic, and political realities that determine what candidates must know or show in order to get the job, survive, and succeed. And each district has a particular organizational structure, a distinctive culture, and a unique constituency that holds various expectations about what kind of leader the district needs. By saying that those selecting Newbridge's superintendent wanted to achieve a "goodness of fit between the Newbridge schools and the community," James characterized just the sort of match that search and selection committees throughout this study sought to achieve.

Conducting the Search in Context

Three important contexts—a district's history, its community, and the organization of its school system—influence the criteria and process of selection.

The Historical Context

The searches described in this book all occurred during a period of great expectations for superintendents as leaders. During the late 1980s and early 1990s, criticism of public education was intense, sometimes strident. At the same time, education budgets were being cut or imperiled. Citizens often blamed the nation's poor economic performance on the shortcomings of its schools. Many took their cues from vocal critics of schooling who urged the public to recognize its stake in education and become involved in school reform. They hoped that superintendents of heroic stature might rescue the schools from devastation and reverse what appeared to be their precipitous decline. Of course, since diverse groups of citizens held conflicting views about what kind of leader their district needed, broad participation often led to selection processes marked by disputes and prolonged debate.

These features of the period between 1988 and 1992—myriad social and educational needs, great expectations of leaders, and intense involvement by many individuals and interest groups—were fairly consistent across all twelve districts described here. The individual histories of the districts varied in important ways, however, which further influenced their search processes. In particular, a prior superintendent's record had a striking impact on a district's selection process. In determining its priorities, the search committee frequently focused on what had gone wrong or what had been lacking under the previous administration, often to the exclusion of what had gone right. Therefore there was little mention of what should be continued, only talk about what shouldn't happen again.

The influence of prior administrations on the selection of a new superintendent played out in several ways. First, the circumstances of the prior superintendent's departure shaped the immediate context of the search. In some cases, sudden and unexpected events required that a new superintendent be hired quickly; in others, the change was long anticipated. Death and serious illness were the precipitating events in two districts. In four others, the sitting superintendent decided to take a new job, sometimes with the encouragement of the school board. Three superintendents retired after having been in office many years. In the remaining three districts, the superintendent was fired or firmly asked to leave. These districts, in particular, were determined to select someone who would compensate for the predecessor's weaknesses, sometimes at the expense of more objective scrutiny of candidates' knowledge and skills. If the prior superintendent had mismanaged funds, fiscal skills were at the top of that school board's list of priorities; if the prior superintendent had a reputation for being aloof or punitive, interpersonal skills were likely to be one of the board's top concerns; if the former superintendent had suddenly departed, the board sought assurances of a longer tenure.

The retiring superintendent in Newbridge was faulted for being too distant and for, as one administrator said, "exhibiting a lack of communication." A teacher in Millsburg said the retiring superintendent there was a "very outgoing, friendly, charming politician [who] lost sight of the fact that quality education was his primary goal and became satisfied with the status quo." In Oakville, by contrast, the school board judged its schools to be in excellent shape and sought to replace its beloved, retiring superintendent with a "clone." This case, however, was unique. All the other districts were less than satisfied—some were greatly dissatisfied—with the work of their prior superintendent.

Unlike matchmaking for marriage, the search for a new superintendent is rarely expected to lead to a permanent relationship, one that will last until the superintendent retires. Therefore, search committees seek a match not only between a superintendent and a particular place, but also between a superintendent and a particular time. Times change, and communities' needs for school leadership change as well. As one principal observed about Andrew Cronin, the newly hired superintendent in the suburban district of Clayton: "I think for now he's what Clayton really needs. . . . Is he the man of the future for Clayton? I don't know."

The Community and Political Context

Since the superintendent's work is entwined with that of local government officials, hiring the right superintendent also becomes the unofficial business of municipal officials and community leaders.

Superintendents must negotiate with mayors, finance committees, and city councils to secure the money they need to run their schools. Contract negotiations with teachers and administrators unions are often linked to prior settlements reached with local fire and police unions. Controversies about sex education, student assignment patterns, or the results of standardized tests spill beyond the boundaries of the schools, affecting civic groups, churches, and real estate offices.

Many mayors will refer to "my superintendent" or "my schools" in interviews, signalling their claim on the public schools. Although some mayors will put their own reputations on the line in supporting particular appointees, others tend to relegate new superintendents to subordinate status in "their" cities and towns. Most municipal officials have lived their lives and built their careers locally; thus they regard most applicants for the superintendency as outsiders. From the start of the search process they assume that it is the new superintendent, rather than they, who must adapt and change. When asked whether he would do anything differently following Louis Antonellis's appointment as superintendent, the mayor of Ashmont said, "No I'm not going to change my approach. . . . I say what's on my mind, and I don't get ulcers—I give ulcers. No, I won't change my approach to him. I don't think there's a need to." Territorial boundaries between school departments and local governments are regularly in dispute. While school officials try to secure special status and guarantees of autonomy for their districts, city officials often treat the schools as any other city agency. For new superintendents, this process of jockeying for position and control begins during the search and selection process.

Mayors and other local officials often play key roles in the search process, proposing criteria, personally interviewing candidates, and brokering agreements when a committee reaches an impasse. Even when such officials are not involved directly, their concerns are usually represented by school officials who understand that local support for public education depends on the new superintendent's

ability to forcefully and effectively advance the schools' interests in
the community. The racial and ethnic diversity of urban communities further complicates the community context of the search.
Sometimes competition or hostility among groups leads to a racially
charged selection process. In the urban district of Millsburg,
African-American and Latino groups allied to hire a superintendent from a minority group, contending that white administrators
had neglected students of color. In Union, an inner-city district
where virtually all the students are African American, there was a
decided preference for an African-American superintendent.
Reportedly, in some districts candidates are not considered serious
contenders if their race or ethnic background does not match that
of the local community. Any finalist in a diverse community has to
be aware of different groups' concerns and priorities, since success
in office often means recognizing schisms and reconciling the differences that inevitably develop between groups of constituents.

Members of the business community also actively participate in
the search processes of many districts, reflecting the growing belief that
business has a stake in the performance of local schools. The chamber
of commerce in Millsburg both financed and greatly influenced the
extensive search process. School board members in the other districts
kept the priorities of business leaders in mind as they made their decisions. How would this person fare with local Rotarians or leaders of
the local business roundtable? Even if board members reject the notion
that public schooling should serve the economy, they must realize that
business leaders have increasing leverage with the local government
officials who control school budgets.

Thus searches often take place within a particular local context
in which municipal officials; leaders of racial, ethnic, and religious
groups; and influential business people participate directly or indirectly to ensure that their interests are represented. Community
members hope that their new superintendent will not only be an
effective educator but also an influential and cooperative player in
the community.

The Organizational Context: How We Do Things Here

Searches are also influenced by the organizational characteristics of a particular school system. Search committees in highly centralized districts tended to seek superintendents who could exercise hierarchical authority, while more decentralized districts favored candidates who could manage the system effectively while granting considerable autonomy to principals and school staffs. Districts that were more formal and rule-bound expected their superintendents to follow procedures and enforce the chain of command, while more flexible districts showed interest in candidates with records of less formal approaches to administration.

The profile of a district's faculty and administration also influences whom search committees hire. Newbridge, where the faculty were experienced but dispirited, wanted a superintendent with a strong record in staff development. In Union and Millsburg, teachers were said to be retiring on the job, and officials therefore sought candidates with high standards for instructional performance.

School systems' values further shape the selection process. In suburban Highboro, where concerns about African-American students' achievement had intensified during the prior administration, the search committee deliberately sought candidates committed to equity for all students. Officials in Ashmont, who had already reduced the size of the district organization, assumed that anyone holding the superintendency would advocate efficiency.

Finally, districts seek superintendents with the experience and skills to administer current and proposed programs. Fernwood, a small-town district that had begun planning a new high school when their superintendent announced his resignation, looked for a successor who could oversee the process of designing and opening a new building. Summit, a city district involved in a school improvement process, was said to want "someone who was big on organizational development and who knew about organizational change and systemic change over time, someone who could commit to planning." Thus the form, norms, and practices of a school system's organization often influence decisions search committees make as they consider the match between applicants and their district's needs.

Defining a Direction for the Search

With so many individuals and interest groups participating in the process, a search committee is unlikely to settle on a detailed set of criteria. Rather, committee members tend to begin by reaching a broad understanding about the direction they want the superintendent to take—whether they want him or her to introduce change, provide continuity, or stabilize the district.

Looking for Change

Two districts, Millsburg and Newbridge, explicitly sought superintendents who would introduce major change. In each district the incumbent was retiring after many years in office, and respondents in both places characterized their school systems' programs as stagnant and outdated. Members of both districts' search committees intended to hire outside candidates; they thought insiders were too invested in current practices and were unlikely to know about educational reforms taking place elsewhere.

Even a principal whose allegiance to the retiring Millsburg superintendent led him to predict that he would be a "hard act to follow" emphasized the need for change: "I did feel we needed a change. I just felt to continue [by promoting an assistant superintendent from within] would be another continuation of the same old thing."

Although there was consensus on the search committees in Millsburg and Newbridge about the need for change, there was less clarity about what that change should be. "The school board," one Millsburg respondent said, "was looking for a new direction in which to take the whole system." Notably, she did not say that the board was seeking a candidate who would take the district back to basics or toward interdisciplinary learning; no particular direction was specified. But in choosing new leadership, Millsburg would definitely be signing up for change.

Both Newbridge and Millsburg wanted candidates who were knowledgeable about the latest educational reforms, even when search committee members had little personal knowledge about the reforms. A union leader active in the Millsburg selection process said, "We were looking for someone who could, in fact, move the system forward to face the challenges of the twenty-first century. We all knew that education was in a changing pattern. . . . And all of the research and all of the literature was telling us that the factory model we were using was not the best and obviously was not doing the job it should be doing."

R. O. Carlson (1972) distinguishes between career-bound and place-bound superintendents, portraying the career-bound superintendent as "one who develops an early commitment to the superintendency and engages in deliberate career planning to achieve that goal. Place-bound administrators adopt a more passive orientation toward the superintendency and are less favorably inclined toward mobility" (Miklos, 1988, p. 64). Newbridge and Millsburg were looking for career-bound superintendents.

Both of the successful candidates were conversant with the latest literature on school reform and had experience introducing change. Anna Niles, the new superintendent in Newbridge, had initiated a strategic planning and management process in her former district, and Ben Moreno of Millsburg had introduced participatory decision making in his.

The successful candidates declared that they were, indeed, change agents. Ben Moreno explained that he wanted to head a school system that would not have to be convinced about the need for reform: "I was interested in going to a place that was ready for the bold steps needed to move very, very quickly." He confronted the school board with this expectation and insisted that members not offer him the job unless they were serious about change. That challenge and his confidence were exactly what local Millsburg offi- cials wanted to hear.

Anna Niles also communicated her strong commitment to change. A central office administrator recalled that "they were look- ing for a change agent, and she presented herself in interviews and the staff visitations that she made as someone who was in the fore in terms of educational practice and theory. She presented certain talents that indicated she would be able to make change."

According to many respondents, each of these districts eventu- ally hired the kind of superintendent it had sought. Looking back, a few respondents described a remarkably precise match between the district's needs and the candidate's qualifications. Most of the time, search committees' expectations were quite broadly framed. They set out looking for change agents, considered what the various can- didates proposed to change, and selected finalists who seemed to best fit their district's needs. As emphasized later in this chapter, however, the final selection was driven as much by intuitive judg- ments about the character and traits of individual candidates as by the particular initiatives those candidates proposed.

Seeking Continuity

While Millsburg and Newbridge looked for change agents, other districts sought candidates who would ensure continuity and steady improvement in their educational programs. Generally those dis- tricts were proud of their schools' accomplishments, endorsed pre- vailing practices, and believed that students could be best served by refining rather than reforming their approach to education.

Three of these districts—Highboro, Clayton, and Oakville— served relatively homogeneous suburban communities that funded public education generously and, over the years, had established national reputations for excellence. They offered extensive and var- ied academic programs, their students performed well on standard- ized tests, and they provided considerable support for students with special needs. Respondents in each of these districts suggested ways their schools might be improved, particularly by better meeting the needs of increasingly diverse student populations, but none recommended abandoning or dramatically redirecting their current approach.

Fernwood, which also sought continuity, served a small working-class town that did not fund education generously. Programs and course offerings were limited, and graduates rarely attended prestigious colleges. The most recent superintendent had initiated positive changes in the district, securing funds for a new high school, proposing a grade reorganization, and establishing the district's Reading Recovery program, which was a model for the region. A central office administrator said he had introduced "a comprehensive plan that really amounted to a renaissance for the school system, and we needed someone who would be able to pull that together and build on it and carry us forward aggressively."

In Oakville, where the departing superintendent also enjoyed unusually high approval, a central office administrator said that the board was "interested, number one, in continuing the kind of leadership they had. They were very happy with that. The board certainly wasn't seeking change. If anything, they were seeking evolution or continuation of what they had."

People in Highboro and Clayton, on the other hand, were dissatisfied with the performance of their departing superintendents. The Highboro superintendent, hired during a period of fiscal austerity, had been asked to tighten up the district, which had long granted autonomy to its schools. In response he had assumed an authoritarian and distant approach to management, communicating indirectly with principals through central office administrators and making moves to standardize curriculum and pedagogy throughout the district. He was repeatedly faulted for having poor relationships with staff, exercising weak leadership, and having a meager influence on school practices. When the Highboro search committee first convened, the members did not talk about finding someone who would promote change; rather, they talked about finding someone who would better understand how to lead the district in the direction in which it had long been heading. One school board member stated, "We're not looking to revamp, but to fine-tune." The prior superintendent's appointment was commonly understood to have been a mistake, his tenure an unfortunate detour in an otherwise positive administrative course.

Similarly, in Clayton the prior superintendent was regarded as an aberration. During his administration the district had drifted, making less progress than it might have, but past successes and the strength of the staff carried the schools along respectably. When the search committee considered what their selection would signal about the future, they too decided to hire someone who would provide continuity and progress rather than dramatic change.

Like the successful candidates in the two districts seeking change, the contenders in Highboro, Clayton, Fernwood, and Oakville emphasized how right they were for the position. They praised these systems' prior accomplishments and presented themselves as leaders who could ensure continuous progress.

Searching for Stability

Finally, six districts had experienced disruption of such magnitude that their search committees primarily sought candidates who could stabilize the system. As participants on these search committees saw it, the primary goal of the next superintendent would be to steady the district and get it back on course. Candidates were assessed for their capacity to reestablish order, resolve differences, and return the system to its former state of equilibrium.

Two of these districts, Union and Ashmont, were in the midst of considerable upheaval while searching for a new superintendent. Union was emerging from receivership. A central office administrator explained, "There have been five superintendents within a three-year period, many of them 'interim-acting.' The district has been riddled with indictments of high-level administrative and supervisory staff. A school board had been disbanded." In its search for a new superintendent, Union looked to outsiders who had no political ties and thus could bring order to the feuding factions within the district. A Union teacher reflected on the choice of an outsider: "She brought a bit of stability to the district. As someone from the outside, she did not come clouded with any of the problems the district had."

Ashmont, too, was in a state of tumult. The prior superintendent had resigned in August after a heart attack. The school board, torn with dissension, had no budget. The teachers union began a twelve-day strike, delaying the September opening of school. Everyone expected that the next superintendent would be an insider, since in the past one hundred years only one outsider had been appointed, and that person's tenure was characterized by one principal as "a shock to the system." And everyone knew local politics would be important in determining who that insider would be. Therefore, in seeking stability, Ashmont looked to its own. It appointed Louis Antonellis, who said he was "home bred" and that he had wanted the job "from the day I came in."

Circumstances were less dramatic in Summit and Riverton, two urban districts that had experienced repeated turnover in the superintendency. Just as these districts had become engaged in reform efforts, the superintendents championing the reforms left for more prestigious jobs. A central office administrator in Riverton observed, "Much of the feeling was, people come, get things started, you buy into various programs, and before you have the opportunity to refine what you're doing, you have a new administration with a new philosophy." The effect of such turnover on staff morale was devastating. An administrator in Summit explained, "We had two interim superintendents and a superintendent who didn't do a good job and left. . . . There was just a lot of distrust."

Counting those in acting positions, Summit had had six superintendents in seven years, the most recent having been asked to leave. Riverton had experienced two recent changes in administration, with the most recent superintendent leaving, as one school board member explained, "after barely four years," which seemed far too short a time to many. Notably, this superintendent's tenure actually exceeded the national average for urban districts of this size. But people in Riverton felt he was leaving just as reforms had begun to take hold. Michael Fullan and Suzanne Stiegelbauer (1991), who contend that real reform requires five years' worth of a superintendent's attention, would agree. The most recent superintendent in Riverton emphasized equity and accountability, instituted a strategic management system, and, as one principal observed, "shook up a lot of people who thought mediocrity was okay." Being the first African-American superintendent in the district, his leaving was a particular disappointment to members of minority groups. This principal continued, "People who had supported him felt abandoned and betrayed, almost as if he had jumped ship. . . . Planting seeds for change takes more than a few years to see fruition of one's efforts, and consequently, most of what [he] had initiated never really came to be."

As a result of this turnover, search committees in Summit and Riverton sought candidates who were likely to stay for the long term. Riverton hired insider Maureen Reilly, who had been promoted up through the system and was serving as acting superintendent during the search. Although Reilly did not hold a doctorate (and many people in the district thought the superintendent should), she did have extensive experience in curriculum and instruction. More important, several respondents said, was the certainty that Reilly would not leave before her contract expired. A central office administrator agreed: "The feeling is that now it's time to have someone who will be here, who has knowledge of Riverton at many different levels and has a real commitment to the community, being a resident of the community." Reilly assured them that she was not a "gypsy superintendent."

Respondents understood the hazards of hiring an insider—the inertia resulting from past practices and the possibility that political debts might encumber the new administration—but they also recognized the benefits of their new superintendent's feeling at home in the system and being "a known quantity." A Riverton school board member observed that with an inside candidate, "There was no need to do the transition thing."

Although Summit had also experienced repeated turnover, the board decided to seek an outsider; it seemed more likely that the new expertise the members wanted would be found outside the district. Board members believed that someone without established allegiances within the district could deal more fairly and objectively with competing community groups. The Summit search committee members were no less worried about turnover than their counterparts in Riverton, though, and they considered carefully the commitment each candidate might make. When Wayne Saunders, their eventual choice, promised to stay for at least five years, committee members were reassured.

Two remaining districts sought candidates who could stabilize their schools after prior superintendents had introduced flurries of programs that seemed to be counterproductive or contradictory. According to a central office administrator in the small, working-class city of Westford, the prior superintendent had "wanted change as his main goal." In promoting change, "he would find pockets where he could institutionalize change or move it and give go-ahead to people, and the system just grew like Topsie. And there was absolutely a loss of central control, lots of duplication of services, but change was what was needed and a lot of change came about."

In Glendale, which one teacher described as "very inbred" ("Everybody in this system went to school in this system; they've known each other since the year one"), people also characterized their former superintendent as a change agent whose reforms had overwhelmed the district. The superintendent was, as one of his many supporters said, "a dynamic, innovative, brilliant, controversial, troublesome, out-of-state superintendent, who was probably the best superintendent we have had in fifty years in this system."

Under his direction the district had embarked on school restructuring and districtwide reorganization, but the changes were never fully implemented. One central office administrator in Glendale observed, "We had eighteen trains going on eighteen different tracks, and it was time, I think, to sit back now and say 'Let's get one train going out of the station at a time.'"

Both Westford and Glendale sought superintendents who would steady the schools, as these respondents' comments attest: "They were looking for someone who could bring stability to the educational community." "They were looking for somebody that could bring control to the system, somebody with experience in Glendale, to bring the system back on track. . . . We didn't need a turn-them-upside-down-type superintendent." The newly appointed superintendents promised just what was needed. A central office administrator in Westford said, "Wells came in with a message that 'I can organize things. I can bring focus to it.' And I think that's probably what sold him to the school board." Though not an insider, Wells had been a successful superintendent in a similar community. Glendale sought an insider who, as one principal explained, "hasn't hopped around the nation" and, as another said, would be "a cohesive force within the community, someone well respected."

Thus these communities, too, made what they believed were successful matches between their districts' need for change and the candidates who applied. Of course, search committees' preferences for change, continuity, or stability were not pure and uncomplicated. Districts that sought stability were not giving up on progress; in fact, achieving stability was seen as the first step in preparing for progress. Those embarking on change were not disregarding the importance of order and continuity, but their attention was focused primarily on moving in a new direction.

From this small sample it appears that districts tend to alternate over time between seeking change and preferring stability. The two districts seeking change agents were reacting to long periods of stability, which had in reality become stagnation. The six districts seeking stability sought to establish order after periods of rapid, sometimes chaotic change.

Matching the Person to the Time and Place

The twelve districts' decisions to promote change, maintain continuity, or achieve stability were defined in response to their particular context—their history, local circumstances, and school system organization. But the personal characteristics of the applicants proved to be equally important in determining whom search committees favored. Notably, committees preferred candidates judged to be compatible with the community's self-image. Search committees wanted candidates who were smart and experienced, individuals who could make a good appearance at public meetings and on television. They sought candidates who were likely to work well with people, specifically local people, and who exhibited enough confidence and strength to take on the difficult challenges facing their district. These more personal judgments about the match between candidates and context were largely subjective, only sometimes discussed publicly, and profoundly influential in the selection process.

How Does the Candidate Make Us Feel About Ourselves?

Search committees critically reviewed prospective superintendents as potential emissaries for their communities. Members paid attention to candidates' social class, race, and ethnicity as well as to their values and deportment.

In assessing a candidate on the basis of class, race, or ethnicity, search committee members wondered privately whether a prospective superintendent could become "one of us." For example, Westford, a small, ethnically diverse, working-class city, had three finalists, two men and a woman. One of the men, the favored candidate of four board members, came from a similar working-class community nearby, where local politics were sharply divided along ethnic lines. The woman, who was the choice of four other members, came from an upper-middle-class suburban community. Several who supported the man said they did so because he understood Westford's old-style politics. As one school board member explained, the town the man came from "is comparable to this town, and that's why I was supporting that particular candidate." The woman's supporters liked her because she was more liberal and therefore, they assumed, likely to be responsive to the concerns of new immigrant groups in Westford. She described herself as a "quadrilingual person" with "an appreciation of diversity and multiethnicity." But she was Jewish, and Westford was a town with few Jews. A principal offered these revealing comments about the town's response to her candidacy: "There is some sentiment in the city that we don't have enough affirmative action vis-à-vis women. And I really thought they were going to go with [the woman]. In retrospect, for some reason, she turned an awful lot of people off. It may have been that she was Jewish, and outspokenly so, although with that name she couldn't hide it very well. But she probably spoke about her heritage. It may have been that she was from an elitist community and [people wondered] what in the world would she know about Westford?"

The school board eventually offered the job to a third candidate, Thomas Wells, who had been superintendent in yet another working-class city as well as the headmaster at an international school abroad. Both experiences enabled him to advance as a compromise candidate who appealed to both the conservative ethnic politicians and the liberal champions of new immigrants. Later Wells explained how he had featured both experiences in his interview with the search committee:

I was able to capitalize on two things: I would gear responses to point out that I was used to dealing with the mayor, that I was used to dealing with city councils, though Westford is more urban than [my former district]. And the second thing was that Westford is now experiencing a significant influx of new immigrants, . . . and so

I emphasized the international character of my candidacy. I was coming from a school where we had children
from forty-six different nations. I was bilingual and had
lived abroad on a number of occasions, and my family
was actively involved and familiar with settings where
we were minorities and were dealing with minorities.

Wells interpreted the community's interest in him to be about feel-
ings of comfort rather than about particular proposals he might
offer: "I think those were more appealing—the city superintendency
and the international, multicultural background—than any particular initiative that I espoused."

Class and ethnicity also proved important when Andrew Cronin,
a highly qualified candidate from a nearby city, applied to become
superintendent in the upper-middle-class suburb of Clayton. Initially
many people in Clayton discounted Cronin's candidacy simply
because of his urban background. A central office administrator said
that many were "predisposed not to like him" when they found out
where he came from. Cronin recalled the school board's decision to
include him among the ten finalists: "If you asked them at that time
why they were including [an administrator from the nearby city] who
is Irish, they would say, 'Well, we just thought that was the democratic thing to do, and it looked like he had a good record and good
recommendations.'" But Cronin's interview went very well—"I just
clicked with them"—and he possessed skills in financial management that people sought. Gradually the search committee's interpretation of his urban experience shifted, and through Cronin's
candidacy those hiring Clayton's superintendent began to reconcile
the district's past identity with the new reality of its changing demo-
graphics. A central office administrator explained that Cronin was
"an excellent match—and the reason, for starters, is that Clayton is
really moving in a much more urban direction. He is clearly someone with urban school experience and an understanding of urban
kids and parents and the issues. We call Clayton an urban-suburban

community. We're hanging onto that suburban piece, and certainly, in terms of our values, they're largely suburban. But clearly the reality is we're dealing with a real mix of children in this town, and his coming, to me, signals an acknowledgement of that in a way that Clayton hasn't done before."

Millsburg had diversified significantly over the long tenure of its prior superintendent, a white man. At the start of the search, members of African-American and Latino interest groups allied to press for the appointment of a nonwhite superintendent. The finalists, all outsiders, included one white, one African-American, and one Latino candidate. Confusion arose, however, because many thought the Latino was Italian rather than Puerto Rican, and considerable dissension ensued within the minority coalition when African-American members expected the Latinos to back the African-American candidate. Eventually the Latino candidate, Ben Moreno, won the job, though doubts lingered about whether he truly represented "the community." Given the great diversity of that community, it seemed no candidate's race and ethnic background could satisfy everyone.

Clara Underwood, an African-American woman, was appointed to head the schools in Union, an African-American community. Arthur Holzman, a Jewish man, was hired by Highboro, a community with many Jewish residents. Insiders, already proven to be compatible with the social and economic character of their communities, were hired in Ashmont, Glendale, and Riverton.

In considering whether prospective superintendents would fit in, committees also paid attention to applicants' values. Often, however, they relied on meager information in deciding what candidates stood for. Typically search committee members were simply seeking reassurance, and candidates' claims—rather than firm evidence about past performance—satisfied them. For example, one member of the search committee in Summit asked the leading candidate, "If you found out you were running a school system that was really two school systems, one for the haves and one for the have-nots, what would you do about it?" The candidate replied that this was the fundamental question in education, and he proceeded to explain how he would address the problem. This, the committee member said, "very much impressed me."

Boards seeking confirmation of their own beliefs generally accepted the word of candidates who espoused the value of diversity or the importance of excellence. Sometimes during board members' visits to candidates' sites, diligent search committee members uncovered evidence contradicting these espoused values and then reported back to the board about the gap between candidates' promises and past actions; but such persistent inquiry was rare, and most boards trusted their intuition in judging the claims of their candidates.

Is This Candidate Smart and Experienced Enough for the Job?

Search committee members tried to judge whether candidates had the intelligence and experience needed for success in a job filled with tremendous demands. They favored candidates who were quick, clever, and experienced in a broad range of administrative responsibilities. Although they valued intelligence, most were wary of pretentiously learned types. According to a principal in Summit, the school board "went with Saunders basically because they felt he was extremely bright. His credentials were very good. He was a graduate of Yale and Harvard." But almost in an effort to disclaim, the principal quickly went on to note that the candidate "also had a tough side to him," having been a hockey player in college and having "done some work in the inner cities." A strong academic record was essential in some communities; it actually became something of a liability in others.

Sometimes districts sought particular strengths, such as administrative experience at both the elementary and secondary levels or a good record working with a teachers union. While evidence of able fiscal management was a common prerequisite during these times of cutbacks, districts often were satisfied with a candidate who could speak confidently about a broad array of experiences. Having seen the finalists in Clayton, a department head was impressed with Cronin's overall intelligence. "He's bright, and Clayton admires brightness. Any system does, but you *really* have to be bright to make it here."

Does This Candidate Look and Sound Good?

The search process is largely a public one. Most of those studied here began in executive session but ended in open session, several under the bright lights of local television. As a result, district officials placed a premium on candidates' ease with the audience and their ability to think quickly and speak fluently. Respondents often commented on how the candidates looked, praising those who were attractive and commanding while criticizing those who seemed uncertain, withdrawn, or rumpled.

Although many search committees gathered extensive information about their candidates through references, phone calls, and site visits, the public interview proved to be the single most important factor in the final selection. Many decisions turned on the candidates' performance in these moments. Successful public interviews clinched the job for particular candidates. Both the candidates and the search committee members acknowledged that these were practiced events in which the questions and answers were rehearsed rather than spontaneous. Nevertheless, public interviews carried great weight. When candidates did not perform well, school board members worried about the effect a weak public speaker might have on the standing of the schools. One principal explained that although the candidate his board eventually hired "didn't get high marks on the interview, everybody liked him because they knew his credentials gave him credibility. They loved the kind of person he was. But it was awkward for him to interview for some reason. And we all accepted that and looked at it accordingly. . . . And the question was, if he's having trouble in the interview process, what kind of image would he project to the public? Would he get their confidence? Would he hold their confidence?"

Similarly, a board member in another district was very disappointed with the leading candidate's interview: "It was the worst interview by an applicant I've seen for a superintendent's job. At that point everyone agreed it was a terrible interview. He made a terrible appearance, and my thought at the time was, 'There's a guy who, if he's ever got to go before the town meeting and present a budget, we're in trouble.'" Search committee members believed that their superintendent's public image would have real consequences for their schools' future. Thus they could not easily ignore a poor performance.

Will This Candidate Work Well with People?

Without exception, the search committees believed their next superintendent should work well with people, since the job demands repeated, often relentless person-to-person encounters. In several districts the prior superintendent was said to have been distant, aloof, and controlling; these individuals had generally been hired to make hard decisions about budgets and jobs, only to be accused of creating poor morale once fiscal cuts were made. As a result, these districts were now determined to find candidates with excellent interpersonal skills.

In several districts respondents said the new superintendent had won the job mainly because he or she was good with people. A respondent in Clayton said, "I think that's why Cronin was hired. His first three concerns are people first, people second, and people always. His emphasis is people, people, people. . . . Is he a great academic thinker? I think not. Is he a great visionary? He's not a visionary person who can look at education in a different way. I think he was hired because he's a people person and he's a very upbeat type of person. Very, very upbeat. [He believes] that people can make a difference."

In Fernwood, where the prior superintendent had the reputation of being authoritarian, Dick Fitzgerald's gentler, more "humanistic" style won him the job. "The town was ripe for it," a principal explained. Similarly, in Glendale, where the prior superintendent's administration was reportedly fraught with "tremendous pressure and tension," a principal said, "Administrators wanted, number one, someone who was pleasant to work with. They wanted someone who had been in the system for many years, someone with wonderful people skills, someone who could bring people together."

Several superintendents were hired explicitly for their skills as peacemakers or mediators. Union, just emerging from receivership, hired Clara Underwood because they thought she could diffuse in-house hostilities and, as one respondent said, bring "quiet to this district in the midst of a storm." In the suburban district of Highboro, which one administrator called "fractured," the school board sought a superintendent who could help them achieve unity. A school board member who praised the prior superintendent nonetheless observed, "One area where there seemed to be a real weakness was in staff relationships. And I said it publicly at the time, and I believe it still to be the case, the most important thing for the new superintendent was to do what he could to sort of beef up staff morale. The previous superintendent, I think, was seen more as a management type. . . . He didn't appear to be a very warm person."

Finally, several districts sought superintendents who would promote greater participation by teachers and administrators in the decisions of the district. As one school board member said, Anna Niles's candidacy offered participation for all parties: "During her interview, she spoke about her prior experience and successes at having done that—including the parents, involving the business community, and her very strong commitment to professional development [for teachers]." A central office administrator believed that Niles's effort to present herself as a leader who could promote participation had worked. "I don't think there's any question that they felt she was a consensus builder. . . . I think at the time that's what this community needed. I think we needed somebody who could make people feel as though they were part of the project." Therefore, search committee members particularly concerned about the limitations of top-down authority considered carefully which of their candidates might engage others most successfully in new initiatives.

Is This Candidate Up To the Job?

There was also considerable recognition that the superintendent's job requires toughness, courage, stamina, and resilience. Here, too, a district's preferences were shaped by current circumstances or by the style of the prior superintendent. Glendale, where labor strife had heightened the board's attention to the need for strong management, hired a candidate whose style, according to one school board member, was "a better match, in the more aggressive style of management, than the other finalist." In Union, which had just emerged from receivership, the newly appointed superintendent, Clara Underwood, said, "They were looking for someone . . . who was not afraid to let people go who weren't pulling their weight, not afraid to speak up to the school board when it's needed, not afraid to involve everybody in the process, not threatened by any faction of the community." Although Underwood seemed confident that she possessed the needed strength, one principal was worried: "I don't know if she has that killer instinct. . . . I mean, you may not have to do it, but the folks have to believe you will. . . . Will she be able to swim in shark-infested waters? Will she be able to survive?"

The search committees recognized that the task of changing schools requires both compassion and tough-mindedness. They conducted their search with the belief that achieving a balance between these two characteristics was both necessary and possible. However, when committee members sensed a weakness in one area, decisions became difficult. For example, in the suburban district of Oakville, a school board member said that the newly appointed superintendent, Mike Ogden, embodied the values of the board—communication and understanding—and that he was the right choice. But the board member asked himself, " 'Should I have taken a stronger candidate?' Because there were one or two men in the group who

were stronger, but I don't think it would have been the right choice.
I think we need a Mr. Ogden here."

Assessing the Candidate as a Person, Not a Professional

In the end, the task of assessing a candidate as an individual was
approached intuitively by search committee members. They could
compare candidates' paper credentials according to objective criteria, but comparing their strengths and weaknesses as people was a
very subjective process. Committee members debated among themselves about the kind of leader their district needed. Most agreed
that, ideally, a superintendent should embrace local values; be able
to bridge differences within diverse communities; be bright and
broadly experienced by local standards; make a persuasive public
appearance, by looking good and sounding convincing; work easily
with others, engendering optimism among staff and confidence
among constituents; and be strong and determined under pressure,
doing what must be done for the sake of the district's children.

None of the candidates could offer all this, of course; thus school
board members had to carefully weigh their perceptions about the
candidates against their priorities for the district. In Newbridge, a
school board member recalled, "We got down to two finalists, and it
was a difference in style. One of the finalists was more lackadaisical.
When you visited his district, you didn't have a sense that there were
a lot of systems in there, but you had the sense that he really knew
his people. He sort of bumbled around. . . . The system was weak.
And at that point in time, given the surrounding circumstances to
the hiring process, and the strike and everything, it seemed that we
needed someone who was more systems-oriented and would move
ahead at a faster clip. . . . Anna Niles was that person."

In Summit, a principal reported that the two finalists had been
"neck and neck. The other one [who was not hired] frightened people." He was "too directive, too specific about judgments, possibly

too forceful about an opinion, a little too organized." By contrast, Wayne Saunders, who received the appointment, "seemed to be a little more laid back, a little more receptive. There seemed to be a feeling that one could work with him. . . . Truthfully, the school board did not want somebody to tell them what to do. I think they wanted somebody they could talk it over with—a discussion partner, if you will."

Many individuals' final votes turned on these sorts of subjective and undiscussed assessments. A school board member in Westford conceded, somewhat cynically, that in the end "you buy a guy and a style." Another respondent defended these intuitive, subjective judgments, however: "You look for a person who has compassion, understanding, ambition. . . . You cannot hire someone you don't trust and someone you don't respect." If you do, he added, "then you're being very foolish." Although many participated in the search, ultimately it was the school board that made the choice. One board member observed, "Whenever a school board hires a superintendent, it reflects that school board that hired him. I think [our new superintendent] was very much what *we* needed at the time."

Final Days and Decisions

As the searches moved toward completion after two or three months, many of the twelve districts encountered unpredictable events that stalled or sidetracked the process and oddly distorted the outcome. Sometimes the search process unraveled rather than unfolded. Favored candidates dropped out abruptly when job offers materialized from other districts. New, negative information surfaced about some, making once-attractive applicants suddenly unacceptable. Local officials used their political power to augment one individual's chances. Sometimes a hearty list of seemingly strong candidates shrank to a short list of two or three, none of whom seemed right. Reflecting on the selection in one district, a school board member said, "I think that he was hired because the other person was so bad." In another district, the short list of three finalists became a shorter list of one when one candidate withdrew and the board discovered that another had been fired from his previous job.

Such accounts lend support to the view that the search process, as it often transpires in this somewhat haphazard way, is not the best way to select a superintendent; it is clearly not orderly and rational. However, one can also argue that the process, with all its uncertainty, public scrutiny, political influence, and subjective assessment, is not unlike the job of the superintendency itself. And for all the unpredictability and irregularity of the process, the overwhelming majority of respondents thought that their district had made a good match in their choice. They had achieved that "goodness of fit" between the person and the context, which, though not always ideal, was usually perceived to be adequate.

Whether these new superintendents would meet their constituents' expectations over time is another matter. What is clear, however, is that the search and selection process is at once an approach to selecting a new superintendent and an activity of self-definition for the school district; each part affects the other. When it is an open process, it encourages many constituents with varied interests and backgrounds to engage in worthwhile dialogue and to influence the outcome of the search. Commenting on the presidential search process in higher education, Birnbaum (1988) states, "Regardless of the substantive outcome, search and selection is an important and necessary process. It provides people with a sense of participating in important decisions and thereby lessens the power differences in the organization. It stabilizes the organization and leads to satisfaction with the social order by confirming the myth that positions are allocated on meritocratic grounds" (p. 507).

By deciding whether the district is to embark on change, maintain continuity, or introduce stability, a school board assesses its past and charts a general direction for its future. By choosing one individual over others, a school board makes an explicit, illuminating statement about the community and its values. By achieving the best possible match between local needs and candidates' interests, strengths, and weaknesses, a school board can open the way for leadership and change. Jeffrey Pfeffer (1978) speculates that leaders' actual influence on organizations may be less than some expect because the process of search and selection limits the "styles of behavior" that are acceptable within the organization (p. 17). On the other hand, the process of finding a match between the candidate and the district may actually be what makes it possible for a new superintendent to lead. Several of the districts studied could have chosen more venturesome, free-thinking superintendents, but there is no evidence that a new administrator who is seen to be out of sync with his or her constituents can lead effectively.

However it is configured and however successful it turns out to be, the search and selection process creates the conditions for change. It sets the terms for a new administration, identifying both opportunities and constraints and suggesting how a superintendent will be expected to lead in the local context. One of the earliest expectations that many newly appointed superintendents face is to define a vision for change. In responding to that challenge, the superintendents described in this book had to decide how best to pursue their educational goals and values within the particular context of their district. This challenge and the decisions it precipitates are the subject of the next chapter.

Part Two

. . . .

Educational Leadership

3

Crafting a Vision

Vision is the sine qua non of today's successful leader, and the newly hired superintendent is no exception. This was not always the case, as Anna Niles pointed out: "Ten years ago, if you talked about vision, they put you in a white coat and took you away. Now if you don't have a vision, they won't even talk to you." Superintendents today, awash in others' hopes for leadership, are expected to formulate educational visions that will inspire and guide constituents as they set out to improve their schools. Bennis and Nanus (1985), who characterize vision as "a target that beckons," explain: "To choose a direction, a leader must first have developed a mental image of a possible and desirable future state of the organization. This image, which we call a *vision*, may be as vague as a dream or as precise as a goal or mission statement. The critical point is that a vision articulates a view of a realistic, credible, attractive future for the organization, a condition that is better in some important ways than what now exits" (p. 89).

The Need for a Vision

Ronald A. Heifitz and Riley M. Sinder (1988), noting the popular demand for vision making today, observe, "It would be quite unleaderlike, according to conventional wisdom, not to come up with any solution at all" (p. 183). In commenting on similar expectations for

college presidents, Richard Chait (1993) observes ironically that
the "new mode" in leadership calls for visions to be "compellingly
attractive views of the future that stir wonderment ('Why didn't I
think of that?') and galvanize support ('Let's get going!')" (p. B-1).

The twelve superintendents in this study did not dispute the
need for school leaders to have vision, but they did not necessarily
have grand expectations of what that vision should be. Dick Fitzgerald, superintendent of the small district of Fernwood, believes the
term "vision" is often overrated. He quipped dryly, "People who
have visions are prophets." Yet, he still argued that it is "critical"
that superintendents formulate visions: "Whether you want to use
the word 'vision,' whether you want to use 'philosophy,' even
whether you want to use 'plan,' I think that somebody has got to
have a sense of what schools should be trying to do." Competing
demands and contradictory prescriptions besiege public educators.
A clear and worthy vision coupled with a coherent plan for change
can focus the efforts of teachers, administrators, and citizens as they
set forth to improve their schools.

There is an important distinction between an individual's educational vision, which might be relevant to any district, and an educational vision crafted with a particular local context in mind. In
explaining their personal *educational* visions, superintendents might
expound on the importance of learning, espouse certain pedagogical approaches, or voice the conviction that "all children can
learn." By contrast, their *local* visions must be tailored to the specific context, defining change for a particular place—for example,
a superintendent might believe teaching and learning should take
place in the museums, courts, and libraries of the district; parents
should become partners with teachers; or resources should be targeted more directly and consistently at classrooms.

The constituents in all twelve districts expected the new superintendent to begin his or her job with a strong educational vision,
encompassing such things as why learning matters, who is entitled to
first-rate schooling, and what kind of learning environment a school

should provide. By the second year, though, they wanted to know how that vision would inform their efforts to improve their schools, what the superintendent's vision for their particular district was.

Bennis and Nanus (1985) say that "with a vision, the leader provides the all-important bridge from the present to the future of the organization" (p. 90). Although these superintendents would likely agree, they were more confident about stating their personal visions than about explaining how might provide such bridges in their own districts. Successful educational leadership depends on grounding one's personal values in context and expressing them in practice.

When asked to talk about their superintendent's vision, some constituents responded with confidence. One central office administrator in Oakville said, "His vision is of a school district that puts the child first." By contrast, constituents in other districts were unsure what their superintendent's vision was. A teacher in Summit searched for a response when asked whether the district's new superintendent had vision: "I think he does and I hope he does, but don't ask me what it is. Well, I think it's important, for one thing, to have vision. It's important to me, and I would like, since I seem to like him as a person and like the way things are going here—I guess I am hoping that he does. In speeches that I have heard, I think he certainly seems to. Don't ask me what it might be."

Teachers and administrators seek to understand their superintendent's vision in part because they truly want to contribute to its realization. A worthy vision orients constituents, enabling them to organize their joint efforts. A central office administrator in Fernwood asked Dick Fitzgerald about his vision. Wary, perhaps, of presuming to be prescient, Fitzgerald responded that he didn't have one. The administrator demurred: "You do. You just don't know it." Vision was very important—"paramount"—to the administrator; he wanted the superintendent to have one, and he wanted to know how he could help him achieve it. Others were concerned more about the practical impact of the superintendent's vision on their work. Since they assumed that every new superintendent's plan sought to incorporate expectations for constituents, they wanted to know what was in store for them, what their new obligations would be.

When superintendents did not explain their visions, constituents often tried to infer them. In Westford, for example, Superintendent Thomas Wells's early plans for change focused primarily on school board operations, leaving teachers and administrators uncertain about what was expected of them. One said, "So, I'm trying to figure where he's going. I really don't know." Another echoed, "I would hope that, as time goes on, he sets some agenda. People are waiting to see what direction he wants to go in." A third ventured a guess: "I may be totally wrong on this, but I think he wants to see education work for everyone." A principal observed, "If I was the superintendent, I'd want everyone to know, 'This is where we're heading, gang.'"

It might seem from these comments that all constituents sit waiting for a new leader to tell them what to do. But, as one Clayton principal explained, he and his colleagues were not "bereft of goals" themselves. Rather, they and their counterparts in the other districts hoped the new superintendents would bring direction to their often disparate efforts and suggest where they should best invest their resources. They also looked to their superintendent for reassurance that their district was moving ahead rather than standing still or falling behind. One Oakville principal explained, "It's very true. Times are changing, and we need somebody in the know in the driver's seat."

Crafting a Vision

Situating a Personal Vision in the Local Context

Given these expectations, how does a newly appointed superintendent, arriving in his or her new district with a personal vision for education and nascent views about what the local schools need, fashion a vision that works for those people and that place? Ronald Heifitz asserts that "leadership is not simply thinking that one has a vision everyone is supposed to buy into. It requires stepping back and finding values among competing points of view, and trying to orchestrate a process whereby these competing points of view begin to clarify a vision that provides guidance and direction" (quoted in Bolman and Deal, 1994, p. 84).

Of the twelve superintendents studied here, only Arthur Holzman of Highboro said his personal vision remained virtually unchanged after he assumed his new post. This seems to have been possible because the district he left served a community with expectations and needs that were very similar to Highboro's. Three of the other superintendents recrafted their visions in response to information they gathered about their new districts before they were appointed. The remaining superintendents who formulated new visions did so after extensive exchange and interaction with people in the schools and community. There was, then, a continuum, ranging from individually conceived to collaboratively conceived visions.

Holzman's personal vision was composed of three core values—respect for human differences, the centrality of the classroom, and the importance of collegiality—and he was committed to infusing the schools of Highboro with all three. In explaining "the centrality of the classroom" to the press he said, "The hardest job in the world is teaching a classroom. If you understand that, the whole school system has to be focused on helping a teacher do all he or she can in a classroom of kids. That's what my job is. Anybody who's not in the classroom and is being paid by the public schools is there to support the classroom effort." Holzman introduced his core values to the community during the search process, explaining to the interviewing committees and school board "what I believed and what I wanted and what I felt was important—and what I was willing to do." If the community didn't accept his personal vision as the vision for change in Highboro, he said that he would withdraw his application: "I wasn't willing to compromise what I wanted to do or to sell it in any way that was anything less than forthright." Dismayed by the impersonal, bureaucratic style of their prior superintendent, the search committee actively sought an individual committed to such principles. They were convinced that these core values could reorient and revitalize Highboro, and so Holzman's personal vision fit the local context from the start.

While Holzman's vision remained constant from one place to the next, Clara Underwood developed a new vision, specifically formulated for improving the schools in Union, while she was applying for the job. It was a personal process, though: "I knew what the district needed, and my vision was not shaped by anybody but me." Throughout she was guided by her own deeply held values about equal opportunity, the importance of high standards, and the power of learning. Having investigated the state of education in this urban district, she discovered that the children were "completely ignored," that standardized test scores had been steadily going down, that "there was a lot of trouble with the school board," and that there was a tremendous number of immigrant children in the district. Consequently, her vision included making sure every child was provided an education that met his or her needs, interests, and abilities; emphasizing enrichment rather than remediation; making parents partners in their children's education; and making Union the best district in the county.

Other superintendents relied on colleagues and constituents in developing their local visions. Anna Niles, the new superintendent in the small town of Newbridge, organized a strategic planning process, involving members of the school department and the community in an array of committees. She planned on having the vision for her superintendency in Newbridge emerge from this planning process. Mike Ogden visited schools and classrooms in suburban Oakville during his first months on the job and reported regularly to the board on what he found. He encouraged teachers, administrators, and parents "to reveal themselves, to share their dreams, their goals, their expectations." Upon entering the district, Ogden said he was unwilling to "articulate strategic plans" and "itemize objectives," because "education's always a rough draft, and you're always revising it. . . . There are so many forces that cause you to change and to adjust." After six months of visiting schools, talking with constituents, and deliberating about the meaning of what he had seen and heard, Ogden described the vision he saw emerging for Oakville. He emphasized that he did not "claim any special ability to read the future," and he affirmed that "leadership is a shared experience. If we rely on a few people in designated positions to provide all the leadership, we cannot progress as much as we can if we unleash the leadership potential of everyone in the organization. A school system is already very different than many other organizations in that it really is a collection of leaders. Teaching is a leadership experience."

Ogden set forth a list of "directions for the future," so named because he intended for them to be "discussed with and responded to by a wide variety of interested parties." His "directions" called upon educators in the district to commit themselves to teaching for lifelong learning, to address the needs of the district's early adolescents, and to review the district's current structures for teaching. Throughout Ogden stressed the collaborative nature of the inquiry he proposed: "If the directions remain only mine, they will not work. They can only have an effect if they are reviewed by others, thought about, argued, and discussed so that the dialogue can lead to a better future for our students."

Building a Practical and Purposeful Vision

In translating a personal vision into one that is meaningful in context, the superintendents considered their districts' history and current needs, the character of their communities, the structure and culture of the school organizations, as well as the formal and informal authority inherent in their new position. By defining a vision that was responsive to the local context, each superintendent could better ensure that his or her vision was both fitting and feasible.

From their constituents' perspective, a meaningful vision had to set a direction about something educationally important, it had to be realistic, and it had to have clear implications for action. Visions were not all perceived to be equal or regarded as worthwhile. Several were vague and called for no more than an emotional endorsement of change; others seemed to celebrate the status quo; yet others were well beyond reach. In his "Blueprint for Excellence," Ben Moreno proclaimed, "We have the capacity and the will to make Millsburg the first city in the nation with an effective school system." Constituents said that Moreno often promised to make Millsburg "the best in the nation" or "the number one school district." Although many marveled at his enthusiasm, the vision did not strike many as achievable. One principal said wryly, "I think that's being very optimistic." John P. Kotter (1992) offers this comment on such unrealistic expectations in the private sector: "When a company that has never been better than a weak competitor in an industry suddenly starts talking about becoming number one, that is a pipe dream, not a vision" (p. 19). When teachers and principals judge their superintendent's vision, however noble, to be unrealistic, they give it halfhearted support, at best.

By contrast, Dick Fitzgerald, personally confident about the power of education to change lives, was not satisfied with students' aspirations in the small working-class town of Fernwood: "Part of our vision has got to be to show kids what's out there, . . . to get them to think about greater possibilities." He faulted the community for having low expectations of its schools and its children. He said the people in Fernwood believed "things are okay the way they are. . . . 'It's good enough for my kids, good enough for my parents, and good enough for me.'" In response, Fitzgerald said Fernwood's schools must at least increase opportunities, if not raise expectations: "If youngsters want to go to vocational school, who am I to say they shouldn't go there? But I don't want them to go there because it's preordained from the time they enter kindergarten that their option is to go to vocational school. So, I think we've got to broaden the menu without denigrating the world of work."

Therefore, Fitzgerald said his vision would involve increased opportunities rather than "getting 80 percent of our kids into selective colleges." The latter goal, he stressed, would simply be "a flop, a failed vision. And no one wants a vision that doesn't work." A realistic vision, on the other hand, could make Fernwood "a place where kids' abilities get challenged," a place where kids "have a sense that they can be a lot of things" and where the schools "challenge them to be more than their parents, [to] see options that their parents don't see."

Constituents also expect a superintendent's vision to be more than a planning process or a collection of unrelated goals. Wayne Saunders in Summit said that goals were not enough: "Goals should operationalize vision. . . . If you do not have vision, your goals will not have the value [they would have] if you did have a vision." In the multiethnic city of Westford, where Thomas Wells contended with urgent problems in bilingual education and the special needs program, respondents did not see his efforts as part of a coherent vision. A principal there, who acknowledged that the superintendent was "addressing what are perceived to be problems in this community," still looked for a broader set of purposes: "No, there is no plan. I don't see a new plan. I don't see a new vision."

Constituents commend visions that they think will lead to constructive changes in educational practice, and they are wary of lofty, hollow pronouncements. In his "Superintendent's Entry Plan," Mike Ogden said, "Our true purpose as a school system is to make it real that every child can learn. It is not our fundamental purpose to separate those who can from those who cannot. If a child comes to us with a disability—physical, emotional, social or motivational—we need to devise instruction that overcomes that disability. We owe that to the child and to the society which needs his or her contribution." Constituents widely praised his message. One principal said,

> It's not a lot of words. I've seen things that are put out
> by districts, their philosophy, their goals—they'll call it
> a vision or the cutting edge or the Year 2000, all that

kind of stuff. He doesn't deal with something that has such little substance to it. His vision is grounded in reality, and it's moving at a pace that's going to make something really happen. We've got good, specific, tangible goals that will take us from point A to point B. And if I were to describe Mike's vision, it's to make sure that that never stops and that we never, any of us, ever leave our own quest for knowledge and our enthusiasm for what we're doing.

In general, respondents believed that a good vision focuses a district's energy on constructive change and brings conceptual coherence to the independent efforts of teachers and administrators in all schools. A Riverton school administrator emphasized that, in conceiving a vision, it is the superintendent's responsibility to direct attention to important educational issues: "The educational issues may never get discussed while political decisions are being made. I think that this is the teaching mission of the superintendent, to conceptualize the educational issues so that people can address them." She believed, however, that the superintendent's vision must realistically reflect the potential of the district: "The great skill of the prophet is not so much in looking into the future but in penetratingly viewing the present." The leader must be able to see, she said, "what kind of flowers will bloom from this plant." An effective leader recognizes and articulates opportunity within context. Clayton's Andrew Cronin agreed: "The vision is being able to capture what's really a potential in the system, what they need. . . . The vision is getting it and then being able to articulate it—and then being able to get financial and program support for it." When leaders' visions are meaningful to constituents, they are well grounded in the present and reach out toward an achievable future.

Superintendents find that, as they craft their visions, prior superintendents' actions constrain what they can do. When there has been a rapid succession of superintendents who each pursued a different vision, new superintendents find they are obliged to propose partial and gradual rather than rapid and radical changes. They must seek to maintain constituents' support by emphasizing continuity and linking new initiatives with past ones. Andrew Cronin, for example, decided not to change Clayton's annual goals, set by his predecessor, and he consequently won the praise of a district administrator: "There's a lot of concern here with superintendents who don't stick with goals and who jerk people around. So it would have been a very bad mistake if he had thrown those goals out and started in a new direction that nobody was prepared to pick up and follow. It would have taken him until February to get any movement. I think he was smart to do what he did."

In addition to thinking about the context of the community and school organization, the superintendents in the twelve districts studied had to face fiscal constraints that prevented them from including in their visions all that they thought their districts needed. A school board member in the urban district of Union said of Clara Underwood: "She's limited by the nature of the budget cuts, the nature of her power structure, as to how much she can gain, how far she can reach into the future."

For most superintendents, therefore, personal values and goals for education are but a starting point for developing a locally relevant vision. Often these require compromise and adjustment before constituents will take them seriously, and superintendents must struggle to decide whether and how to make concessions. Suburban superintendent Ogden reflected on the constraints he faced: "So I find myself navigating between those goals and dreams and hopes that you would have for a school system, and dealing with the limits and realities that are there." Andrew Cronin concurred: "You have to articulate visions you believe in. But you have to articulate visions that the community—the school community—is ready for, ones that make sense to them."

Not All Visions Are Created Equal (or Alone)

What is the appropriate role for a superintendent in defining the vision or agenda for his or her district? Heifitz and Sinder (1988) argue that individuals in positions of authority often feel compelled to assume full responsibility for leadership: "Constituents appear to want answers to their questions, solutions to their problems, security in their surroundings, and a sense that their individual activities are connected to larger purposes and thus are meaningful. And leaders have viewed leadership accordingly: taking stands, providing solutions, having a vision, and interacting with constituents by explaining, supporting, and ordering so that they feel part of the vision and secure in knowing what to do" (p. 183). While some of the superintendents studied moved quickly to provide such direction, others waited, watched, and listened.

The twelve superintendents can be divided roughly into two groups, those whose visions were independently conceived and those whose visions were collaboratively conceived. Ben Moreno, the urban superintendent who prepared a detailed plan for the district before he was offered the job, presented a vision that he developed on his own:

> I tried to, during the interview, paint a picture of my vision—that there was a relationship between the entire community and the school system; that the school system did not exist in a vacuum unto itself; that it represented the community rather than the community representing the school system; that in order for the city to become a viable place, a place of being able to do business and being able to live safely, you had to link up educational excellence; that you could not expect a working, viable community with a good quality of life, with jobs for people, if you didn't make an excellent school system.

As Moreno saw it, his role would be to "link the entire community around the issues of the schools." He was very explicit about what this would imply for programs:

> It was a very defined vision. I was very clear about the things that I felt had to be done to make that happen. So, I talked about site-based management. I talked about parental involvement. I talked about community-business-education relationships. I talked about focusing on the curriculum and changing it for the twenty-first century. I talked about assessment. I talked about the need for testing what we teach. I talked about getting the school to be responsible for its own destiny as a unit. I talked about the function of the central office, being more of a provider of services and resources than a monitor of what people said they were going to do. I talked about a centralized vision being implemented with individual vision, so that I made it clear that the central office was responsible, with the community, for setting the goals and standards that it wanted the rest of the school system to be held to.

Moreno believes that he might not have been appointed if he had been less assertive about his plans: "So, that was the picture that we painted for them, and that's what I think got accepted, and ultimately [it was] why I came." Though Moreno defined his vision for Millsburg on his own, those hiring him believed that the vision matched their district's needs.

This purposeful, solo approach contrasted sharply with that of Andrew Cronin, who worked collaboratively to develop his vision for Clayton by creating an initiative called "Agenda for the '90s," a districtwide effort headed by a diverse steering committee of thirty-five, including educators, parents, and other community members. In preparing the charge to this committee, he drew up a six-page document identifying four areas of focus for the next five to six years, including academic excellence, equity, instruction, and community relations. Cronin explained that it was "the superintendent's responsibility to communicate two things. Number one, the assessment of the major priorities in the system. And two, his thoughts on the directions the school system should go. So, then, to bring people together, to share this with them, and say, 'This is what I've seen. This is what I see as our needs. I want you, as a group, to take this to review it. To consider it. But only use it as a point of departure in developing a long-range plan for your future.'"

A principal corroborated Cronin's account:

> He ran several drafts of that [document] by the principals. He's very careful to do that, gets the feedback before he finalizes something, . . . and he gave a very inspiring charge in the first meeting to all thirty-five or forty of us that were there. He just spoke for ten to fifteen minutes about his ideas and what he wanted the committee to do, and then [he] left. And he said, "I'm going to leave the meeting to you," and it was well done. He gave us a sense that he was with us, but he wasn't going to get in our way, and he was very careful to say that the five- to six-page document was just a point of departure for us to think about.

Notably, constituents in all twelve districts were skeptical about their superintendent's approach, whatever it was. They criticized leaders who drew up their vision for change on their own, because they did not rely on the wisdom of others in the district. Constituents also questioned whether those who appeared to plan collaboratively truly did so.

The superintendents faced trade-offs as they decided how to fashion a vision for their district. While they knew that creating a vision was a critical task for the first year of their tenure, they found advantages and disadvantages both in crafting a vision alone and in creating one with others. From the perspective of constituents, the *process* of designing a vision for districtwide reform appears to be almost as important as the ultimate *content*. Working alone appears to fulfill the managerial demands on the superintendent to create a clear, efficient plan that can be rapidly implemented, while collaborating with others satisfies political demands to seek input and endorsement from a large and diverse group of participants. Often these two approaches seem to be at odds, forcing the superintendent to choose one over the other or create a hybrid of managerial and political strategies.

Independent Visions: Do They Work?

A few superintendents described the advantages of creating a vision independently. First, they believed that conceiving a vision alone allows the final product to be clearer and more coherent, less muddled by the inclusion of countless constituents' agendas. Such clarity enables superintendents to champion a focused set of purposes. Arthur Holzman promoted three core values in his district. One was "respect for diversity," which referred not only to the responsibility of staff to appreciate students' race, ethnicity, and class background but also to ensure that students of all backgrounds perform to high standards. Holzman explained that his willingness to raise the issue reflected a widespread recognition of its importance throughout the district: "It doesn't necessarily mean they bought it, but they understood the importance of this issue and the kinds of behaviors I was expecting that we as adults engage in to help kids understand why it's important to respect people." Ben Moreno also argued that a vision devised by a superintendent alone can foster comprehensive, wholesale change: "I don't think you can change piecemeal. . . . I think you need to attack. You need to find a way of putting on the table all of the issues up front and then finding a way of getting to work on all of the issues at the same time." Bennis and Nanus (1985), who found "no incrementalists" among the ninety successful managers they studied, noted the utility of such an approach: "These were people creating new ideas, new politics, new methodologies. They changed the basic metabolism of their organizations" (p. 23).

Second, designing a plan alone may expedite its implementation. Ben Moreno, who envisioned the schools as a centerpiece of the community's activity and investment, told the urban school board that hired him, "Don't invite me here unless you're interested in change, unless you're interested in doing some very different things." His early and independently crafted vision enabled Moreno to institute a number of significant changes in his first six months, including site-based management and vigorous business partnerships.

Nonetheless, independent visions and unilateral plans have disadvantages for the superintendent who hopes to build long-term working relationships with constituents and then count on them to exercise leadership in making the vision work throughout the district. Such an approach can create overreliance on the superintendent for implementation of district plans. When the superintendent creates a vision alone, constituents often believe he or she will also take full responsibility for its implementation. Ben Moreno recounted his constituents' expectations: "One parent said to me, 'We thought God was coming.' . . . There was a very high expectation of what I could do." Such expectations can lead to disappointment, as Newbridge's Anna Niles observed (also drawing upon religious imagery): "School boards always are looking for somebody who walks on water, and they usually think they've got them; then it's all downhill from there when they find out they don't." Heifitz and Sinder (1988) observe that all "a leader can reliably provide given such expectations is failed expectations" (p. 183).

By crafting a vision alone, superintendents may also inadvertently encourage an undue and unhealthy dependence on them for inspiration, insight, and solutions. Noting their superintendent's strong leadership capacities, constituents may see themselves only as followers rather than potential leaders. (Jay A. Conger and Rabindra N. Kanungo [1988] note that followers' dependence on charismatic leaders is weakened when the followers perceive "opportunities that could be achieved on their own" [p. 333].) Michael Fullan (1992) argues that a school leader should be an "enabler of solutions" rather than a take-charge visionary; he contends that "high-powered, charismatic" leaders who take charge of reforming the schools can be "blinding and misleading" (pp. 19–20). A high school principal in Clayton confirmed that phenomenon: "I have a lot of trouble with the word *vision* because it brings up the conundrum that people who believe in shared decision making face. If they say, 'My vision is . . .' that then eliminates other people's dreaming. If you believe that the school system should be the joint dreams of people, then it's somewhat antithetical for you to say, 'This is the way the Clayton Schools should go.'"

Ben Moreno, too, expressed concern over board members' passive response to his long-range plan: "I gave them the Blueprint for Excellence for their review. They didn't react to it. They said, 'It looks like a good document; let's go with it.' There's still some concern that they didn't develop it." Given the short tenure of many superintendents—one of the twelve studied decided to leave his district after only fifteen months, and a second was a finalist for another job during his second year—the district that relies on the superintendent to define and implement a vision may be helpless when he or she leaves. A leader who does not empower constituents to think through problems, processes, solutions, and obstacles may cripple the district's chance of sustaining future reform.

Third, a community's own vision for public education may not coincide with that of its superintendent. And while visionary superintendents aim to educate the community and move the district forward, a vision that appears to disregard the community's culture, ethos, and desires for its children may not be viable. Without incorporating the perspectives of constituents of different race, ethnicity, and social class and constituents with different roles in the district, a superintendent risks introducing a vision that does not truly reflect the community's thoughts and needs. One principal said, "I think we know what we're about, but it's unclear whether he shares that vision." The implication is clear: if a superintendent does not share in the community's vision for itself, he or she cannot succeed.

Finally, failing to solicit participation in the process of developing a vision may cause resentment, resistance, and backlash. Pressured to make rapid progress in reforming the schools, superintendents may send the symbolic message that progress is more important than process. Constituents who have their own agendas, those who believe that democratic participation is the linchpin of public education, and those who simply want to feel they are a part of the process often judge superintendents by the respect they demonstrate for the ideas of staff and the community. If dissatisfied, constituents withhold support during the ensuing implementation process. Superintendents who impatiently exclude constituents from the process are often seen as arrogant, and their actions are thought to imply that the staff and community have nothing to offer. Cronin, whose district had a long history of participation by constituents, said, "Nobody takes anything from the top down. You must make a process, or you might as well forget it." Another superintendent described the resistance she encountered after presenting her vision for change: "Their standards are very low. So I came barreling in, like a bat out of hell, with all of these ideas about what we need to do. . . . It has caused all kinds of problems." One principal underscored the necessity for widespread community investment in school plans: "He might set wonderful goals, excellent goals that everyone might agree with, but because the people here didn't invent them themselves, they would have been all wrong for Clayton."

Keeping Constituents in the Circle

Despite the attendant problems, an independent vision can enable greater clarity. A collaborative effort, by contrast, can suffer from too many cooks. Incorporating diverse perspectives can enrich a district's vision or strategic plan and stem subsequent critiques; however, it can also blur the vision's focus and dilute its meaning. Anna Niles worried about where her many planning groups in Newbridge would all end up: "People are really taking those themes and running with them. Sometimes it makes me a little nervous." A principal from Clayton, where similar efforts were under way, said, "I fluctuate between being very excited about that and being very disappointed and discouraged. I just don't think it's focused." Collaboration can also cause inefficiency. A Clayton school board member wondered "if there wouldn't have been another way of dealing with their long-range planning. Everybody was trying to do the work. And so a lot of work didn't get done effectively."

Taking the time to listen carefully, promote debate, and encourage others to assume responsibility for proposing solutions may incite impatient demands for more decisive action, especially from constituents unpracticed in collaborative processes. Superintendents who await constituents' input may be portrayed as indecisive and lose the support of the community or school board. After a year of collaboration, Andrew Cronin said, "People were nervous because I wasn't coming on with a program. They hadn't had anybody say to them before, 'I'm going to collaborate with you. We're going to do it over time.'" Superintendents who develop a vision in isolation from their constituents may be criticized for being politically unwise; at the same time, however, those who try to create participatory processes may be faulted for being managerially weak, and their constituents may express dissatisfaction with the pace of change.

The severity of problems, especially in urban districts, also affects the political and moral pressure for rapid results. Collaborative processes may stand in the way of developing urgent, decisive responses. Ben Moreno's vision for Millsburg was that of a school district grounded in its community. But since he believed neither he nor Millsburg's children could wait for others to define a course for change, he mandated school-based management. Clara Underwood wanted all practices to follow from students' needs; therefore she quickly eliminated an activity called test sophistication, which she said was inconsistent with her vision. "Kids would just do mock tests all the time. . . . [The teachers] were doing things that were detrimental to the kids." She moved swiftly and unilaterally to end such harmful practices and to support activities that were consistent with her vision of a district that put children first and provided equal opportunity to all.

Superintendents and constituents who engage in collaboration endorse this approach for reasons both practical and political. First, just as individually designed visions tend to discourage leadership by others, collaboration seems to promote independent thinking and action. By involving a large array of people in the process of defining his or her vision, a superintendent ensures that those same people are invested in seeing the vision through and acting as leaders in its implementation. Thomas Sergiovanni (1992b), a proponent of shared leadership, observes that when teachers exercise professional responsibility there is less need for directive leadership by administrators: "The more professionalism is emphasized, the less leadership is needed. The more leadership is emphasized, the less likely it is that professionalism will develop" (p. 42).

Furthermore, a collaborative process ultimately helps the superintendent get feedback about the vision itself, as well as possible strategies for achieving it. Although Clara Underwood had formulated her educational vision for Union early on, she recognized the risks of continuing to be a solitary leader and encouraged others to join her. A teacher who endorsed Underwood's vision that Union should ensure children's development to their full potential said, "She realized that she couldn't do it alone, not only because she was new, but because she was one person."

In the small town of Newbridge, Anna Niles sought to raise standards for students and teachers alike. She was able to combine her personal vision with a collaborative process for defining reform strategies appropriate for her district. An administrator commended her for fostering broad support through collaborative planning:

> I think her vision in one word is "excellence." And in order to get to that position, I think her plan is to have lots of strategic plans, both systemwide and community-wide. I think her goal would be to make sure that every single student in this town is operating at maximum efficiency and that we provide those youngsters with the best education possible. . . . Strong community involvement is one of her big things—get as many people involved in the process so that you can build consensus. So, when it comes time for a recommendation, you have involved all of the constituencies.

While a few respondents dismissed Niles's effort as a political ploy, others, like this principal, said participation by a diverse group was valuable because it enriched the outcome. They saw participation as necessary because change in such a complicated organization cannot be controlled by one person. As the principal explained, "It's almost like you can't tell if it's her vision or a collective vision. It certainly has her imprint on it. But it really does have a sense of being collectively shaped and articulated."

Collaboration also gives superintendents an opportunity to search out and accommodate opposing views early on, thereby avoiding resistance at critical junctures. A central office administrator praised Dick Fitzgerald for listening to "the teachers and principals, the citizens in the community, and the activists to see exactly what their thinking is." He contrasted Fitzgerald's approach with that of a prior superintendent, who in developing a vision "would have put his brain trust together, developed a model, and then gone out and sold it like he was selling a car."

Finally, inviting participants to envision change signals to the district and the community that the superintendent understands both the community's stake in its educational system and the appropriate role of the superintendent in leading change. Public education's strong commitment to educating future citizens for democracy seems hypocritical in the face of an undemocratic decision-making process. What superintendents gain in expediency they ultimately lose in the form of weak commitment to the vision itself.

The Delicate Balance of Collaboration and Control

The new superintendents in the districts studied all struggled with competing demands. They all had to search for the right balance between control and collaboration, between their best judgment and others' contradictory advice, between the need for patience and urgent demands for reform. Superintendents who took strong positions and acted decisively usually expected others holding contrary views to voice their objections. Arthur Holzman said, "I speak in very definitive terms. I also tell people continually that my opinions are open for discussion. . . . And I will expect people to feel strong enough as individuals to raise questions and to challenge me. And if they don't, if they sit there and are quiet about something and are acquiescent, they're saying 'yes.' I'm real clear about that. If you don't say 'no,' then you've said 'yes.'"

Several superintendents described the ambivalence they encountered in trying to share leadership with constituents. Wayne Saunders in Summit explained: "People want leaders to be understanding and responsive and consultative. On the other hand, they want leaders to say, 'Here's what we are going to do.' And I'm getting signals that people here are looking for both." Although he was far more comfortable with a collaborative approach to leadership, Saunders had decided to act more decisively: "I have consciously been trying to do that this year, which is to say, to try to bring focus to a reduced number of objectives and to develop a sense of program and what I stand for, and to push for making decisions and getting movement in several major areas—school improvement, maintenance of funding for education, and central office reorganization."

There are no certain answers to the challenge of how a superintendent might best adapt his or her personal vision to the realities of the local context. Constituents want to know that their new superintendent has a set of beliefs about public education and how it should work. But constituents also expect the superintendent to be aware of where the district has been, to be informed about where those in the community and the schools think it should go, and to know what might propel or retard progress in the district.

Constituents in the communities studied rejected ready-made visions that did not accommodate local realities. If the superintendent declared what should be done, constituents wanted that superintendent to hear their responses. Clara Underwood drew up a vision for her administration when she applied for the job in Union. Soon after her arrival she squelched the program of "test sophistication," altered school assignments to better serve bilingual students, and formed teaching and learning teams in formerly fragmented junior high schools. If that were all she had done, she would certainly have generated resistance and provoked opposition; but she went further, soliciting input and offering help. Repeatedly, respondents said that Underwood was open and responsive to anyone in the district. She voiced strong convictions and acted decisively, but she did so with an inclusive style that won her broad support over time from her constituents.

Respondents criticized superintendents who encouraged participation and collaboration without stating their own priorities or convictions or who seemed to promote process without looking for answers or moving toward action. On the other hand, constituents were patient when they knew where the superintendent stood, what values and purposes were guiding their joint inquiry, what progress the superintendent thought they were making, and where their efforts might eventually lead. One principal said of Cronin, whose planning process extended for months, "I don't think he gets undue criticism for not knowing the end result of the play, because he says enough things that matter to him. I think people are understanding his values." When respondents discovered that their superintendent's values resonated with their own, they often suspended judgment and granted that leader time to discover the course for change.

Communicating a Vision

A superintendent's vision does little to promote leadership for better education unless teachers, administrators, school officials, parents, and members of the community understand it, believe that it is meaningful, and know what it implies for them.

In the districts studied, visions that were clearly formulated and deliberately promoted were the ones that constituents best understood and most fully accepted. Holzman was emphatic that his message had to be clear and comprehensible: "It's got to be a small number of things. And [you have to be willing] to stay with that small number of things over a long period of time. You can't change the goals every year and expect anything lasting." Holzman conveyed his message in the press; at school board, faculty, and administrative council meetings; and in conversations with staff and parents. As we interviewed constituents throughout Highboro, it was clear that Holzman had been heard, for they repeatedly cited his core values, often emphasizing or interpreting one or another. For example, his call for respecting diversity had prompted new attention to African-American students' academic performance. A central office administrator said, "I think his primary goal is to make sure that every kid, especially the disenfranchised, be it financially, racially, technically—I think it's his determination that every single one of those kids will get the very best that they can get in the system and that . . . everyone in the system is committed to that goal. He says it over and over and over. That's our responsibility. It's a mission; it really is. And . . . it's very clear, very simple when he says it. . . . And there's a zeal in him."

In Oakville, too, constituents confidently cited Mike Ogden's vision about the primacy of children: "He stands for the children and the best they can get." "He has the children of the district at heart. He makes that very clear and very obvious." "One goal, and he keeps saying this, is that every single child can learn." Ogden, like Holzman, did not rely solely on an annual speech or a single news story to convey his vision. As he explained it, "I talk about instruction wherever I go. . . . I try in every way that I can to communicate the message that the heart of the district is not the superintendent's office but is indeed the classroom, and that [in making] decisions, whether they were budgetary decisions or staff development decisions, or articulation of goals or anything else, that the classroom or teaching and learning was the heart of my concern."

This clarity and shared understanding sharply contrasted with the uncertainty and confusion expressed by respondents in several other districts, where superintendents' ideas never emerged as clear and compelling visions. One superintendent sought to raise school standards and students' aspirations. Another envisioned a school district with five partners in the decision-making process: parents, teachers, the business community, a nearby college, and the city government. A third wanted to promote a tone of "valuing, knowing, and supporting the progress of each child" within the schools. But the constituents in these districts seldom knew anything about the superintendent's vision, or if they did they saw it as a piece of a program rather than as a unifying or inspiring set of educational ideas. One respondent said of her superintendent, "She talks a lot about school culture, and yet, I don't really know what she means. I don't have a clear picture of what she has in mind for the system." Another concurred: "When I listen to the superintendent, I hear a lot of different things. I think sometimes it feels like rambling to me." In none of these three districts was there agreement among respondents about what their superintendent's vision was.

By contrast, constituents in Union clearly understood Clara Underwood's message, which she repeatedly explained: "Children can learn. We have the responsibility to teach them. There is not one child sitting before you in that classroom that cannot learn, and they have all different learning styles. You have the responsibility to find out what learning style this child has, and to teach them what they can learn within their style." As one principal said, "She's only about children."

Often administrators assume that a vision must be expressed with compelling metaphors or in catchy slogans. Certainly a strong symbol can enhance the message, but absent originality, clarity and conviction will suffice. The people interviewed were hoping for statements of purpose and vision that were lucid and forthright, ones that made sense of their district's past experiences, current strengths, and future opportunities—visions that told them un-equivocally and often what their superintendent's priorities and plans were.

But knowing the words was not enough, for sometimes con-stituents could repeat the lines of a superintendent's stated vision with little understanding of what it implied for them and their work. For example, Ray Garcetti in Glendale initiated Glendale 2000, a plan for improvement linked to the national goals of America 2000. He saw it as a vision for the next ten to fifteen years, extending well beyond his retirement: "The goal that I've set transcends the super-intendency, transcends the school board, but sets the direction for what we expect to happen for our young people." A few respon-dents, like this teacher, supported his effort: "The national goals are now this district's goals. He's not just running the school system by the seat of his pants, [saying] 'what happens today, I'll deal with it and whatever happens tomorrow, I'll deal with it.' He has put us on a course. And in my view that does show some vision." Many oth-ers, however, found it difficult to translate this vision so that it would have meaning in their schools. One teacher said, "He does [have a vision] on business community relations and Glendale 2000, but I have difficulty in seeing how that relates to everyday goings-on in a teacher's classroom. . . . So I don't quite understand how this Glendale 2000 is going to directly impact the curriculum and stu-dent learning." Another teacher said, "He had this chart with all the goals and everything. Of course, I just think it's what we've been doing anyway for the last thirty years." If superintendents want constituents to assume responsibility for making visions real, they have to offer translations for practice.

Perhaps most important, respondents also expected to see superintendents act on the principles and priorities embodied in their visions. A principal in Union observed, "The proclaiming of a vision is an ambitious venture. Living up to it is another." Mike Ogden, whose vision was widely understood and accepted by his constituents, argued that a vision "has to be witnessed by those people around you." Words, he said, were only a beginning, because "they have to know that what you say is what you mean, and what you mean is what you'll do." Ogden, who had proposed that Oakville educators review their tracking practices, modeled through frequent discussions with teachers and principals the kind of inquiry he urged others to undertake. Throughout the interviews, constituents confirmed the importance of witnessing a superintendent at work on a vision. A teacher said of Clara Underwood, "She's known to follow up on what she speaks about." Another observed that Underwood was closely involved with the weakest school in the district: "She's starting from the school that needs the most work, not wanting to sweep anything under the carpet. She wants to make this school the model school." A third said, "I see in her a deep commitment to children." When a child was shot outside one Union school, Underwood ran several blocks from her office to assist at the scene, an action that did not go unnoticed by teachers, principals, and parents.

What Works

By virtue of their position, superintendents—particularly newly appointed superintendents—have a special opportunity to influence constituents and channel their energy by explicating an educational vision for their district. It is clear from the communities studied for this book that constituents respond to educational visions that are clear and coherent, address important needs and respond to real potential, are shaped to fit the context of a district, and are championed by the superintendent, both in word and deed. Teachers, principals, central office administrators, and school board members listen for a new superintendent's priorities, not so much because they lack their own ideas, but because in the decentralized organization of schools, constituents' efforts to bring about change are often isolated from their peers'. A vision that is well adapted to the district's context can link such programs and initiatives, investing them with larger meaning and broader purpose. Moreover, in a world of ever-scarcer resources and ever-greater demands, those who work in schools invest their souls and time cautiously, knowing that worthwhile programs can be eliminated before the programs ever have a chance to succeed. Consequently, teachers and administrators look to their superintendents for signals about where best to dedicate their efforts. They search their superintendents' statements about vision for information as much as inspiration, for reassurance as much as rededication. Although the term "vision" may seem other-worldly to some, what constituents seek is really quite down to earth.

This is not to suggest that finding and expressing a worthwhile and workable vision is easy; it is, in fact, very challenging. It requires that new superintendents know and express their personal values and priorities for education, look and listen carefully to what is happening in their district, bring to bear relevant knowledge about research and practice, and help provide conceptual order to what may be nothing more than a collection of disparate programs and goals. Superintendents must find ways and times to convey their visions both orally and in writing, and they must demonstrate through their own behavior that they have taken on these goals as their own.

The development of a district's vision is but the beginning of the superintendent's responsibility for leadership, because strategic plans, community compacts, and pledges to educate all children mean little unless they extend to the schools and classrooms, where principals and teachers take them on as their own. The following two chapters further pursue these twelve superintendents' efforts as educational leaders. Chapter Four considers three superintendents who initiated reforms, and Chapter Five examines how a superintendent's educational influence extends through the district and into the schools.

4

Leading Reform

These are the days of school reform, the best of times and the worst of times in public education. New attention to the importance of schooling, increased interest in innovative practices, and sustained public commitment to change coexist with confusion about what works, disagreement about whether reform should be incremental or wholesale, and conflicting expectations about the appropriate pace of change. As we saw in Chapter Three, the visions and plans developed in the twelve districts studied were general ones that committed local educators to achieving higher standards, focusing resources more consistently on children, reconnecting schools with their communities, elevating the importance of teaching, and ensuring that all children, whoever they are, succeed academically and socially.

Whether those visions were developed independently or collaboratively, the school districts looked to their superintendents as their educational leaders, the individuals who would propose specific changes in local practice and give day-to-day meaning to these long-term visions. There is no shortage of solutions to choose from in the educational marketplace—service learning, authentic assessment,

An earlier version of this chapter, coauthored with John Verre, was prepared as an occasional paper for the National Center for Educational Leadership, Cambridge, Mass., in 1993. Material used with permission.

school restructuring, computerized instruction, incentive-based pay. A superintendent has to judge which of the many available reforms are right for his or her district and will enable it to progress toward realizing its vision. Which will truly improve children's educational experience and enhance their learning?

Research offers only partial guidance to those making such choices, and the experts claiming to have "the answer" often disagree. It is not clear whether or when to substitute computers for chalk, collegiality for competition, whole words for phonics, small schools for large schools, or portfolios for final exams.

Then there are important questions about process. How should such change be introduced and sustained? Should it initiate in the superintendent's office or in the schools? Is the district ready for change? Are the teachers prepared to champion the solution, or will they resist, reassuring each other that "this, too, shall pass"?

Any superintendent intent on improving the schools must not only carefully consider the educational merit of any particular reform within the context of the district's overall vision and plans, but also assess the needs of the district and the readiness of those in the schools to make reform work. The challenge of "leading to change" is complicated and uncertain.

Engaging others in change is especially hard today because so many teachers and principals have been numbed by a decade of urgency, blame, shifting priorities, and failed promises. These educators have seen reforms introduced in a flurry of excitement, only to be abandoned suddenly and supplanted by new programs requiring entirely different approaches to classroom instruction or school governance. No reform can succeed without the endorsement and energetic support of teachers and principals, who must not only change as educators but make change happen in their schools. The heady times of school reform have made these people cautious about sure-fire solutions and skeptical of outsiders who claim they have the answers.

The career paths and job requirements of superintendents further complicate their leadership challenge. Rapid turnover, particularly in urban districts, leaves teachers and principals even more skeptical about superintendents' proposals. Knowing that superintendents must make their mark quickly if they are to keep their jobs or find better ones, teachers and principals often resent becoming agents of someone else's career advancement. Fearing that rapid and visible change imposed by a new superintendent may lead to inchoate programs and wasted energy, teachers and others often become cynical and resist superintendents' enthusiastic plans to reform them and their schools. Thus it is essential for superintendents to gain the trust of their constituents. As one teacher in Millsburg put it, "I think that innovation, if wisely approached, can be done easily, if the superintendent has the faith of his coworkers. Otherwise there is resistance. People do not like change, I know that. But I think a superintendent has to win over his colleagues."

What do teachers and principals look for in deciding whether to commit themselves to new proposals for change? What factors determine superintendents' success as reformers? This study suggests that three factors make a difference. First, constituents must be convinced that the proposed reform is educationally worthwhile and locally warranted, that it provides promising answers to important problems. Second, the strategy for implementing the reform must be viable, taking into account the expectations and experiences of those in the district. Third, teachers and principals must believe that the new superintendent advancing reform is credible, trustworthy, and ready to see change through.

Three Cases of School Reform and Leadership

The following three cases explore these factors of successful leadership in educational reform. Ben Moreno, Anna Niles, and Mike Ogden each introduced a program, initiative, or goal designed to change school organization or instructional practice. The teachers and principals in their districts made it clear that, if these superintendents were to be successful as reformers, their educational expertise would not be enough. They also had to possess know-how about the process of change and provide evidence of their personal integrity and commitment.

School-Based Management in Millsburg

Millsburg suffers many of the ills common to small working-class cities in the Northeast. A weak business climate, high unemployment, and shrunken public resources have made day-to-day life hard for the city's largely poor and working-class population of 160,000. The public schools serve almost twenty-four thousand students, with five hundred new children moving to the district each year. The student enrollment profile is typical for this kind of increasingly diverse community—60 percent minority, 10 percent bilingual, 13 percent special needs, 52 percent low income, and 33 percent from single-parent homes. During the course of this study, the dropout rate remained at 36 percent for two years in a row. The per-pupil expenditure for fiscal year 1988 was $3,400, lowest of all cities in the state and well below the state average of $4,200.

After a national search, Ben Moreno was hired to bring radical change to the Millsburg public schools, and he wasted no time in identifying critical problems and instituting reforms. In his entry plan, Moreno delineated the vision, mission, and goals needed to carry the schools into the next century. He stressed the importance of equal opportunity for all students and expounded upon the benefits that greater involvement by parents and the business community could bring to the life of the schools.

The centerpiece of Moreno's reform effort was a decentralization plan that established school-based management in each of the district's forty schools. In each building there would be a school-based management team composed of the principal, elected teachers, parents, administrators, business people, and other community members. Central office administrators developed a training manual and, with the support of the teachers association, conducted a two-day workshop for 150 participants in school-based management. Eventually, Moreno promised, school-based management teams would have discretion in budgeting and program development. However, two and a half years later, only a few teams were functioning well. Many others were at a standstill, stymied by the difficulties of making site-based decisions and coordinating them with those of the central office.

New Respect and Responsibility for Newbridge Teachers

While maintaining many of the characteristics of a small town, Newbridge has both the advantages and disadvantages of a busy inner-ring suburb in a large metropolitan area. Thirty-three thousand residents live within the four square miles of Newbridge's densely populated, solidly middle-class neighborhoods. Though but a few miles from a major city, only 6 percent of Newbridge's residents are people of color. Twenty-six hundred students attend the district's five schools. Approximately 60 percent of graduates from Newbridge High enter four-year colleges, and 15 percent more attend two-year colleges or technical training programs.

In the first months after her appointment as superintendent, Anna Niles instituted an elaborate long-range planning process that included representatives of all segments of the community and eventually produced a strategic plan for the district. This participatory process became the trademark of Niles's administration. The resultant plans included an array of initiatives, such as new recognition of teachers' work, shared decision making in the schools, enhanced multicultural sensitivity, expanded parental involvement, innovative community partnerships, and management reorganization.

Establishing professional development programs and developing new roles for selected teachers in the schools were among Niles's early accomplishments. She established a professional development council that planned and operated the systemwide staff development program; she won approval from the school board to grant tuition for teachers pursuing additional coursework and release days for in-service activities; she created opportunities for accomplished teachers to serve as curriculum consultants; and she integrated professional development with teacher evaluation and curriculum review. Although these reforms were only some of those that Niles launched, they were clearly the ones most valued by staff and the most frequently praised in our interviews.

Eliminating Tracking and Departmentalization in Oakville

In a recent book ranking U.S. school districts, the Oakville Public School District was said to be twentieth out of the top twenty-five in the nation, with an "effective schools index" score of 86 on a scale of 0 to 100 (twenty-eight points above the national average). In the eyes of many of its forty thousand middle-class residents, Oakville schools deserved that recognition; with a per-pupil expenditure of almost $8,000, more than 80 percent of the district's graduates went on to higher education. Oakville, described in a prominent newspaper as a "village that still represents small-town USA," pointed with pride to its public schools.

Mike Ogden was appointed in the fall of 1990 to succeed a highly respected superintendent retiring from the district after holding various positions in the system over thirty years. School officials were pleased to find Ogden, an assistant superintendent from a nearby town who seemed almost like an insider. For the first six months of his tenure, Ogden studied the district by visiting schools and classrooms and talking with students, teachers, parents, administrators, and community leaders.

In January 1991, Ogden publicly presented his Superintendent's Entry Plan, setting forth recommendations for improving the schools. He cited "challenges" and raised "unanswered questions" about issues he considered critical. Among the practices he focused on were the tracking and departmentalization that existed at all school levels. Research and his own experience had convinced Ogden that tracking stigmatized children limited their chances to learn, and that academic departmentalization in the early grades focused teachers more on the subject matter than the children and consequently fragmented instruction. Ogden asked staff and administrators to review these approaches, stating, "Our challenge is to continue to examine our own ideas, practices, and procedures to see if they can be improved." Later he added that "If an organizational structure destroys a student's motivation to learn, we must change it." Committed to developing a collaborative inquiry and vision, Ogden urged others to join in reviewing the current practices: "If the directions remain only mine, they will not work. They can only have an effect if they are reviewed by others, thought about, argued, and discussed so that dialogue can lead to a better future for our students." Within one and a half years, tracking and departmentalization had been eliminated in the elementary schools and were under review in the middle and high schools as well.

Making Sure the Remedy Fits the Diagnosis

A new superintendent is presumed to bring educational knowledge and expertise to his or her district. Although a small number of districts hire generic managers to head their schools, most choose someone who is experienced as a teacher and school administrator as well as knowledgeable about curriculum, pedagogy, and school organization. The plans for change are usually left to these new educational experts, who must assess their new district's programs, consider their predecessor's legacy, identify needs and opportunities for improvement, and suggest changes that will lead to better teaching and learning. The superintendent's success as an educational leader lies in his or her working with others to make accurate diagnoses and propose sound solutions that people in the schools can understand, endorse, and undertake as their own.

Moreno in Millsburg

When Ben Moreno was appointed, Millsburg was perceived to be, at best, a second-rate school district. Many outside the schools, such as business leaders and politicians, thought the district was in dire straits. Test scores were below the state average, dropout rates were high, and teacher morale was very low. When Millsburg's longtime superintendent resigned, community members seized the opportunity to initiate change. The local chamber of commerce financed an extensive and ambitious search process, seeking an experienced reformer explicitly committed to change. A community member, active in school affairs, recalled the effort: "The school committee was looking for a new direction in which to take the system as a whole. The business community became very actively involved and very vocal with their concerns about the direction the school district was taking. We were looking for someone different." A teacher on the search committee agreed: "We were looking for someone who, in fact, would be an activist, a visionary, someone who would see these things and could move us forward." Search committee members judged Ben Moreno to be such a leader, and they were impressed with his confidence and directness.

Although the pressure for a dramatic change in leadership originated outside the schools with the mayor's office and the chamber of commerce, many inside the schools concurred that change was needed. One teacher observed, "We needed something to get us going, to shake us up, to make us aware of what was going on in education and what we were doing. We were very complacent." Therefore, when the new superintendent arrived, teachers, principals, and parents expected a new approach, even if they were not quite sure what that new approach might be or what it would mean for them.

Ben Moreno believed school-based management would decentralize the system, freeing the schools from the regulation of central administrators and enabling parents, teachers, and principals to join together in making the schools more responsive to students. School-based management promised to be a striking change from bureaucratic business as usual in Millsburg, where educational policy had long been centralized, educational practice standardized, and parents excluded from decisions about their children's schooling.

Although many thought school-based management might be good for Millsburg, it seemed foreign to the very people in the central office and the schools who had to make it work. Central office administrators were more comfortable regulating the schools than serving them. Principals were more accustomed to telling teachers and parents what to do than soliciting their advice. Teachers were more comfortable addressing children's needs in classrooms than assuming decision-making roles. Although many thought school-based management might be a worthwhile reform for the district, the district was not ready for it. Nor did people ever fully understand how a new governance system would improve student performance.

Niles in Newbridge

The Newbridge schools did not have severe shortcomings like Millsburg, but respondents repeatedly noted that they were behind the times. The prior superintendent had reportedly done little to promote new practices. After his eighteen-year tenure ended in controversy—a financial investigation and a week-long teachers' strike—one central office administrator observed, "He was a good man, but he was in crisis and had lost his grip on the system."

Constituents inside and outside the system strongly supported hiring a superintendent with a record of reform, but recent events also called for a peacemaker. A central office administrator observed, "Anna Niles was hired to become a consensus builder, to bring people together. We were just coming off a strike." A teacher concurred: "We needed a change. Anna Niles came along, presented a good package. [She was] a very capable person, nice reputation from [another district], and [she] came in as—what we saw as—a teacher advocate. She came to us as someone that wanted to help our teachers. You have to remember, we had a tough situation last spring. We had a five-day walkout."

Niles was hired not only to bring about change, but also, as one administrator said, "to calm the waters, to bring the teachers and the school department together again and sort of heal some wounds.

It would probably make teachers feel that they had a place, an important place, in the educational process in this community."

Indeed, the teachers were ready for new leadership. Although many had excellent credentials, the district had not sponsored staff development or encouraged teachers to develop new instructional approaches or participate in decisions about how the schools should be run. According to one school board member, "Our past problem wasn't that our school system was so poor, it was that we didn't have that level of confidence, partly because we didn't have a leader who knew how to develop it among those constituencies."

Many believed that Newbridge had deliberately suppressed initiative and held teachers in subordinate roles. A central office administrator said, "It was a very top-down system. If you had access to the superintendent, it was all well and good, but if you didn't, you definitely felt closed out." A principal who welcomed the new opportunities for teachers concurred: "It was a real sort of tier system, with teachers being really second-class citizens, vis-à-vis administration." Some of this respondent's colleagues, though, preferred the district's old-style, authoritarian management and were expected to oppose any serious effort to empower teachers.

When Anna Niles became superintendent, many in Newbridge were optimistic about the possibility for change. Teachers anticipated that she would be their champion, securing for them greater professional opportunity and higher status in the district. They believed that if they were granted respect, given opportunities to learn new approaches, and granted discretion in their work, education in Newbridge would improve.

Ogden in Oakville

While the public schools had their critics in Millsburg and Newbridge, virtually everyone in Oakville thought their schools were in excellent shape, and they could point to data supporting this belief. Although some respondents saw room for improvement, there was a strong sentiment when Mike Ogden arrived that the schools were successful and that no major change was needed. A central office administrator observed, "We had a very high-level instructional program going on. And that means Ogden did not have to come in and accomplish a great deal in those areas." Many believed that the school board had sought and found in Ogden a clone of their much-beloved, retiring superintendent. He was welcomed with goodwill, but only modest expectations about what he might initiate; his mandate was to ensure continuity of past practices. But despite the prevailing wisdom that the new superintendent should simply maintain a successful school system, some did acknowledge that things could be better. For example, one school board member said that the district was looking for "someone who would be progressive and continue to look for a means of improving the school system—a fine line to walk."

Though most in Oakville thought their district exemplary, Ogden did not think all was well. As noted above, he especially objected to the district's practice of tracking students and departmentalizing subjects in the elementary schools. But given the community's satisfaction with Oakville's schools, Ogden's proposed reviews of these practices seemed, at first, unnecessary and perhaps even unwise.

Different Histories, Different Needs

These three districts presented distinctly different educational needs, and their new superintendents responded with notably different reforms. Having long endured bureaucratic regulation, the professionals and parents in the Millsburg schools would be empowered by Ben Moreno to define their children's learning needs and shape school practices accordingly. Following a period of professional neglect and labor strife, Anna Niles became a proponent of increased professional recognition and growth for teachers. In Oakville, Mike Ogden found a solid but somewhat complacent district where changes in tracking and departmental organization might well have been warranted but constituents did not expect to have their tried-and-true practices disrupted. The new superintendents in Millsburg and Newbridge entered contexts where the constituents thought reform was needed but past practices constrained their ability to effect change. In Oakville, Ogden entered an apparently successful district where few recognized the need for change, thus introducing the possibility of resistance to reform from the start. It was within these three contexts that the superintendents crafted their approaches to change.

Developing a Strategy for Change

There is an obvious and important distinction between a reform initiative and a strategy for implementing it. For example, there are many ways for a superintendent to introduce alternative types of assessments, ranging from mandating the change in a memo to encouraging staff to attend conferences about portfolios or demonstrations. Constituents in all twelve districts emphasized that they pay attention to *how* a superintendent advances a reform—and that a superintendent's approach is central in determining the success or failure of his or her initiatives.

Moreno in Millsburg

Ben Moreno recalled having carefully considered his strategy for introducing school-based management in Millsburg: "This is September 18th, and you're brand new. Now, how do you go about changing a system into having site-based management? Do you say, 'Let's talk about it, folks,' or do you say 'This is what we're going to do'? That's a very hard decision to make. . . . So about a week after I was here, I told the folks that this is what we're going to do, . . . that the constituency would have a say in site-based management and decision making, but I was not giving them the option as to whether they wanted to do that or not."

The fact that Moreno initiated school-based management—a decentralized, democratic, participatory reform—in a top-down managerial way did not, as some might expect, antagonize the district's teachers and administrators. From the constituents' perspective, that was the way things were done in Millsburg. Past experience provided no precedent for bottom-up reform. Constituents did, however, think that Moreno might have benefitted from listening to them more closely. One teacher said that he and his colleagues had anticipated big changes and figured that they might not like everything Moreno proposed. But this group of teachers had hoped for a greater say in the process: "They just feel that there's not any input from the people on the front lines."

A union leader agreed that others in Millsburg could have made important contributions to successful implementation if only the superintendent had asked them to advise him: "He is a fair person. He tries to do the right thing; there is no doubt. But I really do think that he absolutely disregards process." Another teacher said that Moreno did not adequately explain how school-based management would work: "I think he knows exactly where he's headed. . . . He's got it all in his head, but the rest of us haven't quite caught up to him yet."

Some respondents were ambivalent about the superintendent's fast pace of change, even though they had initially been attracted by his enthusiasm; school-based management was but one of many reforms under way. Still, some of those interviewed endorsed the intensity of Moreno's approach because problems in Millsburg were so serious. As one principal explained, "We need to move with the times in order to help us educate children to be productive and independent citizens, and I think he's adamant about that, and I see him moving in that direction and moving swiftly, you know, because time is of the essence." A teacher agreed, noting that people in Millsburg had not taken Moreno seriously enough when he promised reform: "He really did have the ideas. And he told everyone that was what he was going to do. He was going to come in and change things. I don't think anyone believed him. But if they did, they thought he was going to take baby-step types of things, and he's taking gigantic leaps." Another teacher was more critical: "I think right now he has too many goals. We were due for change, but I think he's going so fast now that everybody's confused."

Given the bureaucratic history of the district, some respondents thought Moreno should have given the transition to school-based management more sustained and systematic attention than he did. A union leader decried the lack of training provided by the district: "We put the site-based management teams together a year ago. There was no training. Training was promised to us. There was no training. The only training we got was the training the union gave them, because we came up with the money from our affiliates."

Others were troubled by the fact that central office policies and practices were not aligned with the new responsibilities assigned to site-management teams. These teachers and principals saw no plan for implementing the complex change. Some criticized the superintendent for failing to respond to their efforts to exercise new powers. One teacher explained: "There are people who were very excited about the site-based management in the beginning. But they put together all this stuff and they sent it down [to the central office], and nobody ever looked at it. . . . On the one hand, he said, 'Y'all come,' but when they came, he ignored them. So there's disappointment, there's disillusionment; he's lost a great deal of credibility."

Other teachers complained that central office administrators interfered with the new powers granted them under school-based management. One teacher described how his council's decision to change the lunch schedule had been overruled by the central office: "You can solve problems through your site-based management committee, and yet, all of a sudden, we get these directives that say, 'You must do this; you must do that.' This is what people are getting worked up over, because [the lunch schedule is] such a small thing, that [we wonder] what's going to happen with something larger."

A central office administrator, too, questioned how these differences would be resolved: "So there's site-based management on one hand where there's a 'shared governance' . . . an 'empowerment' of the local schools for certain kinds of decision making. And as a result of that, there's the movement of those decision-making functions from central office personnel [to the schools]. . . . People are wondering what [the central office] will look like." Critics thought Moreno should have anticipated the complexity of the changes he introduced. One said, "The problem is this: he does not seem to have a plan. He's got the entire system in his head. . . . He has a way of talking about the larger picture, and talking philosophically, but it doesn't fit with the reality. . . . Teachers have a tendency to be literal, and so they see these massive contradictions."

Support for the reform was uneven, and there was strong resistance in some schools. Although many in Millsburg believed that school-based management might improve education and were impressed with Moreno's determination, they also thought the reform would have been better received if the superintendent had recognized that people had to be prepared for change and more engaged in planning how to make it work.

Niles in Newbridge

Anna Niles pursued her goal of increasing the professional status and participation of teachers through a variety of empowerment strategies. Most of these were included in an extensive and detailed strategic plan that teachers helped her prepare. The superintendent held roundtable discussions with teachers, and together they planned a staff development program featuring teachers as paid presenters. The district partially reimbursed course tuition. Outstanding teachers were recognized for their accomplishments, and some took on new roles as curriculum coordinators in the schools.

In these efforts, teachers saw evidence of the superintendent's serious intent to recognize their worth, develop their talent, and involve them in reforming the district. But given the district's long neglect of staff development and the recent labor strife, many teachers were doubtful about the reforms at first. Niles saw their skepticism and made teacher enhancement and empowerment central to her vision. A school board member described the new superintendent's collaborative approach: "She began this program the first day she addressed the professional staff. . . . She has developed a professional development committee, which, of course, she had to work out with the union. . . . The work of that group involved going back to their buildings or back to their departments or whatever the appropriate structure was that they were representing and getting their input. So, she tried to reach deep into her staff to get their recommendations as to what they wanted to see for professional development."

In time Niles found broad support among district staff for the changes she proposed. Teachers were grateful for the new learning opportunities and ready to contribute their time and ideas to school governance. A central office administrator observed, "Anna has really done a lot with teacher empowerment. I think teachers feel they have something to say about what is going on. They have a commitment. They have some ownership to what has been done in the schools."

While this long-term approach to reform elicited a widespread increase in teachers' participation, there were, after a year, reportedly only modest effects on classroom practices. One central office administrator said, "I have seen instances here and there of change, or hints of change that have come from professional development activities. For example, there'd be a workshop on cooperative learning, and in one or two classrooms I might see teachers trying to practice some of those strategies and become involved."

Although teachers welcomed the new opportunities for staff development, participation, and recognition, principals were, as the superintendent observed, less sanguine about them. Niles said that, despite teachers' obvious approval, "there's a lot of resentment . . . from the administrators. Teachers are involved in making these decisions, and [the administrators] don't like it." It seemed clear that Niles's strategy, while winning obvious support among teachers, fell short of gaining full administrative acceptance during the first two years of her tenure.

Given the district's history of authoritarian management, any effort by Niles to introduce these changes by mandate probably would have been rejected by staff members, who supported the changes only as they became confident that the influence they were being offered was real. Instead Niles's strategy was embedded in an elaborate and detailed strategic planning process. When respondents were asked to name the superintendent's accomplishments, most pointed to the changes in teacher professionalism and staff development, but mentioned the strategic planning process and Niles's many other initiatives only as an afterthought. The goal of increasing teachers' professional roles by empowering them, then, was understood to be particularly appropriate in this district, where teachers had been discounted for so long.

Ogden in Oakville

Mike Ogden's goal of eliminating tracking and promoting interdisciplinary teaching was challenging for two reasons. First, as already noted, there was no perceived need for the change in Oakville. Second, the proposed reforms would likely threaten teachers who, having been told for years that their current instructional approaches were exemplary, were unprepared to teach heterogeneous, interdisciplinary classes. Given this context, if Ogden had sought to institute change by mandate he would have encountered intense opposition from teachers, principals, and parents. Alternatively, if he had chosen simply to provide teachers and principals with more freedom in the hope that they might change their practices voluntarily, he would have seen only scattered success, at best.

Ogden's goal, as explained in the entry plan he presented six months after his arrival, was to engage the district in examining the tracking system and proposing alternatives to it. Notably, he did not start by recommending that the district abandon its current practices. Given the widespread belief that he should not revamp the system,

Ogden's approach of gradually engaging teachers and administrators in reviewing the current system seems to have been well calculated.

Upon arriving in Oakville, Ogden spent time learning about the district and identifying its strengths and weaknesses. He deliberately chose to emphasize the strengths. A principal said, "He's not coming in and setting the world on fire with changes. You know he's not coming in with a host of new ideas, that he's not going to right all the wrongs of Oakville. He's coming in being very—he's affirming what's going on here. He's impressed with what's going on here, and it's not an act." A teacher concurred, saying Ogden "would have been very foolish had he run in and started, day one, putting his own brand on everything and changing things. I think he has chosen a very wise course."

Ogden's approach was to influence teachers' and principals' views about tracking and departmentalization rather than to use his formal authority to order a change in those practices. One administrator said that even this gradual approach of leading to change was hard for people to accept, since they "had been steeped in the idea of tracking for many years and [believed] 'if it's not broken, don't fix it.'" But people respected Ogden's knowledge about curriculum and instruction and therefore took his concerns seriously. A teacher described how Ogden influenced her beliefs over time: "When we first interviewed him, I was very much set on tracking; I believed in tracking children. . . . Mr. Ogden, however, felt very different than I did. And over the course of the year, he shared information with us, and we have now taken ownership of a new idea. . . . He kept telling the board that tracking sometimes works to the opposite of what you want it to and keeps children behind."

Although this teacher didn't initially agree, she kept her mind open to what he was saying: "And as I talked to parents, and watched things that happened in school, you know what? I started to take a new look." Subsequently, she told Ogden that she had changed her mind, that "if we expect a little more from children, maybe we'll get a little more from children, instead of expecting less." She credited Ogden with approaching the staff "in a very diplomatic way—a way of sharing knowledge and sharing the idea with us—so that I have finally changed to his way of thinking."

Some faculty members found the pace of change too fast and the prospect of abandoning old practices unsettling. In retrospect, Ogden acknowledged that he "didn't have a full handle on the teacher expectations or the teacher needs." He thought that he might have communicated his concerns and ideas more clearly and could have anticipated the anxiety caused by demands for new teaching practices. In response to these reflections, Ogden sent teachers to visit other schools where they could observe teachers of heterogeneous classes, and he sponsored workshops on interdisciplinary teaching. He also worked with principals to change the organization of their schools to accommodate untracked, interdisciplinary teaching. Again Ogden's strategy was to encourage administrators to assess their own practices rather than insisting that those practices be changed. Within a year and a half after Ogden's arrival, school and classroom practices in the district were notably different. Elementary classes and reading groups were all heterogeneous; elementary academic departments were being phased out. A teacher who enthusiastically supported the changes said, "We're not totally there, but we're on our way. We're definitely on our way."

The changes in the elementary schools were so widely discussed that teachers in Oakville's middle and high school began experimenting with the new methods. A cluster of middle school teachers started to team-teach, and there were instances of interdisciplinary efforts at the high school. Respondents said Ogden's focus on instruction had fueled these changes. A central office administrator believed that the entire endeavor had changed the views and practices of many in the district: "Since last spring, when the movement was made to change some of the grouping practices, or at least [when] people were made aware of the fact that we need to think about changes, . . . I've seen growth within the individual buildings. There is also more sharing between buildings."

Lessons from the Three Approaches

The three superintendents' approaches to change differed notably. Moreno mandated the creation of site councils, Niles empowered teachers to develop as educators, and Ogden persuaded elementary school teachers and principals to review tracking and departmentalization. Although Moreno's mandate meant that there were quick and visible results—councils formed and met—resistance to the reform arose when site teams were not granted the autonomy they expected and proposed changes collided with other district policies. Initiatives to empower teachers in Newbridge worked well, but they had limited immediate impact on school practices and left principals insecure as power and influence shifted. Of the three reforms, the changes in Oakville seemed to have won the greatest acceptance and had the most influence on instructional practices. Though Ogden moved gradually, his influence on instruction and school organization in the district appears to have been real and far-reaching.

Who Is the Person Behind the Reform?

When a new superintendent embarks on districtwide school reform, constituents weigh the difficulty of what they are being asked to do against what they perceive to be the credibility and trustworthiness of their superintendent. Is the superintendent well informed about their schools and classrooms, about educational practice, and about current proposals for reform? Has he or she made a serious commitment to their district? Does the superintendent respect constituents as individuals and professionals? Teachers, principals, and district administrators in the twelve communities studied watched and listened to the new superintendents to discern their values and assess their character. In the end they asked themselves, "Does this person deserve my support?" Thomas Sergiovanni (1992a) says that two important sources of principals' ability to lead are professional authority ("seasoned craft knowledge") and moral authority ("widely shared values, ideas, and ideals") (p. 31). If constituents distrust their superintendent or doubt his or her respect for or commitment to them, they may passively resist or actively defeat reform.

Moreno in Millsburg

Virtually everyone interviewed in Millsburg believed Moreno needed to be bold and determined if he intended to make a difference in the schools. Many contrasted him with the prior superintendent. One teacher said, "I did have considerable contact with the predecessor, and there is no comparison. We didn't have what we needed before." Moreno was widely regarded as an "activist" superintendent, and he was praised for the twelve-hour days and seven-day weeks he committed to the job. One respondent said, "There isn't a person in Central Office that works as hard as he does." People found his pace breathtaking, and having been deprived for so long of such energy and investment, they had great expectations about what Moreno might accomplish. They were convinced, too, that Moreno was knowledgeable about and experienced in current educational reforms. Many believed that their new superintendent's ideas could improve their schools, even if they did not know exactly how. Respondents were also impressed with Moreno's visibility in the community. He spoke in churches, met with the chamber of commerce, held televised speak-outs with teachers, and was regularly featured in the local media. He stopped by schools often.

Still, many teachers did not feel that Moreno valued them or recognized their potential contributions to education. One who criticized Moreno for "shooting from the hip" said, "From the beginning, he gave the impression that everything was wrong with the teachers." She went on to predict, "If he continues at this pace, eventually I foresee morale becoming low, because teachers do not feel that he is working with them; [they feel] that he is working against them. And in some cases, there's a feeling of hostility." Another teacher agreed: "Morale has gone down the tubes. People feel he came in and, yes . . . changes were needed, but it's like the city did nothing right until he arrived."

Faculty and administrators in Millsburg were impressed with Moreno's credentials and professional success, but they were worried and suspicious about his career plans. Few expected him to remain in the district for very long, and some attributed the pace of reform efforts to his impatience, a need to fix things fast and move on. One teacher observed, "It would seem to me that he would want to make a change so he could make a good name for himself, in the field of education. Maybe for a better job . . . I look at his age and I know he's got to make the change real fast. . . . So many changes so fast—it's like making up for lost time. You know, the big move has to come quick."

Some accepted what they believed was Moreno's professional ambition, while others were far more critical and worried. One teacher said, "My concern is that he's going to go to [a larger, urban district] tomorrow. And then what the hell happens here? I don't know. . . . If he walks away now, we're in serious trouble. I just can't imagine that." Bennis (1990) contends that an important leadership competency is "management of trust. . . . The main determinant of trust is reliability, what I call constancy" (p. 21). For the teachers and principals in the twelve districts studied, the possibility of turnover in the superintendency was a major source of distrust and insecurity.

In general, respondents resigned themselves to the likelihood that Moreno's stay would be short; Millsburg, after all, was not a big-city district. But constituents were reluctant to invest in Moreno if he didn't invest in them. Fullan and Stiegelbauer (1991) conclude that bringing about fundamental change in school districts requires "a leading superintendent with a term of five to seven years, followed by another successful superintendent for a further five to seven years, deliberately selected to complement and extend the work of the district" (p. 210). They further observe that "when a school district experiences frequent changes in its chief executive officer, it is virtually impossible to establish an effective change process" (p. 200). Convinced that Moreno had no long-term commitment to their schools and anticipating that the reforms he initiated might collapse with his departure, constituents were less willing to devote time and energy to making the changes work.

Niles in Newbridge

Although Anna Niles made her commitment to teachers obvious from the early days of her tenure, they were initially cautious about investing much in a relationship with her. There was no precedent for such support from a superintendent. A teacher reflected, "In the beginning, I think the teachers were more or less not too sure about attending these [strategic planning] meetings, because in the past it hadn't always been to their advantage to give their input."

Also, Niles's reserved style made some teachers wonder whether she was sincerely interested in their views. Over time, however, her actions confirmed her words. She was often in the schools, visiting classrooms and talking with teachers, who came to believe that Niles was there to learn rather than just to be seen. They were impressed with her obvious interest in their work. One teacher observed, "I just felt that for years it had been 'Do as I say.' . . . I don't particularly like living under that type of a rule. I think that you should be fair and consistent and I feel that that's the way Anna Niles is. She's very down-to-earth; she's open. I feel she moves among the teachers, which I did not see before."

Niles's readiness to take teachers seriously was welcomed by another teacher: "I think people wanted someone they could talk to. I don't think the staff perceived the superintendent as the kingpin. I think they perceived the superintendent as someone you should just be able to knock on the door and walk in and talk to, and say 'What do you think of this?'"

There was no fear, as there had been in Millsburg, that Niles might be an itinerant superintendent on the move to bigger and better places. She had long lived in a nearby community and did not appear to be looking beyond Newbridge. Niles's efforts to develop a five-year plan signaled her intention to stay at least that long. Having endured the stagnation of a superintendent who stayed beyond his time, teachers felt that Niles had made an adequate commitment to the district; they were prepared to work with her.

Ogden in Oakville

Few respondents in Oakville expected Mike Ogden to be as good as their prior superintendent. A school board member explained: "He came in on the heels of a superintendent who had the love of everybody in this district. The superintendent that was here was a man who worked here for over thirty years; as a teacher, [he] worked himself up in the ranks and became superintendent of schools." But constituents were impressed when Ogden exhibited virtues similar to his predecessor's. A principal observed, "Their educational philosophies may be parallel in some areas, in that they are open-minded people. They have vision; they have direction; they have leadership qualities and abilities." As time passed, many concluded that Ogden had superior strengths. Some said he was a more knowledgeable educational leader. A principal thought he demonstrated a "sense of curriculum, a sense of instruction, a sense of education, that far surpasses what [the prior superintendent] had." Another principal observed, "I think he is more academically oriented than the last superintendent. . . . I do not think [the prior superintendent] was as well read or as well versed. For example, we are really looking at whole language instruction—into thematic topics, into cluster teaching—and we're very much out of reading groups and departments and tracking and that kind of thing, which is a new way for us."

Ogden made a concerted effort to spend time in the schools, observing classes and talking with staff members. Teachers appreciated his efforts. One said, "He's a teacher's teacher. . . . I don't recall the previous superintendent coming in the classroom. . . . And I rather enjoy that he sees what's really happening." Teachers noted that there was a difference between a superintendent who visited their schools as a dignitary and one who visited their schools to learn. Another teacher explained, "Being visible doesn't always mean that a person's participating. But I think he's one to participate." Another concurred: "I can talk to him about classroom needs, district needs, staff development. . . . I have the feeling that he does truly listen. He hears what you're saying, and I think probably he'll use it if he can and help you with it if he can."

Finally, respondents felt that Ogden took them seriously. They believed him when he said that teaching and learning were at the heart of his concerns. Constituents were drawn to his optimism and his confidence in them. A school board member explained: "When you have a person in front of you who says, 'You're okay,' you want to do even better. And that's what's happening. And the people here are—they feel that they are appreciated, and they want to do better. You can't do things alone. And he needs that staff around him to accomplish those things that we all want." A principal characterized Ogden's leadership with words and phrases that echoed those of many others: "He's a collegial leader, in the sense that he doesn't just develop an opinion or an idea and throw it at people. He likes other people's opinions. He likes to be challenged on ideas. He's collegial. He's fair. He's open. He's honest. He sets the kind of leadership that is very approachable. I don't think anybody would be uncomfortable with him. . . . It also engenders a confidence. That's a good point, because he builds confidence in other people. He doesn't hesitate to tell you when you're doing a good job, or this was a great idea. He's supportive."

Ogden's knowledge about instruction, his active presence in the schools, and his stated confidence in those who worked in Oakville led the district's teachers to respect and trust him. Many suggested that their positive assessment of him as a person and professional influenced their willingness to question their own instructional practices. A principal described the enthusiasm for his leadership: "He's got a district that is extremely receptive to his presence. He's become an overnight hit. . . . He really has the opportunity to forge a path and lead the way."

Reciprocal Respect and Trust

All three superintendents were respected by their constituents for their educational expertise and their commitment to improving the schools. Niles and Ogden were more successful than Moreno in gaining the trust of district staff, largely because they conveyed their confidence that teachers could contribute to, rather than simply comply with, the reforms. Doubts about Moreno's intentions were further fueled by fear that he did not care enough about the district to see his plans through. Notably, six years later, Moreno continues as superintendent of Millsburg.

What Is the Outlook for Reform?

In simple terms, when constituents believe a proposed reform meets their district's educational needs, when they come to see that a strategy for change makes sense, and when they believe that their superintendent is informed, trustworthy, and committed to the effort, they will respond with support. If they conclude that a proposed reform is out of sync with the district's needs, a strategy is misguided, their opinions have not been sincerely solicited, or the superintendent is unreliable, they withhold their support. In some instances, confidence about two factors outweighed doubts about the third. In no case did respondents support or reject a reform simply on its educational merits. These were different times than the days of Spaulding. Good ideas, in themselves, never carried the day.

Although the factors that influenced constituents' responses in the different districts were distinct, they frequently interacted. In some instances, as noted above, perceived strengths in one area compensated for shortcomings in another. For example, the many needs of the Millsburg schools and the district's history of laissez-faire administration led some respondents to value Moreno's energetic determination and to tolerate his authoritarian approach and lack of attention to them as individuals. Oakville's ample trust in Ogden's character enabled teachers and others to reconsider what they long believed to be sound educational practices.

It is important to understand that none of these twelve superintendents thought the goal of leadership was to simply accommodate and adapt to the local context. To do so would have been to accept the status quo, and each was intent on change. Rather, each superintendent sought to alter the local context, and during the eighteen to twenty months these districts were studied, each did. In Millsburg, education was placed in the forefront of public attention, parents gained a new voice and greater access to policy making, and teachers and administrators felt new pressure to perform effectively. In Newbridge, teachers enjoyed greater status and professional opportunity, a new standard of excellence began to take hold, and there was a new focus on instruction. And in Oakville, teachers and administrators were increasingly open to progressive ideas, collaboration became more common, and beliefs about the value of high expectations for all students began to prevail. Each district was changed as a result of its new superintendent's reform efforts, and any subsequent superintendent intent on making change would confront an entirely different organizational context.

In order to introduce reform successfully, a new superintendent must interpret information about the district accurately and design an approach to reform that makes sense in the local context. What are the schools' strengths? Where are their most pressing needs? What has happened in the past? Who has power and influence? Who must be convinced about the importance of change and the appropriateness of any reform? What are the prevailing beliefs about what works? What are the structures that will make reform possible and likely? A superintendent who does not closely consider the current needs and past experiences of those in the schools is likely to be surprised when disregard, quiet resistance, or outright opposition defeat a reform effort.

Some of the success that these superintendents achieved arose from the match that was made during the search and selection process; constituents correctly saw these individuals as the right people at the right time for their districts. For example, it seems doubtful that Ogden's low-key, affirming approach would have shaken loose the firmly entrenched practices in Millsburg as quickly as did Moreno's confrontations and demands. Nor would Moreno's unflinching criticism of teaching practice have engaged Newbridge teachers in collegial staff development, as Anna Niles's steady support did.

These three cases illustrate why school-based change presents a complex challenge for any superintendent. The local context is always changing, often as a result of the superintendent's own actions (or inaction). Consequently, the chosen approach to reform requires constant monitoring and adjustment. Although mandates may work well at the start of an initiative, a shift toward collaboration may be needed to sustain the changes over the long term. Having altered the local context, the superintendent's approach to leadership must also change. Finally, every superintendent must attend carefully to constituents' changing assessments of his or her judgment, integrity, and commitment. Trust, never more than temporary, can easily be undone by doubts about a superintendent's courage in the face of political pressure, by failure to deliver on promises, or by rumors that he or she is looking for a new job.

In Chapter Five we look more closely at the leadership challenge superintendents face as they try to engage teachers and principals in reform. Successful school leadership requires the development of leaders rather than followers; it is an interactive process, never a one-person show. Teachers and administrators must become committed to making change work in their own classrooms and schools and to creating new opportunities for improvement. Responsibility for reforming the public schools cannot rest on one superintendent's shoulders, but one superintendent can be very influential in leading schools to change.

5

. . . .

Engaging School Leaders in Change

Most new superintendents hope to make far-reaching, positive changes in their districts. After all, school officials choose them because of their promises to enact educational change, stabilize a district in crisis, or enhance current district practices. Few of those selected plan to perpetuate the status quo. Superintendents in this study aimed to accomplish a broad array of goals—improve science education, increase parents' influence, decentralize school decision making, inculcate respect for racial and ethnic diversity, promote collegiality, raise academic standards—all changes they hoped would substantially improve the experience and accomplishments of children in their schools.

Achieving these goals was no simple matter, however. Ultimately, superintendents and their proposals are dependent upon teachers, principals, and others in the schools. One Millsburg central office administrator said of Ben Moreno's ambitious plans for reform, "He's only going to be as good as I am and the principals are and the teachers are. He can't make it work without principals and teachers. He cannot make it work." Teachers and principals must do more than comply with the superintendent's directives, for even faithful compliance with carefully laid plans is not enough to effect complex changes in schooling. Instituting educational reform is not like changing a factory's assembly line; central office administrators cannot simply issue new instructions, sponsor a training session, and expect teachers to make reform work. Because the details of a new approach are virtually impossible to specify for all subjects, grades, and classes, and because teachers must acquire new knowledge, skills, and attitudes if they are to succeed, the implementation of such reforms takes time, shared understanding, and earnest cooperation (Fullan and Stiegelbauer, 1991).

Therefore it is not passive compliance but active, collaborative leadership among educators that improves schooling. Once teachers and principals assume responsibility for change—reinterpreting their goals, redefining their norms, and altering their use of time—they are no longer dutiful followers. Rather, they have become committed leaders, acting on their own and in concert throughout the district's classrooms, departments, and schools.

Influencing the attitudes and practices of teachers and principals from the office of the superintendency is a challenging task. American schooling is decentralized, resisting standardization and encouraging variation from classroom to classroom and school to school. Moreover, a large proportion of any district's staff is protected by tenure, making teachers even less likely to cheerfully conform to centralized directives. In Ashmont, for example, where only 4 of 285 teachers were not tenured, Louis Antonellis could not rely on a strategy of handing down orders from the central office to remake classroom practices. Teachers and site administrators generally believe that worthwhile change emerges from classrooms and schools, not central offices. Many reject—or even sabotage—top-down proposals that are weakly related to classroom concerns or run counter to the generally accepted wisdom of practitioners. "Any movement, change, must come from within," said one Glendale administrator. "It can't come from up top. You can't say, 'We're going to restructure.' You have to get everybody involved in it." Therefore, superintendents who aspire to lead must find ways to engage teachers and principals. To develop a lasting capacity for innovation and improvement in district staff, superintendents must respect local expertise and confront fears of change with support and training.

Opportunities for leadership of this sort do not come packaged with the superintendent's job offer. Instead, after the official welcomes subside and superintendents set out to work with teachers and principals, they are likely to encounter polite skepticism about their motives and profound doubts about their competence. Superintendents quickly discover that the precisely drawn lines of authority on school districts' organization charts provide little direction about how to lead. And they realize that there is far more than physical distance separating the central office from the classroom.

How, then, do superintendents inspire such commitment and ready a district for new approaches to leadership? As we saw in the last chapter, only when superintendents prove themselves to be well-informed educators, wise change agents, and deserving of respect and trust do constituents seriously consider responding to their calls for change. But such commitment is not won in a moment. Teachers and principals may hope that a new administrator will make a difference in their work, but they do not count on a significant transformation in their school when a new superintendent comes to town. Rather, constituents have only modest expectations—that the superintendent will tend to central office business, ensure that the district gets the funds it needs, attend to building repairs, responsibly distribute resources to support good teaching, and protect the schools from undue interference by politicians and parents. In return, teachers and principals intend to carry out their duties—sometimes creatively, sometimes routinely—and meet their obligations. It is a transactional, unspoken treaty that those in the schools expect to make with any new superintendent, a treaty that supports the status quo.

Sometimes, though, superintendents, teachers, and principals move beyond such transactions, establishing reciprocal professional respect and personal trust, relationships that form the basis for collaborative leadership for change. The process of developing such relationships is gradual. Teachers and principals must first be convinced that their superintendent will work hard to provide the necessary conditions for good work in classrooms and schools—sufficient funding, sound facilities, adequate supplies, and protection from outside interference. If they are not convinced of this, they will ignore the superintendent's calls for commitment to larger visions and instead tend only to their own business. If teachers and principals are satisfied that the superintendent is a responsible administrator, on the other hand, they will look for more: Is he present and active in schools and classrooms? Does she respect and understand teaching? Does he make a genuine effort to engage them in new ideas about their work? Does she act in ways that deserve professional respect and personal trust? When superintendents move beyond securing the basics to working collaboratively with teachers and principals, they create collegial relationships that transform conventional school-district hierarchies into organizations where all can lead.

Encountering Indifference and Skepticism

While it may disappoint those who believe in the power of the superintendency to transform the public schools, teachers and principals in the twelve communities studied did not have great expectations about their new superintendent's potential influence on their work. An Oakville principal stated pointedly, "I am not looking to the superintendent to tell me what to do." Respondents often voiced hopes that the new superintendent would modestly improve the circumstances of public education or enhance their own working conditions. While constituents wanted to know what the superintendent's vision implied for their day-to-day work lives, they almost never sought direction from the central office about how to better educate students.

A surprising number of respondents regarded the superintendent as a necessary but somewhat distant evil who could be ignored, tolerated, or humored as necessary. One Westford principal observed, "In the seventeen years I've been in this building, teachers have never approached their work differently because of a superintendent." Skepticism abounded in the twelve districts about whether real change in the schools could ever emanate from the superintendent's office.

Much of this skepticism grew out of teachers' and principals' unhappy experiences with past superintendents, who had tried to reform their schools by setting new standards, imposing new procedures, or presuming to better measure educational outcomes. Teachers in large, bureaucratic districts resented the many administrators assigned to monitor mandates, and they felt far removed from superintendents, even those who might have initiated these reforms with good intentions. This is consistent with the conclusions of Leithwood, Begley, and Cousins (1992), who reviewed the literature on school change and reported that "current school-leaders most often see district administrators and the policies and procedures which they manage as hurdles in their efforts to be more effective" (p. 246).

When teachers in the districts studied did pay attention to requirements from the central office, it was more likely to result from a desire to protect themselves from inspection or intrusion than from a spirited support for change. Although the twelve districts discussed in this book were certainly not all large, impersonal bureaucracies, teachers often spoke as if they were. For teachers, the context that matters is the school, not the district. "What the superintendent is thinking about," one Glendale teacher said, "really is the farthest thing from our minds." A Clayton teacher echoed this sentiment: "People don't talk about him. They talk more about the school. . . . As a teacher, I never felt the superintendent was close to my daily teaching life." Yet another teacher, from Westford, noted that "teachers don't give [the superintendent] much thought."

Except in times of crisis or need, such as a school's losing its accreditation or the threat of layoffs, teachers rarely think about the superintendent's priorities. A teacher from Westford characterized the superintendent's influence as "rather generic." A counterpart in

Summit concluded that "the superintendent is in the distance." Usually such comments were stated with matter-of-fact indifference, but occasionally there was anger and contempt. One Fernwood teacher said he "didn't really give a damn one way or the other about what they pontificate at that level." Comments such as these, common among the teachers interviewed, illustrate how daunting a task superintendents face when they set out to meaningfully influence what happens in their district's classrooms.

The Primacy of the Principal

Not only do teachers feel distant from the superintendent, they also believe that it is the principal, rather than the superintendent, who has the greatest leverage on their work. Research over more than a decade supports this view, beginning with studies of effective schools and continuing through investigations of school-based management. (See, for example, Berman and McLaughlin [1977] and Fullan and Stiegelbauer [1991, pp. 144–169].) Schools are often likened to families, with the principals as parents (historically, fathers, but increasingly mothers as well). One suburban Highboro elementary teacher observed that "each building feels almost on its own. It's sort of a one-family building. You are very much aware of your superintendent in terms of general leadership in the city, but in some ways you feel your principal is the person that you deal with most of the time. In that small school-family setting, the superintendent is not as closely connected."

From the perspective of teachers and principals, the superintendent is akin to a remote grandfather or absentee landlord. Even when school families are dysfunctional, when disorder reigns and the faculty feels besieged, teachers and principals seldom look to the superintendent for help, choosing instead to keep family problems private.

Principals, too, appear to regard themselves as the key agents of school change (see Barth, 1990). One in Clayton likened himself to a star basketball player who could not rely on his superintendent "coach" for advice about the best play during a game:

> I'm the kind of principal that wants to be the Larry Bird or Magic Johnson on the team. I'm in a crunch time right now. It's fourth quarter and I'm behind. I gotta come up with the right play and the best shot. The coach has just told me a play, and I'm not sure it's the right play. I may run it, but that play may not be out there for me. I have to think in my mind and be the coach and the player. So, I'd better be able to take the shot at the right time and win the game. That's what it is for me.

Although some might hear a note of arrogance in this quote, the unique character of schools does oblige principals to exercise independent leadership. If principals were to wait routinely for orders from the central office, the game might well be over before they could influence the outcome.

Principals who regard themselves as independent leaders typically set forth their own visions and plans; often these endure through the tenures of more than one superintendent. One urban principal in Riverton boycotted systemwide meetings on strategic planning because he and his school had already developed their own plan. He playfully described his quiet insubordination: "I've missed every meeting on purpose. And any time they ask me for stuff, I say, 'Well, you know, I've got that [restructuring] stuff. If you want to look at that I'll send it to you, because that's how we've been doing our plan here.'"

The superintendent cannot succeed without the cooperation of teachers and principals, but teachers and principals often believe they would thrive if only the central office would leave them alone. A teacher in Glendale described her independent stance and that of her colleagues: "In this school, we tend to try to do things to be leaders. So oftentimes we approach Administration with 'Let's do this. Let's do that.' We're not looking to them for directives. . . . You're willing to do a lot more if it's your idea than if someone forces it down your throat." One Ashmont principal said, "What [the superintendent] can do for me is to create an atmosphere where I can be a principal, where I can do my job. He doesn't interfere in my school. We're pretty autonomous."

Notably, such recommendations for hands-off management were tempered with a recognition that school districts had to achieve some consistency and order if they were to serve children fairly and well. Teachers and principals conceded that, in addition to providing autonomy, superintendents could legitimately have a say in the activities of individual schools. The Oakville principal who asserted that "I know where I want to go" also acknowledged that "It's very, very easy for me to sit here and say, 'This is my school. I know what I'm doing and this is what I want to do.' But I also have to realize that, while I may be an island unto myself here, this island is part of a group of islands. . . . I think too often that focus is lost, and that's when the superintendent has to come in to keep things together and keep things running smoothly, and it's not an easy job."

Leadership That Transforms

How, then, should new superintendents go about establishing shared leadership with those in the schools? How can they draw upon individual teachers' and principals' inspiration and capture their energy for a districtwide effort to improve education? Theorists, beginning with James MacGregor Burns (1978), have distinguished between transactional and transformational leadership. Transactional leadership implies a relationship that is largely instrumental, one in which subordinates deliberately trade their compliance and commitment to maintaining the system for certain incentives or working conditions offered by their superiors. Barbara Kellerman (1984b) explains:

The transactional leader gives his followers something that *they* want in exchange for something that *he* wants. It is a barter of sorts in which both sides gain and neither side loses. Put another way, the transactional leader satisfies his followers' private needs by engaging them in a relationship of mutual dependence in which the contribution of both sides is acknowledged and rewarded. Thus we follow the transactional leader because it is obvious to us that it is in our own interest to do so. We follow because in exchange for our support, the transactional leader gives us something that we specifically want and/or need [p. 80].

By contrast, transformational leadership moves participants beyond this dependent and calculated association to a relationship of mutual commitment and interdependence. Such a relationship is guided by ideas and values rather than regulated by favors and obligations. Individuals are no longer concerned only with their own condition, but with the general good; they invest personally in the schools and are motivated to act selflessly by the prospect of shared accomplishments (Enochs, 1981).[1] When superintendents achieve transformational leadership, traditional power relations between superiors and subordinates are changed, and the organization is transformed from one focused on maintenance to one that is poised for improvement.

As demonstrated above, however, teachers' and principals' initial expectations of new superintendents are decidedly transactional. Respondents in the districts studied frequently recalled superintendents who had treated them like subordinates rather than partners or who had briefly generated enthusiasm and commitment, only to depart suddenly for new jobs. These administrators left constituents cautious, even cynical, about investing in their successors' designs for change.

In two cases, superintendents interpreted their role as that of a transactional leader, observing that their influence with staff rested on a series of exchanges. Louis Antonellis of Ashmont explained: "I like to service their requests. And if you do that, they're happy. . . . Their requests sometimes are small and sometimes they're big, but if you're there to do that, they'll eat out of your hand, really, and that's the bottom line."

Most superintendents, however, hope for more.

Getting the Basics Right

As noted previously, successful engagement of teachers and principals depends upon superintendents' working hard to secure the basics—ensuring that the schools have the funds and the public support they need, that teachers and principals can work without interference, and that resources are targeted to support classroom teaching.

Mustering Money and Support

With public education under siege and day-to-day life in schools becoming increasingly difficult, teachers and principals look to the superintendent as the school district's outside agent, the person who can secure funds and maintain the schools' reputation with the public. Many in the districts studied characterized the superintendent as education's "cheerleader." One Clayton teacher said that she sought "an advocate for the school system, for money." A Highboro teacher explained she expected the superintendent "to fight the good fight" on behalf of the schools when he meets with the school board and addresses the public.

Shielding the Schools from Meddlers and Micromanagers

Respondents also looked to the superintendent to shield them from school board members intent on micromanaging their schools and from parents seeking unwarranted concessions. A teacher in Clayton said that he wanted the superintendent to "go to the school board as my advocate instead of just coming to me from the school board. I want his strongest focus to be one of supporting me and my needs as a teacher." A Clayton assistant principal summed up most respondents' views: "I don't want the school board interfering with my daily life. I want the superintendent to be there to protect me against that."

Although teachers generally count on their principals to handle parents who interfere inappropriately, sometimes they look to the superintendent as an intermediary. In one of the urban districts studied, where the superintendent agreed to meet with parents at one school, teachers were dismayed by the alliances they saw emerging: "The way he handled the discussion with parents . . . was very undermining. The teachers felt extremely undermined, as though he came into the school and kind of just undermined all their work and their position . . . without really bothering to go in and say to the teachers, 'What's going on here?' and 'How do you feel?' I think there are some vocal parents who he listens to." A Fernwood teacher who asked that her superintendent protect her from interference by parents and school board members was explicit about the exchange: "I will give him loyalty if he gives me loyalty."

Channeling Dollars to the Classroom

The teachers and principals in the districts studied expected their superintendent to prevail in political battles over scarce resources, and they urged that funds be allocated in ways that enhance instruction. Often they insisted that scarce dollars be spent on students and staffing rather than administration. One Highboro teacher was frank: "I expect [school officials] to put their money where their mouths are when they make promises and statements about the quality of education and [about] teaching in the classroom being the focal point, not administration." A colleague agreed: "When money becomes an issue or when staffing becomes an issue, hopefully [the superintendent] will be on the side of the teaching staff, who actually work with students."

Many teachers had very concrete expectations. One teacher from Westford wanted supplies most: "The most important thing to teachers is that they have an ample supply of books, pencils, and all that so they're able to do their jobs." Others wanted superintendents to see that their school buildings were repaired and kept clean. Early on, Andrew Cronin set the stage for transformational leadership by addressing longstanding maintenance problems at Clayton's high school, a move that won praise from teachers and administrators. A central office administrator explained, "He's gone in on the quality-of-life issues at the high school. It has to do with broken clocks and trash and basic lack of respect for property—dirty bathrooms, lousy space for teachers. He was very visible and responsive to the entire faculty in terms of hearing their list of complaints and getting some real action on those issues." A teacher in that school said that these actions signaled to teachers Cronin's broader commitment to the school: "It didn't take that long before I also had a sense that he was responsive to [instructional] needs."

Overall, teachers and principals expressed hope for the superintendent's support in areas where they felt vulnerable or had no leverage—budgeting, facilities maintenance, staffing, and supplies. Respondents explained that when former superintendents had failed to provide sufficient support in these areas, teachers and principals no longer looked to the district office for leadership. One former superintendent's inattention to the needs of the schools was said to "demoralize the district so that . . . people didn't want to work with him, and they didn't. And . . . the school district went down."

Moving Beyond the Basics

Although such basic assurances were all that many teachers and principals in these twelve districts expected from their superintendent, some respondents hoped for more. They sought to share leadership, taking part in a relationship distinguished by respect and responsiveness rather than rank.

In each of the districts where the teachers and principals wanted to move beyond transactional relationships, the superintendent demonstrated from the start a serious effort to deliver the basic support that the teachers and principals thought they needed to do their jobs. Andrew Cronin, who fixed the high school's clocks and bathrooms right away, eventually engaged the school's staff in addressing more complex problems, such as reforming the science program. A Clayton central office administrator predicted, "People will really judge him on the way he interacts with [the teachers and principals] around the issues that are real for them in their lives." Responding to such basic needs is more than a quid pro quo; it signals respect for teachers' work, empowers teachers and principals to define their own needs, and establishes an atmosphere of concern and a foundation for change.

It should be noted, however, that superintendents who succeed in securing the basics for their schools do not automatically win the trust of teachers and principals or engage them in the serious work of school improvement. Superintendents must also become informed about and involved in the work of the schools. They must establish their credibility as educators early on. They must become respected and trustworthy colleagues. These are demanding professional and interpersonal tasks, but the experience of the twelve districts studied strongly suggests that superintendents must work hard to meet these standards if their district's educators, once joined by contract, are to become unified by commitment.

Being Seen and Getting Involved

When asked what they expect from their superintendent, most respondents answered that they expect the superintendent to be visible and to participate in the schools. The superintendents themselves often said that they ought to be in the schools; many lamented that the demands of their job precluded frequent visits, however. One said, "I try to be visible. I don't get into the schools nearly enough. We only have ten schools. There are some that I haven't been in for two months now. . . . I ought to get out more than I do. . . . There are two I've only managed to get to twice this year." Dick Fitzgerald offered a similar confession: "Some of [the teachers] would say, 'Ah, typical superintendent, he never gets out of the office.' I haven't gotten out enough. I still get out, but nowhere as much as I should."

Teachers and principals, often feeling isolated and unappreciated, spoke disparagingly of superintendents who always seemed too busy with bureaucratic or political matters to spend meaningful time in the schools. Teachers and principals valued some kinds of superintendent visibility more than others, making careful distinctions between ceremonial, social, and substantive visits. Those whose superintendent said "I don't get into the schools nearly enough" repeatedly noted his absence. Initially, one teacher had been encouraged by that superintendent's presence at a staff meeting when school opened: "The very first day he addressed the entire staff, which I thought was a good move because everyone was dying to see who he was and what he was going to say." But this early appearance was never repeated. Another teacher complained, "We would see him at the beginning of the year when he greets us, and we might see him at the end of the year when he says 'Goodbye and have a good summer.' In between, [we] never [saw him] on a one-to-one basis. Never." In fact, that superintendent did occasionally visit the schools—for what even he called "flag waving." An elementary school principal observed, "He comes down to festive events but has never stayed long enough or looked under the surface to really understand the problems we have." A teacher raised the same concern: "Administrators come down to the school when there's a science fair. And they walk through this building, and then they view the science fair, and then they leave. They don't go into classrooms, and they don't see what's going on. They have no idea what's going on."

There were at least two superintendents whom teachers generally thought were less intent on seeing than on being seen. One teacher wished that her superintendent would participate more: "He's attended a couple other meetings of the [restructuring] committee. But he never says anything, and he's sort of there and then he goes away. Or he says, 'Gee, I have another meeting, bye.' So, he'll show his face, but . . ." A third teacher chastised her superintendent for visiting schools only for photo opportunities with the local press.

Some teachers saw their superintendent's visits primarily as social calls. One Ashmont teacher said that whenever Louis Antonellis is in her school, "he always makes a point to go into the classroom and to say 'Hello' and 'How are you doing?'—you know, 'What's new?'" Ashmont teachers appreciated the attention, but some wished the encounters were more substantive.

Other superintendents were seen as being engaged in classroom activities. They watched lessons, talked with children, and conferred informally with staff. Andrew Cronin earned high marks for his visits to schools and classrooms. One central office administrator said he was "omnipresent": "He moves around. He's *in* the system in ways other superintendents haven't been—in and out of schools, up and down stairs, in and out of meetings." A Clayton teacher who valued Cronin's regular visits offered an account typical of many others: "He's come to my classroom. He's been out on Parents' Night. He's stopped in another time. He asked what I'm doing in classes. . . . I just feel like he's tuned in." Teachers praised not only Cronin's energy but also his attitude. His being "tuned in" made a difference for these teachers. He had visited the classrooms of virtually all the teachers interviewed, and each had been pleased, a startling response given teachers' well-documented preference for privacy in their classrooms. One explained: "He's a superintendent who does get out and get into the schools, who has the facility for knowing who people are and how to talk to them. He's got an easy way about him. He also can fool around with people in a way that people like. For a while people would say, 'God, I was teaching a class and I turned around and looked up and there was the superintendent.' And people loved that."

Such easy interaction is not the norm; teachers in the other districts were often ambivalent about their superintendent's classroom visits. Notably, though, they valued them nonetheless. A Highboro teacher who thought Arthur Holzman somewhat intimidating conceded, "I get a little nervous when he comes into my class, because he has high expectations—but I think that is good." Her colleague, who concluded that "those few who grumble are kind of overly suspicious," praised Holzman's efforts: "If I'm teaching, he always pops in to say hello. He wanders around. He knows it doesn't bother me. He drifted in and sat down for five minutes. I introduced him to the kids and went right on doing what I was doing. He's very visible. He's around. He's in the schools. . . . He knows where to place himself." Overall, Holzman's frequent classroom observations impressed Highboro's teachers.

Classroom visits by the superintendent proved to be particularly charged events for teachers in districts with no history of such practices. The difficulty was exacerbated in one district where a superintendent offered little feedback about what he saw:

> He comes right in and he says very little to you. He will acknowledge you. You will acknowledge him. . . . You get nothing when he leaves. Once in a while, he has a half a minute and he'll talk to you. I think maybe he doesn't want us to feel that he's evaluating us. But in reality, you can't tell me he isn't. He's counting in his own mind; he's getting a mindset, every time he walks into someone's classroom. He sees certain things, certain activities, or lack of activities, or lack of student involvement, or more teacher lectures. You know that he is beginning to compile all this information in his head.

This teacher wanted a more meaningful response from her superintendent—some notion of what he thought about the class, some personal acknowledgement of her intentions and efforts. This was especially true since the prior superintendent of many years had rarely visited classrooms, and therefore the teacher had no broader context in which to interpret her new superintendent's classroom observations.

A superintendent who is regularly engaged in the life of the schools and classrooms has a tremendous influence on teachers' work, even if that influence is difficult to trace. One Highboro teacher tried to explain what it meant to her when Arthur Holzman paid a visit: "I don't do my daily job any differently; that's my job. But I have more of a sense of pride when Arthur walks down the hall and there's a possibility that he might walk into my classroom. Even if I don't do my job differently, I feel differently about it when he's around, when he's in town. When his name comes up, I do feel differently about it, because I feel different vibes coming down from that position. I don't feel that he's far removed in an ivory tower."

For a number of teachers and principals, the superintendent's active presence in their school conferred greater status on their own work. One teacher said, "You feel that what you're doing is real worthwhile and somebody cares." Others suggested that the superintendent's presence conveyed the district administration's support of teaching. One Summit teacher described how Wayne Saunders's visits to her school convinced her that he was committed to the work in which she was engaged. Initially she was surprised to see him in her school, and she found him impressive:

He wandered through the halls, introducing himself. I didn't know who it was. When he said "Wayne Saunders," that still didn't do a thing for me, because I'm not involved other than in my classroom and my grade. I don't really get involved with the politics of the position. His sense of humor was great. And his interest. He showed genuine interest. So that was the first week of the school year, his first year. I had never met another superintendent before him. And this was the first week. So that right off was impressive.

Saunders did more than visit occasionally. "He also started an advisor/advisee program—his first year, in the seventh grade—and he was a team member in that. He had a weekly group. And that itself showed me that he's not all talk. He's taken an active part. He made a commitment on a weekly basis."

One might expect that regular visits by superintendents to schools would be far less likely in large districts than in small ones, but this was not found to be true in the twelve districts studied for this book. The two superintendents who were said to be least visible headed the two smallest districts in the sample. A teacher in the five-school district of Ashmont said, "The kids should at least know who the superintendent is." By contrast, a teacher in Union, the largest district in the sample (with forty schools), noted that Clara Underwood's visibility was unprecedented: "This is the first time that I have ever known for our students to actually know not only who the superintendent is, but to actually know her."

When superintendents are perceived to be present and involved in the life of their district's schools, teachers and principals are more likely to believe that they share with them a concern for students and their learning. The potential for their working together for better schools thus increases. In weighing that possibility, those who work with children want to know whether superintendents who seek to engage them in change are credible as educators.

Being an Educator First

A new superintendent can gain a local reputation as an educator in different ways. Three of the superintendents studied were promoted from within; they were deemed good educators largely because they had taught successfully in their district's classrooms or been respected principals in its schools. Louis Antonellis, whom some teachers criticized for his lack of visibility, retained a reservoir of respect from teachers who remembered his work as a principal: "Lou was my principal. . . . And you can go down to that building to this day and there's not one teacher that will not praise him to the hilt as far as being a principal in that building. He was terrific. He was on top of everything. He was around every day, but you never felt like he was around to spy on you. If you had a problem, it was solved the next day. If you needed books, you got them within an hour or two. He was good; he really was."

Such reputations earn superintendents dutiful respect in the short-term, but if they are to gain real, long-term commitment from teachers and principals, there has to be more than recollections of past success. Teachers and principals want current confirmation of their superintendent's competence as an educator. Some are persuaded during classroom visits. Arthur Holzman, for example, asked questions and made observations that showed him to be thoughtful about educational issues. One Highboro teacher was impressed when Holzman quickly discerned what was important in her class: "He was just here for a few minutes, but he asked the right questions about the kids and the right questions about the equipment and the right questions about the way that equipment and material would work to better [the kids' education]." Others told of moments when they became convinced that their superintendent grasped the important features of their work. For example, a Clayton biology teacher told of seeking special lab equipment so that she could conduct experiments with DNA. Andrew Cronin heard about her interest, visited her classroom, and told her to contact the grants coordinator, who then found the money she needed. She said, "Actually, I was kind of impressed because he had read up on [conducting DNA experiments] before he came over."

When such events occur they become symbolically important, and teachers talk about them often. The superintendent becomes known as someone whose real interest centers on instruction and learning, no matter how much time he must spend on administrative matters such as building repairs and grievance management. When teachers and principals believe that their superintendents

understand the demands of classroom teaching and support their
best efforts, they are far more likely to entertain the superintendent's
ideas and support his or her goals.

Giving Respect and Earning Trust

Teachers may believe they have the most important job in education, but they also know that others—particularly those in the central office—do not necessarily share that view. The classroom
teacher sits at the bottom of the organizational chart and seldom
influences those at the top. Given their low status in their districts
and in society, teachers are particularly attentive to how the superintendent treats them personally. Once they feel genuinely
respected, they can trust their superintendent's intentions and consider his or her ideas. However, when teachers sense condescension,
they respond with haughty contempt of their own, dismissing the
superintendent as a bureaucratic functionary.

Teachers in the districts studied were outraged by superintendents who disparaged them. A Westford teacher said, "One of the
most infuriating things about the last superintendent—and the way
teachers perceived him—was that they always felt like he was talking down to them." In Fernwood, the previous superintendent had
made it clear that he regarded teachers as an inferior breed. One
teacher recalled, "He didn't socialize with teachers. It was a very
distinct line. One situation when he first came on board was very
clear. He said, 'I am management and you people are blue-collar.'
And that set it off." The fact that he subsequently worked hard to
win higher salaries for teachers did little to compensate for his having relegated them to second-rate status in the organization.

When a superintendent arrives in a district where the teaching
staff is strong but teachers' efforts and achievements have been
ignored by previous superintendents, the new administrator has a fine
opportunity to win teachers' support by acknowledging their
strengths. In Clayton, Andrew Cronin seized upon such an opportunity. One teacher concluded, "He believes in teachers. He believes

that the teachers, not the superintendent, make Clayton, Clayton."
A principal there said that Cronin thought his school was "wonderful, one of the best in the country." And the principal explained that when someone says that, he wants to live up to that reputation, "whether it's a myth or whether it's real." Another principal described how this kind of recognition empowers her to work harder and seriously consider the superintendent's suggestions for improvement: "There's a sense of wanting to please him. . . . He celebrates what you're doing, so you feel good about things that you're doing well. So you're happy to then look at things that aren't going too well and listen to what he has to say and move in the direction that he would like you to go. I never get the sense of being pushed around by him."

A few of the new superintendents studied thought the teachers and principals in their district were ineffective, and they therefore took up the task of improving their performance. It was hard for them to deliver criticism, however, without antagonizing the very teachers and principals whose support they needed to secure. Those in the schools were attentive and responsive—in some cases reactive—to their superintendent's style of interaction. One teacher said of her superintendent that "she tends to believe that we are not the best teachers in the world. Instead of coming and . . . forming her own opinion, she has come in thinking, 'Well, you're adequate or you're below average.'" Teachers in other districts recounted times when the new superintendent sparked their anger by categorically criticizing their work. One complained that Ben Moreno had reproached the teachers in his new district because the test scores of Hispanic and African-American students were considerably lower than those of white students: "He's absolutely right. [But] what he does not know is that in the last three years we made very significant progress closing that gap. . . . The staff goes crazy. I said [to him], 'Well, don't you think you should have asked somebody before you jumped out there?' He said, 'Well, I didn't assign blame to anybody.' I said, 'You don't have to. The implication is that we're not doing our job.'"

Although one Millsburg teacher we interviewed praised Moreno for saying that the teachers were doing some things that weren't good and needed to be changed, many others experienced his public criticisms as a painful, blanket indictment of their work. One teacher concluded that Moreno's outspoken and public criticism had been counterproductive: "The one thing that he hasn't done is won over enough teachers. . . . He shoots from the hip and then he thinks about it afterwards." A teacher who knew that her colleague was participating in this study said, "Be sure that when you're interviewed you use the word *arrogant*." She went on to explain: "There's some very strong feeling about the fact that he's tending to run roughshod over many people." In Ashmont, a teacher contended that his superintendent "operates through intimidation. Most people in the system fear him. You cross him and he'll find a way to get you back." He went on to explain why such tactics were counterproductive: "I think you get a lot more treating someone with respect than you do stomping all over them and instilling fear in them to get them to produce. Because—let's face it—in the long run, people aren't stupid. They know how they're being treated, and they're going to give you back what you give them."

Although teachers were sensitive to their superintendent's public criticism, they did not expect unqualified praise or acceptance. They knew that in any district there are both expert and amateur teachers, the selfless and the selfish. In Union, for example, there was resounding support in the schools for Clara Underwood, who described herself as a "tough person" who would "write up" teachers and principals for not getting results. Respondents there knew that their schools had serious problems; they were willing to hear about them in part because Underwood was careful not to level undifferentiated criticism. Rather, she identified individuals she knew were failing and closely monitored their performance. She dealt with the others confidently and respectfully, and they responded in kind.

Thus it is clear that teachers and principals are both attentive to their superintendent's personalities and discerning about their intentions and actions. One suburban teacher said, "I think the teachers cut to the chase—I think they say [either] 'This man represents me well' or 'I function in spite of this person.' " In those districts where the superintendent understood the teachers' work and respected them as professionals, respondents expressed confidence that their opinions would be heard and that they could contribute to the superintendent's decisions and the schools' success. Cronin, in particular, was said to listen well: "He can make every group, no matter how extreme, comfortable that he understands where they're coming from and have them be respectful of what he's trying to do." As a result of this open and responsive style, one teacher said, "People have immense confidence in him. . . . They see him as fair. They see him as reasonable. They see him as thoughtful. . . . I don't think he has a block of critics." Another teacher echoed this sentiment: "I like having someone I can respect, someone I can agree and disagree with. . . . I like having some personal connection. I like the fact that he knows my name. I like feeling that I have some connection with the top."

A principal in Fernwood said that the previous superintendent "didn't give a rat's nose" about issues that were important to him. The principal had recently raised the same issues with Dick Fitzgerald, who turned out to be responsive—a fact that made the principal take the superintendent's goals more seriously. A Union principal said that Clara Underwood "will consider my point of view. She doesn't close me off. . . . She is a person that you can touch, you can get a response from and you can respond to. She's a no-nonsense lady, though." Another teacher said, "She has a very unique ability to make people feel confident, unthreatened. She gives off a vibrancy, getting people to want to do things. It's very difficult, sometimes, with the problems we face, to just keep on going day after day."

By contrast, teachers and principals criticized superintendents who seemed inaccessible or uninterested in their views. In one urban district a teacher complained, "He needs to be *the* leader, and no one can tell or suggest anything." Another urban principal said that if his superintendent would only solicit his input, "I could make it happen. But he never asked what I thought ought to be done, what I thought would work."

Of course, respondents from the same district had different experiences and therefore different assessments of their superintendent. One school board member thought Anna Niles "should be more of a positive force, showing by example, and patting people on the back, and building them up." A principal saw it differently: "I sort of go through like a little mental checklist when I think if I'm tackling something that I don't feel real comfortable about and think about how she would do it. Because I really respect her enormously. She's one of the things that has made this job. I've wanted to be a principal for a long time, but in addition to that, [I've wanted] to work for somebody that I respect."

Ben Moreno also evoked mixed responses from constituents. He said that his natural leadership style was "to be inclusive, to involve people, to give people a say, to give people power so that they become more responsible, to share with people—and yet also to be very directed toward a goal." He did not think that people seized the power he made available to them, though; he had found constituents more inclined to say, "Hey, you're the boss—tell us what to do." One respondent in Millsburg said that "the image that he projects is one of including people in the process, getting people to understand the process, getting them plugged into participating in the process. But it's *his* process." A union leader decided Moreno responded best to persistent prodding from staff: "You've got to push it and follow through and be aggressive, and then he respects you more or responds better. That seems to be what's happening. . . . He's accessible, that's for sure. More accessible than any other superintendent I've ever known. He doesn't always listen, but he's accessible." When teachers could advocate for themselves, they could collaborate; but when they interpreted Moreno's impatience as censure, they reverted to a transactional relationship, doing no more than the tacit treaty required.

Dick Fitzgerald's experience in Fernwood reminds us that trust is fragile. Fitzgerald replaced an authoritarian predecessor, and he quickly earned a reputation as "one who really cares" when he personally met with each teacher who was about to receive a pink slip. One Fernwood teacher said, "I would trust him." Another confirmed, "He's very honest. You might not like what he's about to say to you, but he is an honest person, and he doesn't try to hide anything." But when Fitzgerald announced after little more than a year on the job that he had accepted a superintendency in another district, teachers were disillusioned. Resentment spread quickly. One teacher said, "There was a difference after he had been here a short while. I think morale went up. . . . There was a feeling of trust. That has now changed, as soon as we learned that he was seeking positions in other places. . . . I feel a little bit betrayed." Fitzgerald's sudden departure would make it hard for his replacement to reestablish trust.

It is clear, then, that teachers and principals, who often hold low expectations about their superintendent's potential impact on their work, are not beyond influence. In fact, in all twelve districts studied, teachers hoped that their superintendent might respect their work, seek out their opinions, and earn their trust and support. They wanted to move beyond the superior-to-subordinate relationship to establish a collaborative, reciprocal association as educators, a relationship in which each might be informed and empowered by the other, leading the schools to change.

The Benefits of Transformational Leadership

What happens when teachers and principals perceive their superintendent to be more than a bureaucratic boss or a transactional leader? The districts studied suggest that when those in the schools perceive their new superintendent to be invested in them and their work, they respond with a new attentiveness to systemwide concerns, a readiness to rethink their priorities, and a willingness to take risks and try new practices. The transformation may be gradual and undramatic, but it is nevertheless important.

Getting Teachers to See Beyond the Classroom

As noted previously, teachers' and principals' attention is typically focused inward on classrooms and schools rather than outward on their entire district. One of the superintendent's greatest challenges is to enlarge that field of attention so that those in the schools see beyond their students and classrooms to consider districtwide issues that affect everyone's teaching, such as assessment, promotion, text-book selection, curriculum development, personnel practices, and approaches to special education.

Reciprocal trust is liberating. When a new superintendent gains educators' confidence and shows confidence in them, they tend to assume a broader perspective on their work and show more interest in districtwide initiatives. One Clayton principal said that since Cronin's arrival she felt "quite confident in talking about the system, defending the system, more so now than I did a couple of years ago." A Highboro principal explained that during the prior superintendent's tenure she had felt that her role was to "hunker down and protect my school. Now I look at my role as being more involved in the total system, that I'm part of a pulling together to create a better school system." A teacher in Highboro said that she was "much more open to volunteering to participate in citywide efforts" than she had been under the prior administration, and that it was due to the new administration, "because the cast of characters has changed." A Union teacher said that she and her peers had new insights about how their work in classrooms contributed to greater achievement in the entire district: "The teachers really feel that they are contributing a lot to what's happening in the district to improve education. That's what I gather from them. The respect that we have for her, based on who she is, as a person . . . she

encouraged us, sometimes, when we were ready just to give up. . . .
We are not by any means out of the woods, but I think we have
come a long way."

These teachers began to believe that they should move beyond
the transactional expectation that the superintendent should just
provide the basics—funding, supplies, and security—in exchange
for a good day's work. They started to see that by entering new, collaborative relationships with their superintendent, they could invest
in the system and improve the lives of the children in their school
and others.

Helping Teachers and Principals Invest Wisely

Given the perpetually short supply of time and money in public
schools today, teachers and principals must inevitably choose where
to invest those scarce resources. Much of what superintendents
sought to do by their various plans and goals was to reorder the priorities of those in the schools. Sometimes this meant asking teachers and principals to rethink how they organized their schools and
classrooms; sometimes it meant helping them rediscover what truly
mattered.

An Oakville principal who prized his autonomy as a school
leader praised Mike Ogden's efforts to influence where he invested
his resources: "We're more focused than we ever were. And you
know, I'm more focused because of him. There were things before
that I'd come up with, these brainstorms, you know. I love new
ideas, and no matter what I came up with [under the prior admin-
istration] it was just accepted—'Oh fine, good, give it a try.' But
Ogden really questions, . . . he really makes you think things out.
I've grown, I've definitely grown just through working with him."

In Union, Clara Underwood's influence on the priorities of the
faculty and administrators in one school was reportedly profound.
The principal explained that the new superintendent had led her
to focus on children: "I support her because I know that she's about
children. And I haven't always been about children that much

myself. . . . She's even got *me* thinking about children." And Underwood's influence did not stop there: "I'm looking at curriculum. I'm looking at subject matter. I'm looking at teachers in terms of strengths and weaknesses. Now we are talking about staff development. That's where we are going to be going next." Teachers confirmed this principal's account, describing how her leadership had changed. One said, "She works with the staff in a more cooperative manner than she did before. She is not willing to be the recipient of negative information that works against her administration and her leadership. She's not in conflict as much as she used to be with the union. . . . She has a very different leadership style. . . . She takes time, and she listens and she weighs situations more than she ever did before." Such accounts of dramatic change were unusual, but there were many reports of teachers and principals rethinking how they organized their work, reconsidering their approaches to children, and rebuilding their relations with one another.

Enabling Collaborative Risk Taking

Leadership is about change, and as our respondents' accounts have repeatedly demonstrated, change is difficult to achieve. In the conservative culture of U.S. schools, it is far easier for principals and teachers to repeat what they have always done—even when it no longer works—than to venture forth and experiment. Certainly some teachers' and principals' negative reactions to reform are warranted—many innovations are flashy and foolish, and some are wrongheaded and disruptive. Given public education's failure to meet the needs of today's students, however, teachers and principals cannot simply continue to do the same things in the same ways. Recognizing this, the new superintendents studied here initiated many programs to promote improvement. Their experience illustrates how teachers and principals approach innovation when it is introduced as a genuinely collaborative process.

In some cases teachers and principals had ideas about how they might improve their schools, but they needed encouragement and resources to get started. In Clayton, Andrew Cronin created a culture of support for school-based initiatives. A central office administrator observed, "He empowers people around their own ideas, and there are plenty of people with ideas in this town." In Fernwood, a teacher contrasted the response of principals working for two very different superintendents. Under the prior superintendent, she said, "most of the principals were . . . the best way to describe it is 'uptight.' They felt a great deal of pressure. . . . They were in charge; they made the rules. They did what he said, whether they really agreed with that philosophy or not. Since Dick Fitzgerald they're more relaxed, they're more accessible, they're more willing to listen to your opinion, they're more willing to try new things." Under the previous administration, the principals' anxiety was quickly transferred to teachers, limiting their ability to experiment. The teacher explained that the principals "didn't do anything unless they got his approval. Period. They might hear your idea, but if they didn't think it was something he was going to buy . . . it was a dead issue." With the new, more collegial superintendent came a relaxed and accommodating approach to innovation. The teacher continued: "I don't think that's the case now. Being autocratic stifled creativity in the teaching staff. Fear is a great motivator, but it's a very negative motivator. . . . What happens is that people begin to live with fear after a period of time, but they will not produce for you. They will not become creative for you." Trust between the superintendent and educators in the Fernwood schools was the foundation for transformational leadership that would empower them to work together productively.

In Union, where Underwood urged those in the middle schools to restructure into clusters, staff members initially dismissed the idea. One teacher said, "People find change difficult. Some of the people here are squealing because of change; some of the people here are welcoming change. . . . In the opinion of most staff members—and I'd say most administrators—the attitude was 'Here's another fly-by-night idea, here today and gone tomorrow.' And they tended to ignore and not even pay attention to it." Another Union teacher, however, said that her colleagues eventually took Underwood's proposals seriously. She attributed the change to her new superintendent: "It's from Ms. Underwood and no one else. She came in and was faced with some decisions, and she handled them immediately, and people realized that she was fair-handed and didn't sit on any hidden agendas. And so people decided, 'I'll lay it on the line.'" Resistance steadily subsided. "And so now there's very few people standing there shouting out, 'No, No, No,' and there's more people saying, 'How can I get involved? How can I get on the bandwagon?'"

Teachers change their teaching practices in response to superintendents' initiatives. As we saw in Chapter Four, Oakville's teachers and principals eliminated tracking and departmentalization in their elementary schools. In Highboro, teachers and principals attended intensive workshops on cooperative learning, a strategy that Holzman believed would prepare teachers to meet the needs of diverse groups of students. A Highboro teacher said that she had been influenced by this initiative: "I think that cooperative learning could be effective, especially for students who don't like to learn very much. It might be another way to pull them in. It's not dramatic. It hasn't changed dramatically what I do, but it's been useful. I do a few things [now] that I wouldn't have done before the whole system was pushed." Such change is noteworthy in a district known for its teachers' fierce defense of their professional autonomy.

In the districts where the new superintendents were more than transactional leaders—where they invested themselves personally in the schools—teachers and principals exhibited more open-mindedness, energy, and goodwill than did those in districts where the superintendent claimed to have the knowledge, ability, and authority to single-handedly improve the schools.

Understanding the Challenge Ahead

Tracing the path of superintendents' leadership in public education is complicated because so many events and influences intervene between the central office and the classroom. What became clear from respondents' experiences with both current and past administrations is that few superintendents make the difference in educational practices that they hope and expect they will. Sometimes they fail; sometimes they move on before the results are in; often they hobble along without good information about how they are doing. While more than half of the new superintendents succeeded in moving their relationships with teachers and principals beyond basic transactions, only three or four could be said to have approached transformational leadership, where personal commitment is genuine and mutual, authority and responsibility are shared, power is dispersed, and influence is reciprocal.

The reason, in part, is that the odds are stacked against new superintendents from the start. Teachers are suspicious of formal authority, wary of being abandoned, and absorbed in their work with children. They prefer investing in what they know rather than submitting to the dubious judgment of the latest administrative expert. Sometimes superintendents confirm teachers' doubts by remaining aloof, failing to learn about their schools, ignoring the wisdom of practitioners, making unfounded or unqualified judgments, or treating staff as underlings rather than colleagues. In other cases, though, new superintendents belie conventional expectations by first addressing basic needs for funding, supplies, and security and then proving to be attentive, well-informed, responsive educators who respect teachers and principals and win their confidence by engaging them in meaningful, if difficult, discussions about their schools and how to improve them.

If meaningful reform is to extend throughout a district, teachers, principals, and superintendents must agree about purposes and priorities. If teachers and principals are to change their ways and exercise consistent leadership in pursuit of districtwide goals, superintendents must do much more than decide and decree. Those in the schools want support rather than direction and engagement rather than neglect.

In developing a capacity for meaningful change, superintendents must exercise not only educational leadership but political and managerial leadership as well. As political leaders, superintendents must discern patterns of power and influence in their constituents' struggle for greater control of resources, and they must work on behalf of the schools to secure sufficient funding and maintain control locally over important educational decisions. Then they must build coalitions for support and improvement among those with an interest in the schools. Chapter Six examines the local political context in the twelve districts studied for this book and the political challenges their new superintendents faced from school boards, municipal officials, and teachers unions.

Note

1. Thomas J. Sergiovanni (1990, pp. 30–40) identifies four stages of leadership that engage the principal and teachers in school improvement. The first, "bartering," is transactional, while the second and third, "building" and "bonding," are transformational. The fourth, "banking," routinizes school improvement efforts.

Part Three

· ·

Political Leadership

6

Political Contexts and Constituents

Curiously, those intent on educating the public's children often hope to do so without touching or being touched by politics. Though they realize that interest groups influence programs, loyalties bias resource allocation, and coalitions gain concessions that individuals cannot, many educators persist in believing that politics is beneath them. Arthur Blumberg (1985) explains the reasoning underlying this reaction: "Education is for children, the thinking goes. It is too important and sacred a societal function to be mixed up in politics, whether that politics is public and partisan or involves the covert, astute manipulation of competing pressure groups in a community or on a school board. Educators should maintain a position untainted by the political battles that occur in the community and consciously seek to ensure that the schools will be unscarred by those battles" (p. 46).[1]

Typically, those who hope to bypass politics conceive of it narrowly, envisioning smoke-filled rooms, old-boy networks, shady deals, and ethnic factions. However, politics is central to the work of today's superintendents, who cannot succeed as educational leaders without also being active political leaders. They must build coalitions, negotiate agreements, and force concessions when necessary, all without hitting political land mines that may cost them ground. To be "above politics" is to be outside reality. Educators may not want to admit this fact, but they do recognize it. As a teacher in

Westford said, the superintendent "could come up with an idea that might be sound educationally, might make a lot of sense, but if for some reason someone on the school board—a politician—had an ax to grind, that person could very well defeat it. Politics are involved. You need those five votes." Thus, no longer free to choose whether to enter the political fray, superintendents must assess the political context of their district and decide how best to work within it. Today's superintendents can no longer rely primarily on the authority of their position to run the schools (if they ever could), for politics pervades virtually every aspect of public education.

The prominence of politics in education has risen in recent years, for several reasons. First, public funds have shrunk while students' needs and society's expectations continue to grow, causing competing groups to draw battle lines over funding. Second, in response to alarming reports of the schools' failings, there is an increasing conviction that public education is, indeed, the province of the public rather than the professionals. Given this urgency, many actors both inside and outside school districts now claim the right to say what is to be taught, how it should be taught, and how it should be assessed. Third, the increasingly complex ethnic, racial, linguistic, and economic diversity of U.S. communities makes it hard to reach an accord on what the schools should do and how children should be served. Competing groups struggle to determine whose children's needs will be met, whose culture will be validated, and whose values will be sustained. Finally, as in other American institutions, conventional authority structures within education are routinely challenged. Many teachers and principals, once assumed to be the subordinates of school boards and superintendents, are now union members supported by strong labor organizations and strict contract language.

The political context new superintendents enter may well include unscrupulous practices such as patronage, exclusion, and coercion, but it also features the best traditions of democracy, with decision-making power in the hands of legislative committees, school boards, faculty senates, and individual school councils. New superintendents who hope to lead effectively must think and act politically. They must understand the historical relationships between various groups and individuals in their district, assess both their own and others' power, anticipate what matters to various interest groups, advocate for funds with various municipal officials and legislative groups, and adeptly negotiate with an array of actors and organizations. The issue for new superintendents is not whether to engage in politics but "what kind of politics will prevail here?" As Arthur Blumberg (1985) asserts in his study of school superintendents, "One thing about today's superintendent is almost a given. Whether or not he is partisan in his politics, in order to survive he must indeed be a political animal—or behave like one, even if he is not so inclined" (p. 19).

None of the superintendents surveyed for this book contended that it was possible to work effectively while being detached from politics, although clearly there were those who would have preferred it that way. Several felt politically naive and acted in ways that left them and their schools vulnerable. Others, like Dick Fitzgerald, enjoyed the role of the constructive politician. But even he acknowledged the hazards: "I am a good politician, I hope, in the best sense of the word. . . . I'm very creative at finding solutions, and I always think there's a solution out there. . . . Thomas More is my hero, so that tells you something. I hope I don't lose my head at the end."

Why Superintendents Need to Be Political

As political leaders, the twelve superintendents we interviewed had varied purposes. First, they sought to build coalitions of strong public support for their districts' schools, staff, and programs. Demographic changes over the past two decades have diminished the number of taxpayers with school-age children in many districts. One suburban Highboro teacher observed that "28 percent of people living in Highboro have children in the schools, and that's not a good number." Moreover, dramatic reports of schools' failings diminish taxpayers' confidence in public education, leading to contentious, often unsuccessful levy campaigns.

Superintendents also work to ensure continuous, adequate funding for their schools. This means organizing coalitions of local leaders to petition legislators in the statehouse, bargaining with the mayor, asking teachers to represent the schools' interests at town meetings, or challenging a finance committee's inadequate budget allocation for education. They must use their political acumen to see that coherent educational programs are developed in their schools. Such change, which requires more than a superintendent's directives, rests on participation by a broad spectrum of parties. A Riverton school board member explained, "As a school board member who wants to get something done, I know that I cannot get it done alone. Neither can Maureen Reilly. Anything that she wants to do, she will need the cooperation of a number of people." As districts decide about a range of issues from curriculum to student assignments, the superintendent must solicit views, orchestrate deliberations, and reconcile differences in the interest of educational progress.

Finally, superintendents exercise political leadership in allocating resources among programs and schools, teachers and administrators, and instructional and extracurricular activities. In doing so, the superintendents in the twelve districts studied were routinely besieged by individuals and groups vying for influence. Superintendents who understood the political implications of their decisions and could plan their strategies to improve education with those implications in mind fared better than those who did not.

Respondents told of past and present superintendents who tried to distance themselves from politics. Ironically, in the end, politics drove the course of change in their districts. City officials, for example, often treated the schools like the fire and police departments, subjecting them to municipal standards. Patronage determined who was hired and promoted, and a few powerful individuals or interest groups controlled decisions about resource allocation. Conflict endured, important issues remained unresolved, and in the end, superintendents often lost their jobs. One principal in the small town of Fernwood recalled a superintendent "who was driven out of town. . . . He just didn't have it politically. He was not a shrewd politician. He was not a politician. . . . He was an educator." This account and many others suggest that political insight and action are essential companions to superintendents' educational leadership. If the superintendent stands back, someone else's politics will prevail.

Operating in the Political Landscape

When beginning a new administration, superintendents must first interpret the local political context. Is it a strong union town? Are there "camps" on the school board? Who has pull with state legislators? Who are the power brokers? Do less-privileged students have advocates? How are resources divided? Does school policy result from open debate or closed deals?

Local contexts vary a great deal. These twelve new superintendents had to be quick studies of their new political landscapes. One Oakville principal explained how important it is for a new superintendent to astutely assess local politics: "He has to understand the power structure as it exists in Oakville. If indeed it's the Federation of Teachers that holds power, then that's the group that he's going to have to deal and reckon with, and he's going to have to realize that. If they're not the base of the power structure, and it turns out that the Association of Administrators and Supervisors is, then he has to take a different thrust."

Superintendents also have to reconcile their own leadership style with their district's political realities. Each individual comes to the job with a different set of inclinations, talents, and experiences. For some, educational politics is engaging and exhilarating. For others, deciding how best to approach the job is not easy. One

newly appointed superintendent said he was just no good at politics. He said that sometimes not being politically astute "can be disastrous. '. . . You sort of don't know whose toes you're stepping on.
You just kind of forge forward. Everybody is related to everybody. I
have no idea of some of the connections. I find out something new
every day. I have to be really careful."

In addition to reading political signs and deciding how best to
marry one's talents and values with local demands and opportunities, new superintendents must establish their own base of power by
building alliances, developing influence (and a reputation for having it), and contending with challengers who may be bent on making them look insignificant, ignorant, or ineffective. A number of
the new superintendents we interviewed tried to be visible and to
achieve prominence in their communities. A central office administrator in Millsburg recalled that when Ben Moreno arrived, he had
to make political choices: "Do you go to the parents? Do you go to
the teachers? Where do you go?" Moreno chose to meet first with
parents and community people, but he quickly moved on to teachers. His vision called for schools to be the rejuvenating force in the
community, and he sought to inform citizens, parents, and others
with a stake in the schools and enlist their support. For new superintendents these are not either-or choices, since they are obliged to
find their political way amid an incredible array of actors and
groups, ranging from the teachers union to the PTA, the central
office administrators, the custodians, the Rotary club, and the
mayor's staff. In order to make these connections and situate themselves as individuals to be respected and reckoned with, the superintendents we interviewed hosted lunches, spoke at community
meetings, answered questions before unexpected cameras, and
responded to myriad requests and inquiries. They faced such time-
consuming challenges within the early months—often the early
days—of their tenure.

Although respondents did not suggest that a superintendent
could succeed on political savvy alone, many believed that politi-

cal ineptitude could be ruinous. One teacher in Fernwood predicted, "The community is going to see what he wants to do and how he plays the political end of the town. I've seen superintendents come in and, once the honeymoon period was over, just go downhill. They made enemies somewhere in the town, and it was just over."

Types of Political Contexts

While politics was prominent in the work of all twelve superintendents, the local political context varied notably from town to town. There were important differences in how political groups organized and vied for their share of scarce community resources, influence, and control. When distinct political groups or parties competed over educational issues, *partisan politics* prevailed. When group membership was more fluid and alliances were ad hoc, *participatory politics* predominated, featuring the complex, changing interactions of interest groups and individuals. When programs rose and fell, jobs were offered or eliminated, or funds were allocated or withheld on the basis of personal affiliations, *patronage politics* eclipsed all other political interactions. These three strains of politics could be found in varying proportions in all twelve districts, but one usually predominated and thus commanded the new superintendent's attention and challenged his or her expertise.

Partisan Politics: Ideologies and Alliances

In four districts respondents said that relatively stable, partisan patterns dominated political interactions; key actors were known to be members of distinct political groups that had vied over the years for control of local education. In Glendale, a decidedly Democratic city, school board actions reflected larger patterns of local party loyalties. A school board member there observed, "We are a nonpartisan school board, which is the biggest oxymoron I have ever heard. . . . It means that we have no political parties in our elections. We run nonpartisan." But, he explained, "The only way you can be elected 'nonpartisan' is if you are a registered Democrat in Wards 1 through 8 or a Republican in Ward 9." In Westford, where school board candidates ran for office by electoral wards, there had long been a 4–5 split between liberals and conservatives, with elections causing the balance of power to shift back and forth over time. In Riverton, local candidates for all offices ran on one of two slates sponsored by conservative and liberal coalitions that had competed actively for more than twenty years. A school board member emphasized that although some members would occasionally cast crossover votes, "there are still clearly two sides of the aisle." Similarly, school board members in the city of Summit were identified either as "progressives" or "traditionalists," with these informal labels again designating liberal and conservative views.

Superintendents of districts with strong partisan politics found that, despite frequent conflict, the balance of power changed little over time. In Westford, Riverton, and Glendale, superintendents were expected not to disrupt that balance but to manage it. A central office administrator in Riverton said that his boss, Maureen Reilly, "does a pretty good job of walking the fences. She has leanings both ways." A school board member there assumed Reilly's personnel appointments would preserve the political order: "I expect that there will be some points thrown in both directions, with the balance ultimately reflecting the political balance of the city."

When a new superintendent was hired on a split vote, his or her initiatives were likely to succeed as long as the balance of power on the board remained the same. If the split was decidedly one way (4–1 or 5–2), the superintendent appointed by the majority could expect consistent support for his or her programs, since those programs were likely to reflect the majority's priorities. When the split was closer (5–4 or 4–3), however, and a majority vote was not routinely assured, the superintendent had to pay close attention to shifting alliances that might affect the outcome on any issue. Counting votes became a preoccupation. Often, supporting a controversial program or appointing a candidate who did not enjoy the firm backing of the majority presented a major political challenge. For example, Maureen Reilly, an insider in Riverton who had been appointed on a 4–3 vote, nominated as principal a man known to be a liberal, progressive educator. She thought he would be the best match for that particular school, even though he was not the choice of all those who had hired Reilly. As one observer noted, "There were some very strong pressures for her to move away from that choice and that decision, but she hung in there with it." Once appointed, the new principal recalled the "enormous pressures" brought to bear on his boss: "I'm sure it took a great amount of courage. She didn't do that on a whim. I remember her calling me in to tell me that she had made her decision and that she was putting my name forward. After she congratulated me, she said, 'It's going to get rough. I hope you're going to hold in there with me.' I said I was up for it if she was." Another Riverton principal, who characterized his newly appointed colleague as "just extraordinary," praised the superintendent for holding firm but predicted she would pay a price for her courage: "That decision must have been a very, very difficult one. It's not just that you cut an arm off and it goes away when you make a decision like that. It stays around and rots for years and years. It is not the decision that is difficult; it is the price that you will pay. You pay a very heavy price for these decisions."

Sometimes when competing camps were nearly balanced in strength, the school board appointed a compromise candidate as superintendent. Members reasoned that such candidates have no clear allegiance to either political group and thus could maintain the balance of power or bridge the distance between competing groups by mediating between coalitions. Wayne Saunders, an outside appointment whose urban district was split between "progressives" and "traditionalists," adopted such a strategy to ensure that the traditional values of working-class families would be fairly represented: "The progressive group is overrepresented on the school board of nine. . . . We would have only two people who really consciously represent the working families of Summit. What I'm trying to do is keep the traditional educators and the progressive educators in some effective constellation." Saunders thought that if he alienated one group or the other he would have "nothing much to work with" and would spend all of his time "trying to placate the alienated group." Therefore he decided that "the way to educational development in Summit is to do things that represent a consensus that both groups can accept." Anticipating that any change bearing the stamp of one group would generate opposition from the other, he fashioned compromises and smoothed the edges between the groups, so that ultimately both groups could say, "Here are changes that we can embrace within the total community." The fact that Saunders was an outsider seems to have made it possible for him to maintain trust with both sides.

Therefore, political leadership within partisan contexts calls for several approaches from new superintendents: effectively representing the interests of the partisan majority, lobbying to secure the needed votes when support is not routinely assured, and serving as mediator in reconciling differences between competing groups. The challenge is to make sound educational choices given a political context marked by stark divisions and ongoing conflict. Such leadership requires far more calculation and creativity than simply taking sides.

Participatory Politics: Issues, Agendas, and Interest Groups

In five of the districts studied, where actors and interest groups affiliated in response to particular issues rather than according to long-term alliances, participatory politics prevailed. These superintendents spent their time building coalitions in support of their initiatives and managing the interactions of competing interest groups as varied as hockey parents, local business owners, and special education teachers. Constituents in these districts expected their superintendent to be attentive to multiple perspectives and skilled at building consensus among activists with different agendas.

For example, in suburban Clayton, a town characterized by one school board member as "a politically sophisticated community," the prior superintendent was unable to engage in the participatory politics of the town. Consequently, he withdrew to his office, becoming a distant and ineffectual manager. He was, one respondent said, "way out of his league in that regard." By contrast, his successor, Andrew Cronin, was skilled at managing complicated interactions, building coalitions, and mediating among diverse interest groups. One principal praised him for being able to "get things done" in a complex political environment: "He has an ability to respond to a lot of different constituencies. . . . Particularly in this day and age, you're always dealing with essentially competing constituencies . . . within a town. And you need to take every one of those constituencies seriously and make every one of those constituencies feel that they are being heard. And I think he does that well."

Another principal noted how Cronin deliberately maintained an open process: "He has not established any type of 'in' group for himself. He's kept himself very broad-based, and I think he should keep doing that, just so nobody sees that there's a cabal. An 'in' group might make people feel they didn't have access."

Superintendents entering more participatory districts had to forge inclusive decision-making processes. Still, constituents did not deem them successful leaders simply because they heard out various opinions, understood different groups' priorities, and brought together adversaries. Their success depended on the outcome of those efforts, on whether their deliberations produced coherent solutions to educational challenges.

Patronage Politics: Loyalties, Connections, and Paybacks

In districts distinguished by patronage politics, alliances are formed, positions taken, and resources distributed on the basis of personal connections, including family, race, ethnicity, neighborhood, and age-old friendships or feuds. As with partisan politics, patterns of patronage politics are predictable over time. There are often invisible, but inviolable, boundaries between the insiders who grew up in the district and the outsiders who settled there as adults.

Constituents expect a superintendent who has lived and built his or her career within the district to dispense favors and mete out penalties in predictable ways. One assistant principal described Riverton as "a very political city in which the school board had a great deal to do with the appointments at all levels. . . . There are close, even incestuous, connections between people in this city." A school board member in Westford recalled, "When I came into the picture there was—and I use the words advisedly—tribal war-fare among a couple of the members of the school board, and every issue was decided on that basis. The superintendent was unable to deal with that, and he took sides; and it was a disaster for the school system."

One teacher in Ashmont described the ethnic patterns in the city's politics. He said there had never been "an Italian mayor in this city. You will see Italian councilmen and Italian aldermen, but the mayors have always been Irish." The local newspaper publisher in Ashmont recalled that years ago "there were a lot of rascals around," and "they wanted $100 or $200 apiece to get the necessary three votes on the teachers' appointments."

Interviews suggested that patronage politics had not disappeared in Ashmont—it had evolved. The current superintendent was appointed during the first ten minutes of a board meeting, without prior announcement of the docket item. According to one principal, this event was so predictable that it "did not upset anyone in house." However, subsequent program cuts by the superintendent caused resentments to simmer and charges of patronage to fly. One principal warned, "Right now, things are pretty testy. There's a lot of name-calling—things like that, you know. I don't know where it's going to end, but I see destruction. . . . Someone's going to get hurt pretty soon, because it's getting very personal, and it's not very professional." By all accounts, such animosity was not uncommon in Ashmont. A teacher there accepted such politics as "a given. You understand that those are the rules that they play the game by. And I don't see how that will ever change."

Constituents in all twelve districts judged superintendents to be ineffective leaders when they submitted to the pressures of patronage by actively campaigning for their favorite school board candidates or rewarding their allies with financially advantageous decisions. One Ashmont school board member whose faction had recently lost seats on the school board said, "I'm bitter that this goes on, that education takes a backseat to politics, that everything that goes on is politics. Antonellis has his position today because of politics. Many of the decisions he makes are because of politics. And so far as I'm concerned, it shouldn't happen. . . . When I see people using the public school system for their own personal gain, it disturbs me."

When superintendents did not lose their educational and ethical bearings but managed patronage politics on behalf of better education by brokering agreements that advanced the interests of all children, constituents praised them. Such superintendents began with what they believed to be the "right" values and then proceeded to advise board members and community leaders about responsible courses of action. One Riverton respondent called this "working the politics of the city on behalf of the schools." It is difficult for any superintendent to take principled stands in an environment charged with expectations of favors and paybacks. One Ashmont principal described this turbulent environment: "Someone owes you a favor, or you owe them. Then they call in your favor, and then this aggravates somebody else on the other side of the board. They fight over people getting jobs, everything. Everything's a fight."

Notably, the data suggest that in a district laden with patronage politics, a superintendent appointed from outside the district may be more successful at making good educational decisions, because hometown superintendents are widely believed to enter office with political debts. Maureen Reilly's being known for successfully "working city politics" made her constituents ever suspicious that patronage was at play in her administration, and some repeatedly questioned her motives. A school board member, convinced that Reilly owed her appointment to a local politician, observed, "I have some worry about Maureen's political ties. This kind of appearance of patronage makes the job harder for her as a leader." Therefore, although the superintendent of a district where patronage politics thrives might responsibly work local politics on behalf of the schools—as Reilly did in appointing a controversial but highly regarded principal—it appears that a new superintendent's capacity to lead may still be compromised by others' doubts about his or her motives and by rumors about deals.

The twelve sample districts can be sorted almost evenly among these three political contexts—partisan, participatory, and patronage politics—but none rests exclusively in just one. Thus superintendents must be versatile political leaders. For most of the superintendents studied, the political context was workable, even comfortable, largely because the search process had eliminated candidates who lacked the locally requisite political experiences, habits, and skills. For three superintendents, however, the fit was less satisfactory; they found themselves having to adopt new ways of thinking and acting that sometimes seemed awkward. After two years, all three still held their positions, but none was secure.

Political Leadership in Three Arenas

Superintendents exercise political influence as they talk with teachers in schools, listen to parents in PTA meetings, and solicit support from the business community. Often the politics at play in such settings is subtle rather than strident, geared toward building alliances, encouraging action, or winning support for the schools. In fact, many might not even call this politics, just good personal and public relations.

In the districts we studied, there were three groups—the school board, local government, and the teachers union—with whom interactions were explicitly political. Members of these groups vied openly for scarce resources and control over decisions, battling over questions like, How many local tax dollars will be spent on education? How many education dollars will be spent on teacher salaries? Who will determine the curriculum? Who will select personnel? Notably, the key participants were elected officials whose constituents—local citizens or teachers—expected results. As Thomas Wells said of Westford's school board members, "They need to look at [any proposal] and to feel it and to taste it and to chew it and to determine 'Where is this going to go?' and 'How is this going to make me look?'—because they were elected here; they are elected officials."

Interactions among these three groups complicated the superintendent's political leadership in the districts we studied. School boards negotiated with teachers unions, for example, but they were dependent on local government to fund the settlements. Teachers unions endorsed school board candidates, some of whom had promised to seek the superintendent's dismissal if elected. Mayors or local legislative groups controlled the bottom line of budgets, but they had to rely on school boards to spend the money well. These superintendents' challenge as educational leaders was to encourage all participants to recognize their shared interests in supporting the schools and then take those common interests into account as they pursued their particular political goals.

The School Board

Theoretically, school boards are in charge of school districts and hire superintendents to run them; they set the policies that superintendents must implement. However, as anyone involved with school district politics will testify, the relationship is seldom that simple or unidirectional.

Since school boards hire and fire superintendents, technically they hold the upper hand. As Thomas Wells reminded us twice in one interview, "They vote on your job." Many board members are well-intentioned, but others are simply self-interested. Whatever their intentions, few school board members are educational experts. Some represent the interests of only a certain group of students, such as the gifted and talented, or of groups with particular goals, such as purging curricula of liberal values or reducing school budgets. Sometimes school board members have no real interest in education and only want the position in order to climb the local political ladder.

Since school boards are seldom unified groups, superintendents must be careful about taking sides. In districts dominated by partisan politics, a superintendent may be expected to side with the majority who hired him or her; but in others, suspicions of favoritism often preclude that possibility. One school board member in Fernwood recalled an unsuccessful superintendent who had "caused friction on the school board. He would get close to two or three members and there would be like a cabal against the other three members." The superintendent's challenge is to lead this disparate, sometimes self-interested assembly of policy makers so that they act wisely and responsibly on behalf of the district's children.

The prospect of frequent turnover of board members often makes the superintendent's work with the board even more uncertain. Soon after several new school board members were elected in November, Arthur Holzman observed, "As of January 1 we're going to have one-third of the people with no investment in my being here anyway, who bring to the board no tradition of how a board operates."

Ironically, although they are hired by school boards, superintendents are expected to lead them. If they fail to do so, board members will act independently—even irresponsibly—with potentially disastrous consequences. As one seasoned administrator said, "I have found that school boards will fill a void wherever there is one." Failing to work closely with the board may result in flawed and inconsistent policies, publicly damaging showdowns, day-to-day intrusions into school practices, personnel appointments made with little regard to merit, and resources allocated without attention to need. The school boards in the twelve districts studied ranged from a polite group of individuals who their superintendent said "don't talk enough" to a raucous assembly whose televised meetings were called by one respondent "the best show in town." Superintendents ranged from one who reportedly had no say in school board business to one who controlled his board's agenda and lined up the votes well before the meetings.

All twelve superintendents faced similar challenges with their school boards: establishing appropriate and workable boundaries between the board and the central office, avoiding destructive public conflict, framing problems in ways that would elicit attention and action, promoting orderly and constructive decision making, converting political opponents into allies, and fostering collaboration among adversaries. The following three examples illustrate these challenges and highlight the strategies superintendents employed in dealing with them.

Helping Board Members See Beyond Their Wards

In Westford, where the school board is elected by wards, members often act as if the schools in their wards are theirs. Some even volunteer daily in their ward's schools and expect the principals to consult them about routine decisions. The wards generally correspond to ethnically homogeneous communities, and patronage politics is common in the district. Before coming to Westford, Thomas Wells had worked successfully in a comparable city where ethnic groups influenced politics. But he had never seen board members claim such proprietary rights over particular schools. The ward-based focus in Westford discouraged the board from sharing responsibility for all the schools in the district. Wells's goal was to move the board and the district beyond parochialism: "I would hope that the incidence of promoting narrow perspectives or viewpoints in school board meetings will become less prevalent than it is now," he said. Where initially Wells had been determined to eliminate ward-centric behavior, eventually he accepted it as inevitable, understanding the logic behind the members' actions: "They're supposed to represent that ward, and they need direct access to agents of the school department in the ward, not simply through the superintendent."

Recognizing Westford board members' need to be ward-based but wanting to expand their perspective, Wells set out to foster individual relationships with each member and provide accurate and balanced information about both school-specific and districtwide concerns. He started by inviting each board member to lunch: "I would ask them what particular concerns they had, and then I would get my own across." Wells was careful to treat each member equally, playing no political favorites and attending no political fund-raisers. In matters of substance, Wells promised to provide the board with "honest recommendations based on my best judgment." He wanted the members to know that they could vote as they wished but they should not flex political muscle in an effort to influence his recommendations.

School board members warmed to this approach. As one member explained, keeping all the members of the board informed proved to be very important: "You'll always know what's going on. Before, you were always in the dark." Another said, "Even if Tom Wells disagrees with you, he makes you feel respected. If he has the absolute opposite viewpoint, he'll be honest with you about it and tell you he did his review. But he does it in such a respectful way that it's a conversation. It isn't a conflict."

Over time, Westford board members took more responsibility for districtwide goals. One woman reflected, "School board members, a lot of times—all of us—become entwined in politics rather than in what might be best for the system, and it's a temptation. . . . I think Dr. Wells needs to be strong, he needs to be the guardian and remind us, 'You need to do what's best for the system, and not do it just in words but with these recommendations.'"

Teachers and principals were impressed with the progress Wells made in Westford. One said, "Those of us on the inside, knowing the division that was on that school board, [were impressed to see him] come in and patch that up and apparently win a majority. They haven't turned him down yet on any major crisis." Wells had managed to meet members' personal and political needs while at the same time remaining unbiased and advancing sound policies. After two and a half years, Wells's job was secure, and his initial four opponents had become strong supporters: "I feel good about that. In garnering their support, I didn't alienate the other five. I was developing a consensus with the school board."

Leading Under a Contentious, Divided Board

Anna Niles inherited a contentious, divided board accustomed to intervening in the routine decisions of her predecessor, a superintendent of many years. Niles was hired as a change agent, and the majority of board members relied on her to make change happen. But they also expected to closely monitor what she did along the way. Niles moved ahead with programs to improve the schools, despite opposition by a minority of board members. The majority, she observed, were "excited about the things they see as possible changes." But Niles also saw "conflict within the school board between people who are influenced by the old-time, old-town way and people who want change."

As an outsider in a district of insiders, Niles gained only cautious acceptance of the change she introduced. When a position opened for an elementary school principal, many residents and school staff assumed that, in keeping with local custom, it would be filled from within the district. But Niles considered personnel decisions "probably the most important decisions" a superintendent makes. Thus she committed herself to hiring the best candidates, recognizing that "if the school board won't support that, you might as well pack up."

The board rejected Niles's recommended appointment of an outsider for the principal's position by a 4–3 vote. According to a newly appointed central office administrator who was himself an outsider, this "was what you could call a broadside. It was a major event. . . . [It] would have been quite explosive to eliminate the local candidate early in the process. But little did I know that when the school board had the two candidates juxtaposed, they would say, 'We want that one.' It was quite a shocker."

Of the four members who opposed Niles's recommendation, two strongly supported the inside candidate with, as one central office administrator said, "a real, real strong, organized, full-court press." Two additional board members were unhappy with Niles's independent approach to her job and allied with the opposition on this vote. The new central office administrator recalled that these two board members were "not happy. Niles says A and they say B." The vote about the principal, the administrator said, "was the perfect case in point. We could have brought Jesus Christ in last night, and I think two of those people would have voted no." Underlying this dispute was dissension within the board and a strained relationship between Niles and certain board members. The same central office administrator concluded that the 4–3 vote that night represented "one of those classic situations of politics making strange bedfellows. There was an alliance among four people who normally would never, never vote on the same side of an issue."

Eventually the school board relented, largely because state law prohibited them from appointing someone the superintendent had not proposed. A principal described the scene: "It felt like *Showdown at the OK Corral*. They said, 'Okay, you've twice submitted this name. What will you do if we reject it again?'" When Niles said that she would continue to submit the name, one dissenter changed her vote, and the superintendent won a highly publicized victory. Still, it came tagged with a substantial political price. Another principal predicted, "I don't think the school board will forget. I think she put them in a difficult position. . . . That was probably her riskiest single moment."

The history of school district politics in Newbridge presented Niles with special demands. According to a board member, the trouble had started during the prior superintendent's term, when the board "became way too involved in running the schools. The school board needs to take a big, giant step backwards." This respondent argued, however, that pulling back was "hard to do. When you can't count on the information that you're getting, when you learn from bitter experience that that information might not be very good or was manipulated, then you get involved in the details where you don't belong, and it's hard to let go."

Several board members suggested that Niles should keep them better informed, engage them in developing policy, and take responsibility for teaching them to work together. One administrator said, "She's not been forceful and aggressive enough in engaging them around the problem that they have of not getting along with each other—all of those relationship things that continue to foul the processes that we have, and to retard progress." By the end of our study, Niles still had difficult work ahead.

Changing the Priorities of a Stepping-stone Board

The school board members in the inner-city district of Union were only incidentally concerned about education. According to the superintendent, Clara Underwood, many on the nine-member board were there "for political reasons. They see it as a stepping-stone to someplace else in politics. Some of them truly care about education, but that's very few." This was the sort of board that seasoned administrators warn novices to avoid if they hope to survive. When Underwood arrived, the board granted her a one-year contract somewhat reluctantly. Underwood told them, "That's fine. You'll be begging me to stay." She quickly found out, however, that board members' first priority was "little petty stuff," and it became her goal to make it education instead.

In dealing with the board, Underwood discussed educational issues frankly. "I'm refreshing to them," she said. "They've not been used to this. . . . They have not been used to someone saying, 'No, this is not good for kids. This is what we have to do.' It's just very new to them." A central office administrator emphasized that educational values rather than political expediency always determined Underwood's positions: "She would not bow down to political pressures. She is soft-spoken, but she is very forceful. And very forthright. She would not hire or take recommendations for hiring anyone that she felt could not do the job."

Underwood was widely endorsed as a skillful politician. One principal, who said that Union's school board is "a political beast," added that "she is also." Another principal contended that a person in Underwood's position has to be political: "You need five votes. So you walk a tightrope of trying to understand what it is that they are saying and what they really mean, and at the same time you try to maintain your principles. You have to see that education goes on in your schools." Like Wells, Underwood had to deal with members one at a time. As a central office administrator explained, "This board is fragmented. If they spoke with one voice, then she would answer to just one individual." But the board members did not, and consequently Underwood's strategy for garnering five votes was to secure them one by one. A board member explained: "When I talk to her about things, she gives me her time and her attention, and she will work with me as an individual. She never talks to me about other school board members and their ideas and what it is that she is doing with them."

Board meetings in Union were, by several accounts, chaotic. One member said, "We have a school board that is not up to its task. . . . You read our minutes and you'll see. We don't discuss issues." According to one central office administrator, the superintendent persisted even when the board didn't want to deal with her agenda, "listening to them, staying until one o'clock in the morning at working sessions, trying to get things done." If the board rejected her proposal, Underwood would just "reissue it the next time they [met]. She's not going to stop because of any pitfalls they open." After two years, Clara Underwood had won broad support on the board, moving from a bare majority in her 5–4 appointment vote to a unanimous three-year contract offer after two years. As one board member said, "That says a lot."

Leading the Board

As these three examples illustrate (and much additional data from the interviews confirm), superintendents must deal with school boards as distinct organizations and with board members as distinct individuals. There was wide agreement among respondents that superintendents should inform and advise but not coerce their board; that board members' individual needs differ, and legitimate ones deserve the superintendent's attention; and that boards must set aside time for learning to work together with the superintendent, particularly when there is frequent turnover or when the positions board members take are defined by patronage or partisan affiliation. Notably, the data from the interviews suggest that a superintendent who exercises leadership with his or her school board—providing valid and timely information, promoting independent thinking, valuing individual differences, encouraging group responsibility, and taking a stand on important issues—is as much a good educator as a good politician.

The Local Government

Whereas school boards were once relatively independent bodies, today local officials regularly participate in decisions about school budgets, salaries, and programs. Fiscal crises during the last decade have forced superintendents to contend with the mayors and finance officials who allocate funds for the schools. In one of the states included in this study, school districts had fiscal autonomy until 1982, when a referendum capped taxation and mayors won the power to control school districts' budgetary bottom line. Increasingly, local officials have challenged the rights and fiscal judgment of educators. In this state and others, questions have emerged among educators and local officials about who really should control school programs, resources, and personnel appointments. All of the districts we surveyed faced cutbacks; consequently, negotiations between school and local officials often focused on how large budget reductions should be and how teachers' salaries should compare with those of other city employees. These difficult questions increasingly brought school and municipal officials to a face-off as they vied for greater control over scarce resources and important decisions.

In several of the districts, local officials held school board seats as well. In three districts the mayor was ex officio a member of the board; in one of those, a city council member also voted on school policy. Fifteen years ago city officials kept a respectful distance from school business; today, however, many monitor district activities and intervene regularly. Superintendent Garcetti said that in Glendale "the mayor and his group of people" don't trust the school department. "We are the largest consumer of tax dollars in the city. . . . We consume 44 percent of the budget. So the city looks at us as a department. . . . We look at ourselves as autonomous and not responsive to any political interference." In Ashmont, a working-class city where the repeated cry of citizens was said to be "low taxes, low taxes, low taxes," the mayor bridled under the state law restricting his control over educational spending: "We do not have a legal capacity to tell them what to do with that money. So they could come in and tell me that they needed $10 for apples when I really wanted to spend it on oranges, and there's very little I can do about it." This mayor believed, however, that ultimately he had greater leverage than the school board, because what school officials did one year would have "a great deal to do with my response to next year's budget. They have to justify—as any other department would, to this office and to the people that advise me on financial matters—why they need a particular amount of dollars."

Over and over, the superintendents we studied tried to protect their budgets and staff from cuts, while mayors, finance committees, and city councils tried to reduce the tax dollars spent on education. The superintendents became vocal advocates of education and searched for ways to negotiate agreements with city officials without making unwise or unnecessary compromises. Several superintendents described the challenges posed by this increasing interdependence. As Pfeffer (1981) explains, interdependence "means that the potential for both conflict and cooperation exists. The interdependence creates conflict because the goals and values within each of the various interacting organizational units may not be consonant. The potential for cooperation and coalition formation exists because organizational participants are used to working with and through others in order to get things done" (p. 154).

Standing Up to the Mayor to Protect the Budget

In the working-class city of Westford, the mayor has the final say on the size of the school budget. He also has a seat on the school board, along with a Westford council member. When the mayor told Thomas Wells to recommend a million dollars in budget cuts, Wells refused, proposing instead a 13 percent increase in school funding. The mayor was furious, contending during his interview that "his superintendent" should never have taken such a stand. The superintendent analyzed the problem in retrospect: "He felt that I had boxed him in. He would have preferred that I'd gone to him and said, 'How much can you give us?'" Wells, however, stood firm in support of the schools: "People are worried about the new mayor because he is the guy passing out the dollars. I think that they are looking to me to influence that mayor in a way that will . . . minimize losses and maximize damage control." Wells had considered his options carefully, and he decided to play to the public on the issue. Teachers and administrators supported him. One said, "He has been outspoken on educational issues, particularly fiscal issues, which past superintendents have been afraid to do. They're not always courageous enough to stand up against the mayor or against the aldermen of the city when it comes to fiscal matters. He's been very plain."

Still, such courage may not always pay off. For if the money is not there or the mayor doesn't have the political power to commit more funds to education, the superintendent will be blamed for undermining the mayor and still pay a political price for his courage.

Taking Public Action to Restore Budget Cuts

In Fernwood, a small-town school district with a history of modest school budgets, Dick Fitzgerald assumed his position believing that educational finances were secure. Soon after arriving, however, he learned that serious mismanagement of municipal funds had threatened the schools' future. Five minutes before a town meeting in the fall of his first year, Fitzgerald heard that the local finance committee had proposed a cut of $500,000 from the district's already tight budget. Dismayed at the distrust implicit in such a sudden turnaround, Fitzgerald vowed to "pack the next meeting." A central office administrator described the effort to mobilize opposition: "We went around to the buildings [to recruit staff] and packed the meeting. They restored the cuts. He could have run for mayor the next day; everybody was very supportive. It was a phenomenal response that [the finance committee] gave to him, because they had never been communicated with like that before. No superintendent had ever sat down and told them what was going on."

Fitzgerald had to make a convincing case to skeptical public officials, and in doing so he carefully built coalitions with politicians throughout the town on behalf of education. One teacher praised his effort and success: "I see him working with the selectmen. I see him working with the school board. I see him working with the finance committee. It seems like he's trying to pull it all together. It seems like he's being the magnet and saying, 'Let's get unified, people, and let's all work toward a common goal.'" Fitzgerald won great admiration in town for bargaining successfully with a finance committee that, according to one principal, has its own vested interests. By organizing a strong, broad-based coalition of teachers to demonstrate at the meeting, he gained power to negotiate in the future on behalf of the schools.

Demonstrating Political Leadership on Behalf of Education

Superintendents obliged to enter their local political arenas have to become adept at distinguishing between concession and compromise and between belligerence and bargaining. They have to learn the priorities of mayors and other local officials and influence those individuals' perception of the schools. The superintendents in the districts studied recognized their increasing interdependence with politicians and devised ways to work collaboratively with them while protecting and advancing their own educational goals. A few superintendents could expect to present their cases in fair hearings and receive reasoned responses to their requests. More, however, found that they had to enter the political fray, take impassioned stands, mobilize community support, and participate in public show-downs when negotiation failed.

Teachers Unions

Collective bargaining laws empowering teachers to organize and negotiate have changed the power relationships in many school districts. While superintendents are technically teachers' superiors on the organizational chart, in the labor-management arena such distinctions have little use. For by their number alone, unionized teachers have the power to initiate coercive demonstrations and job actions that cannot be ignored. Superintendents who hope to lead their districts to better practices need teachers' consistent sup-port, support that is virtually impossible to secure when labor-management relations are hostile or when union leaders repeatedly discredit the superintendent. Therefore, establishing productive (if not cordial) working relationships with union leaders is essential for new superintendents, and the political skills of building coali-tions, fashioning compromises, and trading concessions are central to effective leadership.

Notably, however, a superintendent cannot act as an independent agent in dealing with a teachers union. Any agreement has important implications for others, specifically the school board, which formally negotiates with teachers; city officials, who fund union contracts; and principals, who must administer the agree-ments day to day. Therefore, in exercising political leadership with the union, superintendents must attend to others' interests as well.

Of the various political relationships observed in this study, it was in superintendents' interactions with teachers unions that they were most likely to be granted a period of grace. Although four superintendents took office during times of labor conflict—just after a strike, during a strike, or when a strike was threatened—each was held blameless for the strife and was empowered to try and resolve the conflict. The other eight superintendents were all granted time to develop working relationships with their teachers unions, although sometimes this period seemed more like a cease-fire than a honeymoon.

A new superintendent's relationship with the teachers union is inevitably influenced by the history of the district's labor relations. While the superintendent might be new to the community, union leaders invariably are not; often they have been active teacher advocates in their districts for a decade or more. Labor leaders in the districts studied, though careful not to attack a superintendent early on, sometimes ignored calls for a clean slate or a fresh relationship, particularly when the district had a history of hostile bargaining or contentious job actions. Conversely, districts accustomed to amiable settlements and informal contract management were likely to be put off by a new superintendent who talked tough or touted aggressive managerial tactics.

When the superintendents in the districts studied found labor relations in their new districts to be cordial, they tried to maintain or improve them. If the previous superintendent had been a union adversary, the new superintendent generally pursued a more cooperative relationship. None sought to harden positions, provoke opposition, or wield authority for show, and well over half set out to make labor-management relationships more collegial. In response, teachers unions in districts with histories of conflict generally offered new superintendents the chance to forge new, more constructive relationships.

Disarming Distrust and Building New Relationships

Fernwood superintendent Dick Fitzgerald was himself a former union president, with a reputation for collaboration. His predecessor had stressed his managerial authority as superintendent and had angered union leaders with his haughty criticism of them and their work, reportedly pointing out early in his tenure that teachers were "blue-collar labor."

Fitzgerald met informally and frequently with union leaders, and they were disarmed by his candor and collegiality. One said, "In my current role and because of the relationship he's established, I'd just call him up and say, 'Gee, what do you think about this?'" Another explained, "We all work together. We're all part of the same group. We have our different roles and different positions, but he's accessible." A third emphasized that Fitzgerald was flexible but not without principles and limits: "In some of our meetings he's willing to bend, willing to listen, willing to really negotiate. . . . Other times, he'll come across saying, 'No, no, no. This is the way I want it.'"

Labor relations were relatively calm and steady in Fernwood as Fitzgerald and union leaders developed new understandings and practices. Fitzgerald's political efforts to build a base of trust enabled him to advance his educational agenda. During the first year he eliminated the department-head positions in the high school, consolidating them with systemwide positions. The change saved money and gave different teachers an opportunity to lead. Any superintendent intending to eliminate such positions is virtually assured of a belligerent union challenge. While there was anger among some at Fernwood High School—the move had "caused quite an upheaval" one union leader said—and there was talk of taking the issue to arbitration, organized opposition was muted largely because of the friendly and respectful working relationship between Fitzgerald and union leaders. One said, "If you asked me for a strict union view, I'd give you a very hard union line on that. But all of it was not negative, I'll be honest with you." By making this change, Fitzgerald effectively removed from positions of power several department heads who had undermined his efforts to improve the school. One union leader said Fitzgerald "did the people in this building and myself a big favor by doing what he did."

Because Fitzgerald had developed trust with union leaders and was seen to make sound educational decisions, he was able to take constructive action without incurring intense labor opposition.

Seeking to Minimize the Impact of a Contract Dispute

Ray Garcetti, a Glendale insider, assumed his role during a period of prolonged, unsuccessful contract negotiations. "It's been," as one teacher explained, "a year of conflict between the teachers union and the school board." There was a brief strike in September that ended with a tentative settlement. Members of the school board who opposed the negotiated salary increase refused to ratify the agreement, however, leading the union to file an unfair labor practice charge on behalf of the teachers. Meanwhile, school board members threatened layoffs if the teachers did not forego the raises, a move that one teacher likened to "extortion."

Throughout, Garcetti distanced himself from the conflict, insisting that negotiations were the responsibility of the school board, not the superintendent. A principal said that Garcetti "kept a low profile," trying to support teachers without undermining the board, a difficult maneuver that fueled doubts about his motives and loyalties. Most teachers held Garcetti blameless for the impasse, which had originated well before his appointment. One teacher said, "They know it's not really Ray's fault. They blame the school board." However, some teachers thought he should have taken a more active role. One asked critically, "Is he really pushing to get this thing settled? The man's hired by the school board. We know who he has to back. . . . I don't think he's going to the mat for us."

Garcetti's efforts to boost morale among teachers by praising their work and avoiding the labor conflict worked only in the short term. A central office administrator noted that the superintendent was being held responsible for the conflict even though he didn't have control: "We have to go into the buildings every day with a lot of unhappy teachers. And he's done a good job of morale building there. It hasn't turned around miraculously, but it's not as bad

as it could have been." Ultimately, though, Garcetti did not intervene in an effort to resolve the dispute, which over time became
extremely hostile and damaging to the schools. While Garcetti was
able to work cooperatively with union leaders he had known for
years, he had not developed a good political alliance with either the
school board or the city administrators who held the means to settle the contract dispute.

Mediating a Strike Settlement

An eleven-day strike was under way in Ashmont when the school
board moved quickly to offer the superintendency to Louis Antonellis, an insider in the system. Some respondents contended that the
union went on strike deliberately to ensure Antonellis's appointment, but others saw him as a successful mediator who entered the
scene and ended the job action. Throughout there were complicated interactions among the union, the new superintendent, the
school board, and the mayor.

When the prior superintendent resigned after a heart attack in
August, Ashmont had no contract with the teachers and no budget for the schools. A majority of the school board members were
proponents of Antonellis, then the assistant superintendent. Several of his opponents on the board, including one candidate for
mayor, faced a primary election within two weeks. Some individuals said that the school board members up for reelection believed
that a strike might enhance their public image as principled officials
unwilling to make concessions. Teachers, seeing no serious effort by
the school board to reach an agreement, struck on the first day of
school. Meanwhile, the mayor refused to fund teachers' annual pay
raises until the school board approved a budget.

One week into the strike, the school board, needing Antonellis's administrative skills to prepare the budget, made him a meager
contract offer at the beginning of a regular meeting; there was insufficient board support to offer him a more attractive package. The
meeting room and hallways were jammed with teachers demanding

a contract settlement and with television reporters expecting news about the strike; much of Ashmont watched the engrossing proceedings on cable TV. Given ten minutes to decide, Antonellis accepted the offer.

Several days later, the chairman of the school board, an opponent of Antonellis, lost in the primary election. The union president recalled, "It was the next day after the election that the rest of the members buckled in. By then we had already gotten our guarantee from the mayor that the raises would be funded."

Some, like this respondent, said that the settlement was inevitable after the election; others contend that Antonellis was the mediator who ended the job action.

While Garcetti steered clear of the labor dispute in Glendale, Antonellis earned his reputation by moving into the center of the strike in Ashmont. He explained the situation: "All negotiations then went through me, because they wouldn't talk to each other. Then it bogged down so bad that they brought an arbitrator in to try and resolve it, and actually, between the arbitrator and myself and the attorneys for both sides, we were able to pull the thing through and get it resolved." Antonellis was widely praised for his success. One principal's comments were typical: "He started off with a strike. I think he did a really magnificent job handling that, for a new superintendent, in really holding things together." Union leaders, too, granted the new superintendent special protection in his new role. One said, "I worked very hard to make sure that, during the strike, Mr. Antonellis was not painted out to be the bad guy, because we weren't really at war with him as much as we were at war with the school board and the city government itself. So I was very up-front with him; he was very up-front with me." Thus, Antonellis began his tenure credited with having supported teachers and headed off a major crisis.

Developing a Labor Management Strategy

Four superintendents, including Garcetti and Antonellis, were involved in serious labor disputes during their first two years in office. Others, like Fitzgerald, dealt with only ordinary labor-management responsibilities—grievance appeals, jointly sponsored staff development, layoff notifications. Whether intentionally or inadvertently, the superintendents were establishing the personal affiliations and patterns of interaction that would define labor-management relations over the course of their tenure. Some built relationships that were informal and spontaneous; others chose to be more reserved and faithful to their roles as managers. Respondents often speculated that upcoming negotiations would reveal the wisdom of their new superintendent's strategies. A principal in one district called bargaining "the acid test." A central office administrator dubbed it "the potential Achilles heel, not only for him but for anybody in his role."

Given that none of the newly appointed superintendents participated in a full round of labor negotiations, it was not apparent whether they were better off in the long run maintaining distance from labor leaders or actively fostering cooperation with them. Certainly the local context—the history of labor relations, the experience and intentions of union leaders, the fiscal realities of the community, the attitudes of school board members and local officials—led superintendents to take different approaches in labor-management interactions. The success with which individuals resolved short-term problems suggested that it was important for new superintendents to develop respectful, fair, and firm working relationships with union leaders. And as we saw with Garcetti, if superintendents are to be influential in larger labor issues, such as collective bargaining, they not only have to work productively with union leaders, they also have to effectively influence the priorities of the school board and city officials.

Political Leadership: A Prerequisite for Success

The political demands of the superintendency are many, requiring new superintendents to draw upon a wide range of analytic, strategic, and interpersonal skills. Superintendents must first consider the political features of their districts in light of their own strengths and shortcomings. They must ascertain the character of local politics, identifying the competing interests, sizing up the players, and making connections. They must attend to the particular political demands of school boards, local governments, and teachers unions, discovering how to lead people who are not subject to their authority but have far-reaching influence on the schools.

Throughout, the superintendent must be guided by clear purposes and strong principles. Politics in education is beguiling for some people and can become compelling on its own, without regard to their values or goals. It is possible to become deft at playing politics and skilled at winning, while doing little for schools or children. However, when respondents in this study praised their superintendents for being politically adept, they did so because they believed that adeptness served a constructive educational purpose.

When respondents criticized current and former superintendents for their politics, it was either because they regarded these individuals as inept politically or because they saw them acting politically for poor or paltry purposes. Respondents expressed contempt for superintendents who seemed motivated by self-interest, using politics to enhance their own power or career. They respected those who, however reluctantly, used their political skills to improve the schools. It was such superintendents whose leadership constituents admired and whose example they followed. In the next chapter we look closely at the political leadership of one such superintendent, Andrew Cronin, who sought to increase excellence and equity for the students of Clayton.

Notes

1. Tyack and Hansot (1982) report that "administrative progressives" during the early 1900s "sought to 'take schools out of politics' and to shift decision making upward and inward in hierarchical systems of management. . . . One day, in this dream, political conflict over edu-

cation would become as futile and unnecessary as witch trials; the experts would run everything to everyone's benefit. This was their own version of a millennial future" (p. 107). Neustadt (1990) reports that there is "a yearning in our national electorate for political leaders 'above politics'" (p. 162). This desire for purity, then, is not confined to education. Pfeffer (1981) identifies a "schizophrenia with which concepts such as power and politics have been treated in the literature. Power and politics are fine for understanding and diagnosing events on a national or governmental level; at the level of formal organizations, however, power and politics are considered to be either pejorative terms or illegitimate as analytical concepts for use in understanding bureaucratic or rational systems of decision making" (p. 8).

The Politics of Equity and Excellence

Some communities are known for their industries—electronics, mining, textiles. Others are distinguished by their recreational opportunities—skiing, horse racing, river rafting. Yet others are recognized for their historical sites—battles won, ruins found, or feats achieved there. Clayton, an inner-ring suburb of a large city, is known for its schools.

Public education is not just an attractive feature of Clayton; it is the reason people move there and stay. Schools are the residents' major source of pride in their town. One administrator explained that "in Clayton you get a private-school education in the public sector. We have a number of tuition students because the parents realize they'll get a quality education but the students will still be part of a heterogeneous population. That's what makes Clayton so attractive."

Touted twenty-five years ago as a "lighthouse district," Clayton is still highly respected for its schools. But as one assistant principal explained, it is the comprehensive high school that garners the most attention: "This high school has to be the jewel in the crown. People move into the community and pay exorbitant taxes because the high school is perceived as providing an excellent education. Without the high school, nothing separates Clayton from other towns." A central office administrator confirmed this view, calling Clayton High School "the flagship" and "the most important product that we are peddling in this town. . . . It's an extraordinary educational institution."

Once homogeneously white and upper-middle-class, Clayton has become much more racially, ethnically, and economically diverse during the past two decades. Now the home of immigrants from around the world, speaking languages as varied as Spanish, Hebrew, Russian, and Chinese, its neighborhoods feature ethnic shops of all kinds, patronized by people from many cultures.

Having long regarded itself as a liberal community, Clayton takes pride in this growing diversity, which many say is the source of Clayton's strength. But diversity has also introduced new challenges for Clayton, which are intensified by increasing fiscal problems as demands for social services grow but resources remain constant. "For a long time," one veteran principal explained, "Clayton has been a generous community, and people had gotten accustomed to getting what they wanted. And they want the best." Whereas once the people of Clayton believed that all people's needs—even their hopes—could be met, there are now intense discussions about priorities and complex strategies for dividing a fixed pie. These deliberations often center on the schools, both because they claim such a large share of the local budget and because education is so central to the community's sense of itself.

For Clayton educators, proud of their schools and worried that they might be slipping—or even just perceived to be slipping—the challenge is often framed in terms of equity and excellence. How can Clayton maintain high standards while meeting the needs of all its students? The new superintendent, Andrew Cronin, explained it this way: "Clayton has changed from a suburban system to a truly urban-suburban system, with an economic and social mix that is unbelievably different from what it was twenty-five or thirty years ago. The question behind it is, Can you keep up the quality with this economic and social mix and ethnic mix? . . . What I have to prove is that you can do it." Cronin, previously an associate superintendent in a large urban district, was attracted to Clayton for both the reputation of its schools and the diversity of its population. He envisioned a public school system that would deliver on its promises of excellence and equity, ensuring not only equal opportunity but also equal success. One principal said, "He is committed to educational excellence for all of the constituencies of the town, and he is struggling to achieve that. It's not an easy thing to achieve. It's terribly complex."

Corralling Competing Factions in Clayton

In leading the schools toward realizing a vision of excellence for all students, Cronin had to engage many participants both inside and outside the district. Clayton is a town of lively and intense participatory politics, where citizens expect not only to be heard by their local officials but also to influence the decisions they make. Ronald Heifitz aptly characterizes the kind of leadership Cronin had to undertake: "Leadership is a political activity of corralling competing factions with conflicting definitions of the problem, getting a coherent definition of the problem that takes into account more, rather than fewer, points of view" (quoted in Bolman and Deal, 1994, p. 83). By every account, Cronin had a remarkable ability to corral competing factions; his political instincts were keen.

Experienced activists and strong interest groups vie to shape policy in Clayton's schools and local government. In their annual town meetings, citizens vigorously debate controversial proposals. School board members are highly educated, well-informed, and serious about their work. A central office administrator explained, "Everybody thinks they're right and their idea is more powerful than the next person's. It's a big prima donna town. No one feels they can't come into my office or the superintendent's and tell us how to do our jobs."

With so many self-appointed experts, such varied interests, and such a diverse citizenry in Clayton, Cronin had to be attentive to what one administrator called an "awesome" array of constituencies.

The political order, he explained, "could break down in different places, and you have to be astute enough to know where and how to deal with it. . . . And you can't make everyone happy all of the time. You know that, so [maintaining] the balance is important."

Many respondents described Cronin's political acumen, widely agreeing that his strength lay in his ease with people, which enabled him to gain support for his positions. As one principal put it, "He is a real charming guy and he really likes people." A teacher said, "He's a wonderful politician. He's smooth as glass. That's a wonderful attribute—not to be abrasive. . . . I don't feel as if I'm being conned. He makes everyone feel important. He never looks bored. He has a rare sense of humor. He's not stuffy." Like many others interviewed, one school board member wanted us to understand that he regarded Cronin's political style as constructive, not controlling: "You could say that it is manipulative. The trouble is, 'manipulative' has a very pejorative tone to it; but it's shrewd, it's effective." (Tyack and Hansot [1982, pp. 144–152] described similar qualities in Frank Cody, a politically successful superintendent of the Detroit public schools beginning in 1919.)

From the early days of his administration, Cronin's attention to people ranged well beyond those in the school district. A central office administrator said Cronin was "very smart about other people in town. He gets a quick read on people, and he's very respectful of other people's work." She observed that he drew upon the goodwill he had banked while visiting town and school officials during his first weeks on the job: "I don't see anybody out to get him. He's done so much to make them feel reassured." This demonstrates what Richard Neustadt (1990) calls "prospective power." In his study of U.S. presidents, Neustadt concluded that "presidents did not think hard enough, carefully enough, beforehand, about foreseeable, even likely consequences to their own effectiveness in office, looking down the line and around corners" (p. xviii). But Cronin, by all accounts, did.

Over time, competition for scarce financial resources intensified in Clayton. School officials thus increasingly stressed the importance of promoting alliances among their constituents, both in the school department and beyond it. As a central administrator explained, they needed people to "really, really work hard for their schools" and start to "think bigger than their own small school agenda." The school department was fiscally dependent on the town and had to win approval for its proposed budget each year. At the same time, advocates for better roads, improved police protection, and lower taxes also staked their claim on the community's tax dollars. A central office administrator observed that Andrew Cronin's political skills were critical in this larger municipal arena: "You really need someone who can work with other members of the town's governing structures. . . . It's not a gentlemanly enterprise. And previous superintendents, frankly, were completely killed by that aspect of the job." Although participatory politics in Clayton was polite by many districts' standards, interaction was intense, and demands for leadership in the schools and beyond were great.

Three Issues of Excellence and Equity

Three major issues emerged during the first two years of Cronin's superintendency which tested him as a political leader. Each raised questions of equity and excellence, and since Cronin's goal of providing all students with a first-rate education had become emblematic of his administration, the stakes for each were perceived to be high. The first, a campaign to fund a new school building to serve the town's poorest neighborhood, was a cause that he identified early and personally championed. The second, budget cuts that threatened to decimate school programs, he foresaw and addressed with a politically purposeful plan. The third, a community protest about academic standards at Clayton High School, surprised Cronin, and he reacted with uncertainty, seeking to protect teachers' professional autonomy while sponsoring a forum for open debate among competing coalitions of citizens. These three issues, which overlapped chronologically and interacted politically, illustrate both the complexity of participatory politics in Clayton and Cronin's strategies for political leadership in the district.

Winning Approval for the New Kennedy School

Controversy over the proposed new Kennedy School predated Andrew Cronin's administration by many years. Several of his predecessors had become embroiled in it and had seen their initiatives soundly defeated by local voters. Notably, Kennedy enrolled students from the poorest and most diverse neighborhoods in the town. This was the only elementary school housed in two buildings. Located several blocks apart, both buildings were, as one respondent said, "very old and in very poor shape." For many the shabby state of the Kennedy School presented shameful evidence that Clayton cared more about wealthy white children than about African-American, Latino, and white working-class and poor children.

Accounts differed about the extent to which the run-down facilities compromised the quality of teaching and learning at the Kennedy School. One principal argued that a new school should be built because "it is desirable and fair, not because the kids aren't getting a quality education. Kennedy does a lot for its kids." Other respondents, though, said the program at Kennedy was also inadequate, and that the decrepit building was simply symptomatic of Clayton's disregard for these students' educational needs. They argued that a new school would not only symbolize the town's commitment to all students but also provide the occasion for an academic and social revival at Kennedy.

In 1989 Cronin took on the challenge of winning approval for the new building. He articulated the challenge as one of providing equity, telling the press that the Kennedy School was "a third-rate facility in a first-class town." Some respondents said that Cronin, as superintendent, didn't have a choice in the matter, that he had to advocate for the Kennedy School, but no one thought success was likely. It was potentially a big win for Cronin, but it would not be tallied as a significant loss if he failed. Many said that the Kennedy School suffered because political influence was not equally distributed across town and that people didn't expect Cronin to succeed. One principal said, "If he doesn't get that built, I don't think that will hurt him politically. And that's unfortunate, but it's because that school doesn't have the political backing to make it an issue." Another principal expressed similar doubts: "Andy won't be measured by whether he gets a new Kennedy School. Nobody's ever been able to be successful as far as that's concerned." A central office administrator who labeled the prolonged controversy "a quagmire" remarked, "If he can orchestrate *that*—well, no one's been able to do it." With obvious enthusiasm, Cronin took on the issue of the Kennedy School, calling it the most significant challenge he would face during his second year as superintendent. One central office administrator, noting that Cronin wanted his superintendency measured by his success with the Kennedy School, said, "Whew! That's really putting himself on the line."

Overcoming a History of Failed Attempts

The history behind this controversy was hardly encouraging. The most recent and carefully orchestrated initiative occurred in 1977, when a referendum to build a new school for $2.5 million failed. By all accounts it was defeated because the Kennedy community was politically weak and unorganized. In Clayton, as in many other communities, political power depended on wealth and social status. After the referendum for the Kennedy School was defeated, two other Clayton schools succeeded in winning the votes needed to renovate and enlarge their facilities. Two principals contrasted these victories with the defeat of the 1977 referendum. One said that the referendum for renovating his school passed a year after the Kennedy proposal had failed. When asked to explain the different outcomes, he said, "Politics, I suppose. [This is] a bigger neighborhood and they went out and sold it. [Our school] is more of a community school than the Kennedy is. It serves a wider community. We serve the senior citizens and the music schools and adult education. It's really a community school. It's centrally located. So we generate a lot more

enthusiasm and [serve] a lot more constituencies." Another principal characterized the success of the second school-renovation project, which was located in a wealthier and more influential
community with greater political influence than Kennedy: "They got
a new wing. Kennedy School can't get anything. How does it happen? Politics. [The people in the other neighborhood] knew what
they wanted and they got it. And they put the pressure on the right
people on the school board. They said, 'This is what we want and
you'd better get it.' Kennedy School can't do that."

According to the *Clayton Chronicle*, the 1977 referendum failed
not only because proponents represented it ineffectively, but also
because others who actively opposed it were concerned about their
taxes and unconcerned about whether Kennedy students were well
served. One parent from the Kennedy neighborhood said that opponents used scare tactics to defeat the referendum by telling elderly
voters throughout the town that they would not be able to afford
living in Clayton if the $2.5 million initiative passed. When Cronin
again raised the issue in 1989, the *Chronicle* editors castigated "those
who lacked vision [in 1977 and] spearheaded a vitriolic political
attack on the plan." Editorial writers concluded: "Recent history
teaches that Clayton's voters have difficulty standing tall when
buried in fear, misinformation, and predictions of financial disaster."
The message was clear—it would take the courage and conviction
of a strong leader to help Clayton move beyond this past.

Cronin not only had to overcome doubts fueled by past failures,
he also had to contend with current economic conditions that were
even less propitious than in 1977. Voters had passed a statewide tax
cap severely restricting revenue needed for the project; approval
required endorsement by two-thirds of Clayton's voters, and only 20
percent of those voting still had children in the public schools.
Moreover, new property evaluations promising higher taxes had riled
the voters and impelled them to oppose all new proposals for public
improvements. Not only were non-Kennedy residents unenthusias-
tic about the referendum, many Kennedy supporters were dispirited

and pessimistic. An official of the teachers union said, "Teachers at the Kennedy don't believe that change is possible. They don't believe that this will happen. [Cronin will have to] let teachers know that we're finally trying to right a wrong. He will have to convince the teachers that they're going to have to take a risk."

Cronin's strategy for the Kennedy campaign combined his publicly stated commitment to the cause with a comprehensive drive to win support. He guided the issue through deliberations of review committees; he reframed the issue to make the new school seem locally necessary and financially prudent; and he built alliances with likely opponents and personally educated voters throughout the town.

Taking a Stand for Equity

Given the failures of the past, Cronin firmly stated his commitment to build the school so that constituents and other school officials would not doubt his resolve. A central office administrator said that Cronin was "grieved by the inequity and [saw] it as his job to make that school as good as every other Clayton school." One principal, who heard Cronin champion the issue at a board meeting, was convinced that this superintendent meant to succeed: "He made the best political speech I've ever heard a superintendent in Clayton make. . . . He said that he wants his superintendency to be measured by his ability to turn the Kennedy School around. . . . People were shocked, and then they applauded. I think he's really focused on the Kennedy School and that he has the need to raise the issue everywhere he goes. He's really taking it seriously. It's a high-gain position for him. If he doesn't pull it off, most of the community won't care. But I feel he's really committed."

Cronin convinced many that his words were not empty rhetoric. A central office administrator explained, "He's not pretending that he wants a new Kennedy School. There's such a difference between Cronin and the way previous superintendents have behaved." Many respondents saw in Cronin's strong stand political courage amid indifference.

Not only did Cronin voice unequivocal support for the new building, he also encouraged improvements in the program at the Kennedy. One central office administrator commented at length on the superintendent's active sponsorship of reform at the school: "He's doing much more than talking. He's mobilizing forces. . . . He's pulling in [the assistant superintendent] and two of her best coordinators. And that is progress, because to mobilize the best available resources in town is a very powerful statement." Cronin made it clear that he intended to right past imbalances. "He's giving them money that nobody else is getting. . . . He's making sure the other principals know that Kennedy School is going to get everything, because it's been left out and he's not going to tolerate it. So nobody need come to him, because nobody is going to get anything ahead of Kennedy." This administrator saw in Cronin's advocacy "a very important message to the rest of the principals," who were accustomed to working as entrepreneurs on behalf of their schools.

While Cronin signaled to the principals that they should hold off seeking special concessions for their schools, he also sent a message to those at the Kennedy School that their school mattered and that he would support their efforts to improve it. When the teachers held a retreat for program development, central office administrators, including the assistant superintendent, covered classes. By putting his imprimatur on school reform at the Kennedy School, by investing money and contributing his staff's time, and by apprising other principals about the new order in the district, Cronin set the stage to demonstrate the need for a building in which a revitalized Kennedy School staff could realize its goals.

Analyzing Options and Convening a Cause

Cronin believed that good data and analysis would support the case for the new Kennedy School. On his advice the school board commissioned architects to study the problem and recommend alternatives. The board chair called their published analysis "the most responsible report in the fifteen-year history of the Kennedy School [struggle]. . . . I don't think this rigor has ever been brought to bear regarding the Kennedy." Clayton had few palatable choices: one of the Kennedy buildings could no longer be used safely, and the second facility was not large enough to house all of the students. Therefore the town would have to renovate the substandard building, reduce the size of the Kennedy School, or build a new school. The board eliminated renovation as an option, because the costs would exceed those of new construction. They were also unhappy about the prospect of creating a smaller school, which would require redistricting students who did not want to leave the Kennedy School. The embattled community was determined not to be divided. Moreover, redistricting would have a domino effect on enrollment patterns throughout the town. Clayton residents were very attached to their neighborhood schools; the board could never sell that plan.

Having this clear and comprehensive analysis of the options in hand, Cronin chaired an ad hoc advisory committee of the school board to study the report. In February 1990 the advisory group recommended construction of a new building. Knowing that approval depended on winning broad support among Clayton's policy makers, Cronin said, "I'm meeting with the town council and the school board, and we're forming a townwide committee. This is really a leadership group." According to one administrator, this new organization, the Partnership for a New Kennedy School, included "the best twenty people in town who are really outspoken, who are leaders, who are perceived as representing strong constituencies." Including groups as wide-ranging as the conservative Clayton Civic Association and the liberal Clayton Tenants Union, the Partnership raised nearly $20,000 to promote the cause.

Members of Clayton's town council were convinced by the Partnership's arguments and impressed by the strength and breadth of its membership. In response they voted unanimously to put the referendum on the ballot. One said, "[Keeping] the status quo at the

Kennedy School would violate community standards and thus would be unacceptable." The chair of the town council adamantly opposed any general referendum to increase operating funds for the schools, but he supported this targeted initiative: "It is crystal clear that what is at stake here is not a new Kennedy School but the integrity of our elementary educational system. . . . I firmly believe a new Kennedy School is the future of Clayton. . . . I don't think there'll ever be a more important issue than this." The referendum would ask voters to approve a $13 million bond to build the school; this was a large sum during financially tight times, and it would require broad endorsement.

Persuading the Public

The zeal of Kennedy School advocates was countered by their adversaries' vehement opposition. Both camps framed the issue as one with broad-ranging consequences for all residents. The president of the Parent-Teacher Organization proclaimed, "It's a quality-of-life issue in Clayton. . . . Clayton's whole identity is tied up in education." The *Clayton Chronicle* agreed: "This is a question that will have a serious, long-term effect on the town, not just the school system." Opponents raised specters of financial disaster: "It's a watershed vote. If you go ahead and get enough people approving the construction of a new school, you're inviting the economic destruction of Clayton."

Proponents, led by Cronin, set out to educate the public and persuade voters that a vote for the Kennedy School was a vote for a strong and prosperous Clayton. One advocate, anticipating that the campaign would be won person by person, told a *Clayton Chronicle* reporter, "Any plan that we have is going to be one of education. I see a lot of evening coffees and presentations. Nothing will supplant sitting down in people's living rooms." Cronin, assuming the role of educator, escorted a dozen elderly residents from several housing complexes to the Kennedy School so that they could see the need for a new building. The newspaper quoted him as telling these citizens, "You have the power to vote 'yes' and help us build a new Kennedy School. It's up to you to save the [district's] continuity and community."

In December 1991, Clayton voters approved the referendum by a two-to-one margin, with fifteen of sixteen precincts in the town supporting the measure. Cronin, ecstatic about the victory, was quoted as saying, "This may be my most gratifying moment in twenty-seven years of public education. This vote is a clear and enlightened message from the people of Clayton about the value of education and their concern for the future of our young people." He had resurrected what was thought to be a lost cause and convinced groups that had been at odds to work together for its success. He made it his issue—an educational priority and a political challenge. By reinterpreting the meaning of this issue so that citizens believed it embodied both educational and civic interests and by educating residents widely about their stake in the future of the Kennedy School, Cronin succeeded in demonstrating that he could lead the town to stand behind its espoused belief in equity.

Building a Budget in Tight Times

While working to build support for the new Kennedy School, Cronin also faced budget cuts imposed by the state's tax cap, which automatically reduced revenues for public education in Clayton until they reached a mandated level. The challenge was clear: Clayton would likely have less money for several years in succession.

Anticipating recurring budget cuts, the school board hired Cronin for his reputed fiscal wizardry. His future reputation would depend on how he handled this issue. He would have to secure a fair share of resources for education while overseeing the distribution of cuts within the schools. Unlike the Kennedy School campaign, where Cronin chose to define and promote the cause, this issue came ready-made. Many saw it as a no-win proposition.

Enrollment declines in Clayton made it hard for the school department to claim the same share of town dollars it had received in the past, let alone more. One teacher characterized the problem this way: "There are fewer kids in the system, and more importantly, a lower percentage of people in the town have children. So the investment of the community may not be what it was. We have a lot of 'over 65's' who, rightly or wrongly, feel they've done their part. They've raised their kids; they've had their time. They've spent their taxes, and they do not necessarily feel the same commitment that they had when they were twenty."

Countering a History of Having It All

Once again, history and local values shaped what was possible. For two decades, the school district had added programs and improved services. As the president of the teachers union explained, "I think the biggest thing Cronin faces in our culture is the view that more is better." People believed Clayton could be "all things to all people" because the town had seldom faced hard choices. In the past, she said, school officials had accommodated most requests: "You want this course and that course? Okay, we'll offer them both. You don't want them offered only one time? Okay, we'll offer them twice." Now, though, "People have to make some choices." Those in the schools would have to take on big questions about "what kind of system we need this to be." Fundamental values embedded deeply in the culture of the Clayton public schools would once again be tested: "It's going to be very tricky for Cronin to deal with this [expectation of] 'all things to all people,' because that's how Clayton has defined itself—excellence, period."

Looking for Cuts While Demanding Quality

Cronin had to be not only a keen budget analyst but also a savvy and creative politician. An assistant principal aptly portrayed the test ahead: "He'll be measured by how he makes the transition, how he deals with the reality of maintaining standards as the monetary base erodes over the next few years, how he handles the bickering, and how he keeps people from being pitted against each other. He'll be measured by how he pulls the system through that time." It was no small order. Externally, Cronin had to secure the funds to maintain high-quality schooling; internally, he had to recommend cuts that were both educationally sound and acceptable.

Under state law the town controlled the size of the school department's budget, requiring Cronin to deal extensively with Clayton's bureaucrats and formal decision-making bodies. His keen political instincts had been honed in his prior district, where the politics of patronage and partisanship were vigorous and hard-edged. He quickly adapted to this new setting of participatory politics. A central office administrator recalled his approach: "Andy arrived and realized that he had to begin immediately to work on the budget, because the forecasts were bad. He knew he had to work with the town's people and get everybody cooperating and working together." Although Cronin recognized that the budget process was ultimately a zero-sum game, he entered the local scene not as a competitor but as a collaborator. "He came in with a lot of political savvy about how you go about doing this—make friends in all the right places, speak with people, meet with people." He did this early in the fall, she said, thus "creating a competent veneer that just preceded all the budget work. So when they met in December, he'd already done a lot of the groundwork." She stressed that Cronin had gained people's confidence with his good communication skills and his willingness to spend time with people, creating "a cooperative spirit all over town."

Facing the first round of budget cuts, during the 1989–90 school year, Cronin and his school board managed to convince the elected officials to split the town's projected deficit of $823,825 so that the schools would assume only 30 percent of the loss. Given the huge cuts that nearby school districts encountered, this agreement gained Cronin a reputation early on for "pulling money out of hats." A principal expressed unqualified admiration: "The man is a master. . . . I don't know how he does it." Another principal saw evidence of Cronin's commitment to education in his success with town officials: "He has a strong belief in the schools in general, because somehow he manages to get the maximum amount of money devoted to the schools." Another principal, who observed that the Clayton Public Schools had not "taken hits" in previous years, recognized that "this hit is not as bad as the other towns'." He saw Cronin publicly "walking this line of trying to appear to be a strong proponent for the schools" but knowing "it isn't as bad as elsewhere, so he can't yell too loudly."

At one session of the town meeting, someone began to question items in the proposed school budget. The meeting was adjourned because of the late hour, and before it reconvened five days later, Cronin had provided every member with a detailed memo about the state of the schools and the wisdom of the budget proposals. A school board member marveled at Cronin's quick and thorough response: "He seems to be masterful at giving people the kind of information they need but not overwhelming them." By all accounts, he again made a strong case for the significance of education in Clayton, relying on persuasion rather than coercion to get the best possible budget for the schools.

Cronin was candid about his success, saying he had wanted to avoid what those in the schools called the "fire alerts" of previous years—word would go out that big cuts were on the way, and those in the schools would feel the pain of making difficult choices, only to discover that the actual reductions were modest compared to the alarming forecasts. Cronin explained, "Everyone would be in here two, three days a week listing a million and a half, two million dollars' worth of cuts, and everybody felt they were being emasculated or effeminated, or whatever. They were losing it. I didn't do that at all this year. I tried to be very steady." Rather than scaring school administrators with a worst-case analysis, Cronin said he "went to town administrators and said, 'What is really going to happen?'" Because they trusted him, they told him. "I knew what was going to happen, and I built in a $247,000 cut that pinched but didn't hurt. I could have come up with a million-and-a-half- or two-million-dollar list, and we would have been in a panic. I did not want that." A teacher said that her colleagues respected Cronin for not having "yelled 'wolf' too early." Cronin chuckled about the reputation he had earned by simply getting and acting on accurate data: "If you asked 'How's he done on the budget?' people would say, 'He's worked marvels.' I haven't worked marvels. I just got better information than they've had in the past." But clearly he had access to that information because of the personal and professional relationships he had built with town officials months earlier.

Sharing Responsibility for Paring the Budget

Cronin asked administrators to recommend cuts in their programs. A central office administrator recalled that Cronin's expectations were clear: "Way back, he had everyone hand in their budget requests to him with cuts. He was very tough. He insisted on cuts, so people weren't allowed to come in with adds except in mandated programs. He didn't allow even maintenance. They had to cut." According to this individual, Cronin had an eye toward town officials when he made this demand. Just as he had received good information from them about the extent of his obligations, he wanted to be honest in his requests. "He didn't want to cut publicly from inflated budgets. He really wanted to demonstrate politically that he was being a responsible fiscal manager." Cronin's strategy had "a tremendous impact in town. His budget looked trim, responsible, and it continued the feeling of goodwill. So nobody nitpicked."

Once program directors and principals had submitted their preliminary cuts, Cronin called them together to explain their individual decisions to small groups of administrators from other schools and programs. He wanted the participants to look beyond their particular interests and share responsibility for the whole district. Several respondents said that the experience was informative and constructive. A principal explained: "It was very good. . . . It said a lot of things without him having to say them, like 'There's a whole lot more out there than you know' and 'If you say such-and-such is of vital importance to you, then you also have to recognize that . . . whatever that person across the table from you wants, he can't have. I want you to see that person, and I want you to hear that person's view. I want you to hear him talking passionately and professionally and strongly and philosophically about his position.'" According to this respondent, the discussion was frank and free of posturing: "He allowed that kind of conversation to go on, and it was extremely productive."

One reason that such meetings succeeded was that the participants believed Cronin had been honest with them, and they responded in kind. He was careful to include teachers in budget deliberations, since they would likely be affected by the cuts and he would need their support. He called all Clayton teachers together in January and explained the budget process, an unusual move since the district's teachers usually convened only in September for a ceremonial meeting before school opened. A principal recalled, "Everybody gathered together, and he talked about what the cuts were, what he was going to have to do, how he was going to try to achieve those cuts, and he was very honest." The bad news was well received; people anticipating cuts were relieved to have them explained. Moreover, having been informed of the details, "they didn't feel like there was something hiding over there." The effect, according to one principal, was calming: "People said that if anybody could make teachers feel good about losing a job, he [could]. And I think it comes from real strong personal attributes that he has, which are his openness, his link with individuals. He does make strong personal ties with individuals that they respect a lot, and that has a kind of carryover."

A teacher who agreed that Cronin had been "very forthright and forthcoming" appreciated that the process had been open: "It made us feel that we should all feel free to share with him any of our thoughts or ideas. So I felt that he's been not only intelligent about it but also inclusive and very, very open."

The teachers union, too, supported Cronin's open approach and joined him as a partner in the budget-making process. The president said, "People have [to expend] enough energy trying to deal with what's coming down, never mind being surprised by the people you're working with. . . . So what we're trying to do is use fair play and no surprises."

Following Cronin's lead, principals encouraged teachers to consider different options for cuts and to make their views known. The high school principal said, "He allowed much input into the decisions, and likewise I prepared opportunities in the school for a lot of input from the other administrators and faculty. So it wasn't a big surprise when [the budget] came out." Cronin's leadership and influence moved through the system.

Respondents widely credited Cronin for designing an open, informative, unifying process. One principal said, "He has spent a tremendous amount of time going over these budgets. He's met with the principals. He's met with the program coordinators. He's met with the teachers. He's met with parents. You know, he had the PTO presidents' group in, talking about budget cuts. It has been as open a process as it possibly could be."

Although Cronin was attentive and responsive, he was candid in stating his priorities and confident in making hard decisions. A principal recalled, "It was clear to me all along that he really knew what it was he was doing. He was spending a great deal of time hearing everything that everybody had to say, but he had a framework in which he was working. And that made people feel really comfortable."

In meeting with the faculty, Cronin explained that, as an educator and as their superintendent, he cared most about protecting instruction from cuts. A teacher said, "He listed for us his priorities. . . . He's going to do everything possible not to cut teaching staff but to look at his own administrative staff. . . . [He had] five different categories of cutting, with the teachers being the last of his categories. . . . I admired him for standing up there in front of all of us and saying, 'This is what it looks like.'" Cronin's message carried important political meaning for teachers. Building a budget might be a political process subject to the tugs and pulls of various interests, but in his administration it would be anchored by a strong commitment to instruction.

Principals also appreciated Cronin's readiness to make educational judgments. One said, "I think he has been straight with us. . . . He has heard people, but he has also made clear what his own agenda is. . . . He has been willing to say, 'I'll listen, but there's a point where I'm going to make a decision—and this is what's up for discussion, and this is what's not up for discussion.'"

After the budget was prepared, Cronin petitioned city officials for more funds. A central office administrator said that he succeeded at this where others might have failed because he had earned a reputation for being responsible. She said, "The town watched him and were complimentary about how he handled the process. They watched him shape the process in a cooperative and responsible way. He was very successful in getting through what I think is the murkiest and most dangerous part of the job. It really was a mine field."

Confronting a Second Year of Cuts

In Cronin's second year budget deliberations proceeded in much the same way, but the projected cuts were greater. Cronin again created an open, participatory process and made his priorities clear: the classroom was to be affected last. But in the end, it did not remain unscathed. Presenting the budget, Cronin expressed disappointment that, when such extensive cuts are required, "You lose much of what is special in a system like this."

Reflecting on Cronin's performance after two years, the teachers union president—not generally a superintendent's strongest advocate—offered only praise: "This is a man who presented a cut list of $1.5 million and sat through a budget hearing and, at the end, got a round of applause for being a sensitive person in creating the budget. And this is the man who, the other day, after adding back $32,000, got an A+ from the school board on his job to date."

Resolving the Social Studies Controversy

In December 1989—just after Cronin had warned Clayton about the prospect of devastating cuts in the 1990–91 budget and begun orchestrating the effort for the new Kennedy School—over one hundred angry citizens crowded into a school board meeting and denounced the elimination of Advanced Placement European History from the social studies curriculum at Clayton High School. Although the controversy centered on a particular course, it raised deep questions about who decides what is taught and how the schools can best respond to the academic needs of a racially and ethnically diverse student body. The issue seemed to once again force choices between excellence and equity in a community ostensibly committed to achieving both.

Rethinking Revisions, Inviting Reaction

Since 1982, well before Cronin's arrival in Clayton, a curriculum review process had been under way in Clayton High School's social studies department. Its purpose was to reinvigorate the curriculum by adding a new, global perspective. Those conducting the review had solicited parental involvement during the early stages, when goals were set. But it was teachers in the social studies department who completed the substantive work of the committee, designing new courses and revising course requirements. The proposed curriculum, endorsed by seventeen of the eighteen members of the social studies department, was approved by the school board in January 1988. It was not until 1989, however, that parents and students paid attention to the changes, in particular the substitution of Advanced Placement American Government and Advanced Placement Comparative Government for Advanced Placement European History. AP European History, taught for years in lecture style by the same member of the department, attracted seniors applying to the most prestigious colleges in the country. To parents of those students and others who aspired to high academic achievement, AP European History had come to stand for excellence at Clayton High School.

In the 1970s Clayton's central office included strong districtwide subject specialists, but with the resignation of the superintendent who had created and championed their positions, the school board eliminated them. Since then the process for developing and reviewing curriculum had been vague, with new part-time curriculum coordinators exercising far less authority than their full-time predecessors. Some influential parents began to complain that they had no more than token roles in curriculum review at Clayton High School. The principal said that their complaint was justified: "The citizens were involved to help write the philosophy of the school and set the general tone, but they didn't necessarily see what courses were going to come of that." When a small group of vocal parents protested the decision to cut AP European History, several school board members claimed not to have understood what they had approved in 1988. Cronin, aware of the political hazards in this dispute, decided that the decision warranted another look.

In 1989, when the school board reconsidered the matter before a packed meeting, they again approved the revised curriculum; public reaction was swift. The *Clayton Chronicle* reported that "Many parents see the vote as an outright assault on intellectually challenging courses at CHS and see the need for greater parent input in the curriculum." An editorial writer contended "It would be no exaggeration to say that the decision of school officials to delete the advanced placement course in European history represents a 'closing of the mind' in Clayton. There is something profoundly disturbing about the words of the assistant superintendent as she couches this unwise decision in an appeal for more 'ethnic and cultural diversity' in the curriculum."

Opening Up the Debate About Excellence

For Cronin, who had committed his administration to maintaining quality education for all students, the controversy was particularly disturbing. He wanted to endorse the teachers' efforts and educational judgment in redesigning the curriculum, ensure that the department's most demanding courses were of interest to students from all backgrounds, and fortify the reputation of Clayton High School as a first-rate institution. It was not obvious how these goals could be achieved simultaneously.

Politically, opposition to eliminating the course was formidable. A community watchdog group called the Committee for Quality Education was organized by local activists, including local professors and textbook authors, to "protect the right of schoolchildren to a rigorous academic education."

Teachers, too, were concerned about academic quality, but for them the issue also raised crucial concerns about academic freedom. Most teachers, inside and outside the social studies department, believed the new curriculum was educationally superior. An English teacher who believed her department should make similar revisions said, "Somebody has to say, 'The back of European literature has to be broken,' and there has to be world literature; there has to be some recognition that other parts of the world exist. Too many kids are sitting in classes thinking, 'We never read anything from my part of the world.'" An assistant principal agreed, saying that although "the traditional staff would say there's been an erosion of academic standards," that hadn't been the case: "There's been an understanding that the population has changed, and we've had to modify the curriculum to accommodate the diversity of the high school. I don't think we've watered down the curriculum at all."

Cronin created an open, participatory process that allowed all voices to be heard, but the voices soon became strident and uncompromising. The high school principal met with teachers, parents, and school board members in an unsuccessful effort to negotiate a compromise. Cronin tried to remain neutral, but at a school board meeting in March he suggested that the autonomy of high school departments had not been balanced by adequate administrative oversight. He acknowledged that parents should have a role in curriculum review: "We need a process that is fair and clear and that has accountability at the highest level." At the same time, Cronin was wary of the vigilant and aggressive Committee for Quality Education, stating in the press his hope that members would not "tear down the teachers, curriculum, or schools because of a fixation on one issue." He voiced confidence that they would "work constructively, as do many other groups and individuals in Clayton. I hope we can reach out and work with one another."

The high school principal, saying that Cronin had tried to "keep the discussion going," saw his facilitating role as appropriate: "I don't think he's tried to put any limits on the discussion, except that it should be a civilized one." Moreover, when no resolution emerged from the intense debate, Cronin did not step in and settle the matter, as many on both sides of the dispute had hoped he might. Instead he asked a professional mediator to facilitate discussions among "representatives of key constituencies—staff, students, parents, and others." The dialogue was to address "the social studies curriculum, philosophy, academic freedom, and the roles of the various constituencies." He further asked for a "moratorium on curriculum inquiry" while discussions proceeded.

Staying Above the Fray and Looking for Compromise

In the end, AP European History was reinstated by a school board vote of 8–1, to be offered alongside AP American Government and AP Comparative Government. Incoming freshmen who wanted to take both sophomore European History and the senior-level AP course would have to take a third social studies course with a broader focus.

Constituents offered mixed reviews of Cronin's leadership during the controversy. Some praised his success in remaining neutral and encouraging constructive discussion among the parties. A central office administrator said that "he managed not to have a single ball of mud thrown at him throughout the whole AP thing. He really kept above it. . . . He didn't bite; he didn't write to the papers; he didn't make big speeches. . . . He sort of walked a very clear middle road as the leader." Others thought he should have guided the process more closely, as he had with the budget review. A principal wondered why he had opened it so wide: "Andy Cronin is a very good listener. He has very good political instincts. One wonders why he didn't stave off the AP conflict. It seems that it got somewhat out of control. *I* don't like to lose control, and I don't think *he* likes to lose control."

There were also those, particularly among the teachers, who contended that Cronin should have taken a clear, public stand on the issue, that there was no compromise satisfactory to all parties. They wanted his political action to be guided more obviously by his educational judgment—but no respondent could say for sure what Cronin's position had been on the matter. A principal said, "It makes it difficult for the rest of the people involved in that controversy to respond, because they want to know where he stands." A school board member reported, "We were not clear where he came out on that one." She thought that the mediation process might simply have been a "tactic to delay. . . . At least he is saying, 'I'm doing mediation. You will be interviewed; your voice will be heard.'" In the end, however, Cronin never took a position on the matter, and she didn't know "where he really came out." As a school board member looking to Cronin for educational leadership, she wanted to know.

The Issues Interact

Reviewing these issues one at a time, it is hard to convey how charged and complicated the day-to-day politicking was, with events occurring simultaneously. Cronin needed support from all constituencies for both the Kennedy School initiative and the budget. He could not risk alienating powerful citizens in the town over the curriculum revision. The local paper reported that "Cronin clearly would like to go into budget negotiations with the strong backing of parents, school board members, teachers, and administrators. 'I was hoping for a strong compromise,' Cronin said this week. 'I'm concerned that there are some parents who are so angry over the AP course that they may interfere with the budget process.'" There was also the possibility that teachers, fearing lay-offs as a result of budget decisions, might oppose the expense of constructing a new Kennedy School.

Cronin recognized how these three issues were related, how action in one area might have repercussions in another. His established goals were to build a new Kennedy School and to pass a budget that was sufficient, sound, and widely supported. It may be that the risk posed by alienating either the teachers or strong advocates of AP European History was one he simply decided not to take.

Cronin as a Political Leader

Respondents gave Cronin very high marks for political leadership overall. He was first and foremost a personal politician, enthusiastically selling the schools, listening attentively to many views, building support within the district, building coalitions across the town, and encouraging cooperation among many people and groups who were not natural allies. His success as a leader depended not only on his winning concessions but also on his building a townwide commitment to education and a districtwide capacity for making difficult choices in a context of diminishing resources. Others had to take up their share of responsibility for political leadership if Clayton's schools were to continue to provide an excellent, equitable education.

Respondents were particularly impressed with Cronin's handling of the Kennedy School initiative and the budget process. In both these situations he took forceful, principled stands and achieved his purposes by working collaboratively with an array of participants, encouraging them to lead with him. They were less satisfied with Cronin's approach to the controversy over the social studies curriculum. As a facilitator, he seemed skilled in that he kept people talking until an agreement emerged. But some thought his solution—reinstating the course while sponsoring two others intended to replace it—was educationally and fiscally unsound, a compromise that forfeited principles of excellence and equity for the mere appearance of excellence. They would have preferred his support in developing and defending a multicultural curriculum of high quality.

Ronald Heifitz (1994) explains that any authority figure has three strategic options in deciding where to place himself or herself in relation to an issue: "(1) circumvention, with the risk of backing into a potential crisis; (2) frontal challenge—getting out in front and becoming the 'bearer of bad tidings' by introducing the crisis; or (3) riding the wave—staying just in front of the crisis, anticipating the wave and trying to direct its power as it breaks" (p. 166). Andrew Cronin seems to have ridden the wave with the Kennedy School, carried out a frontal challenge with the budget crisis, and backed into a crisis with the curriculum dispute.

Cronin's accomplishments as a political leader were educational: he moved the district closer to realizing its vision of providing excellence and equity for all students. By mobilizing broad support for the Kennedy School and convincing competing groups that they had a shared interest in building a new school in the poorest section of town, Cronin helped Clayton remain true to its principles. And in doing so, he strengthened both the district and the social fiber of the community. By developing a structured but open budget process that required participants not only to advocate for their own programs and priorities but also to respond to the needs and expectations of others, Cronin guided the district through a course of decision making distinguished by the best features of political deliberation and action. The fact that he won the respect of constituents both inside and outside the schools demonstrates that he was adept at working the political boundaries between the district and the town.

As noted above, Cronin's handling of the social studies dispute won less confident endorsement and generated some genuine disappointment. That the controversy did not derail the Kennedy

School initiative or the budget process was a plus. That Cronin did not take a clear and strong position on this issue, as he had with the Kennedy School and the budget, suggested to many that his stance represented political action, devoid of educational purpose. Although Cronin's neutral stance may have been warranted in that it protected other initiatives, it did not provide the district with the educational leadership that many thought it needed.

The political challenges and opportunities Cronin encountered in Clayton were unique to the town's context. This was not a place where patronage or partisan politics held sway; in comparison with Ashmont and Union, Clayton's politics are tame. Still, the fact that the district was not splintered by age-old feuds or rigidly divided by ideology meant that Cronin could use the political process to advance his educational agenda. Although the political climate in Clayton more likely enabled progress than obstructed it, the superintendent's task of providing political leadership was no less demanding.

The features that distinguished Cronin as a political leader—his openness and amiability, his deftness at building coalitions, his role as educator of the public, and his efforts to devise workable compromises—are features that would serve all new superintendents well, whatever political context they confront. Just as political leadership must join educational leadership if superintendents are to bring about constructive changes in the schools, so too must managerial leadership support reform. The next two chapters consider the importance of managerial leadership and examine these superintendents' approaches to managing their district organizations.

Part Four

. . . .

Managerial Leadership

8

Managing to Lead

As Warren Bennis and Burt Nanus (1985) see it, managers and leaders are different people: "Managers are people who do things right and leaders are people who do the right thing" (p. 21). Managers, though competent and dependable, are nevertheless pedestrian, inhibited by the rules and procedures of their organization. Leaders, by contrast, are imaginative, passionate, and freewheeling, if sometimes unpredictable and unreliable. Abraham Zaleznik (1992) sets forth a similar distinction, arguing that "where managers act to limit choices, leaders develop fresh approaches to long-standing problems and open issues to new options" (p. 129).[1]

Such distinctions between leadership and management may be cognitively and rhetorically satisfying, but they misrepresent reality by suggesting that managers cannot lead and leaders need not manage. Perhaps some entrepreneurs can thrive while disregarding the routines and structures of their organizations, but it is inconceivable that school superintendents could succeed by doing so. School districts, like other government agencies, are bureaucratic organizations, formally controlled by elected bodies. James G. March (1978) observes that "much of the job of an educational administrator involves the mundane work of making a bureaucracy work. It is filled with activities quite distant from those implied by a conception of administration as heroic leadership" (p. 233). School boards delegate their authority for providing educational services to the superintendent, who is expected to appoint staff, allocate resources, and oversee teaching and learning. The superintendent may foster creative teaching and nurture innovative programs, but if the buses do not run or children are unaccounted for, he or she is judged to have failed as a manager, not to have succeeded as a leader. School districts, therefore, are widely understood to be variations on a bureaucratic theme, some looser and freer than others, but all organized hierarchically and assumed to provide at least a modicum of uniformity, order, and accountability.

Despite this presumption of order, a superintendent cannot rely simply on managerial authority to produce good teaching and learning, for school districts and schools are also decentralized organizations that defy close control. Individual schools differ as much as they resemble one another, and two classes conducted side by side in the same school may feature practices as different as expeditionary learning and traditional lectures. Given the discretion teachers exercise, superintendents' opportunities to control their practices are tenuous at best. No superintendent has the knowledge, cognizance, or time to direct all educational activities, and few teachers and principals are willing to comply with detailed directives from the central office or tolerate close inspection of their work. More importantly, though, no superintendent could possibly prescribe appropriate practices for all principals and teachers, whose students vary widely and who must respond creatively to the exception rather than adhere routinely to the rule. Superintendents must rely on those in the schools, not only for faithful compliance with district guidelines and procedures, but also for their initiative, creativity, and imaginative adaptations of formal expectations. Everyone from the superintendent to the teacher has to lead by managing and manage by leading.

Fullan and Stiegelbauer (1991) make a similar point in reviewing research on the work of school principals. They see two problems with making sharp distinctions between leadership and management: "First, [this image] casts the management function as dull and carried out by different people. Successful principals and other organizational heads do *both* functions simultaneously and iteratively. It is also important to note that when we refer to management we are not talking just about management for stability, but also management for change" (p. 158). John Gardner (1990) makes comparable observations about a broad range of organizations: "I once heard it said of a man, 'He's an utterly first-class manager but there isn't a trace of the leader in him.' I'm still looking for that man, and I am beginning to believe that he does not exist. Every time I encounter utterly first-class managers they turn out to have quite a lot of the leader in them" (pp. 3–4).

Each new superintendent enters the position with a substantial measure of formal authority for use in maintaining and improving schooling. Although the scope of that authority varies from district to district, all superintendents are expected to formulate and submit budgets, oversee the appointment and evaluation of teachers and administrators, authorize and review curricula, commission task forces, develop plans, and hold subordinates accountable for their work. In turn, the school board holds the superintendent responsible for outcomes. Therefore, each new superintendent must decide how best to exercise the authority that comes with the job in order to achieve a wise balance between order and variation, compliance and independent initiative—and through that balance make the system work better for children.

In all twelve districts studied for this book, superintendents necessarily made decisions, allocated resources, and evaluated performance; no superintendent sought to evade such demands or to act freely without meeting his or her formal obligations. In each district, constituents expected and accepted some measure of top-down management. Virtually everyone agreed that their district had to be managed and that the superintendent should be in charge, though there were widely divergent views about what areas the superintendent should manage and how absolute his or her authority should be. There was a continuum, ranging from very formal, bureaucratic organizations to those that were more informal and loosely structured.

In the most bureaucratic districts, the superintendent delegated authority to central office administrators and, through them, to principals. Authority was treated as a scarce commodity to be husbanded wisely and parceled out carefully. Decisions were made in predictable ways and tasks carried out according to recognized procedures. Teachers and administrators emphasized the importance of clarity, compliance, and the chain of command. Respondents seldom distinguished between management and leadership in describing their superintendent's careful and deliberate exercise of authority. Rosabeth Moss Kanter (1983) aptly describes this kind of highly structured organization, characterized by what she calls "segmentation," and explains how it blocks innovation:

> [There is] a structure finely divided into departments and levels, each with a tall fence around it and communication in and out restricted—indeed, carefully guarded. Information is a secret rather than a circulating commodity. Hierarchy rather than team mechanisms is the glue holding the segments together, and so vertical relationship chains dominate interaction. Each segment speaks only to the one above and the one below, in constrained rather than open exchanges. The one above provides the work plan, the one below the output. Preexisting routines set the terms for action and interaction, and measurement systems are used to guard against deviation [p. 75].

In the more informal of the twelve districts studied, authority was widely dispersed throughout the organization. Principals, teachers, and central office administrators made independent decisions that were not determined by established policy or their superiors' orders. Formal relationships were blurred; activity flowed across levels of the system. Superintendents seemed to deliberately and publicly ignore the chain of command and to encourage creativity far more than compliance. Those in the schools were expected to act on their own, often outside conventional channels, boundaries, and routines.

While the formal, bureaucratic districts tended to be static and conservative, permitting little room for variation and discouraging experimentation, the informal ones were quite dynamic. And though the informal districts might seem confusing to the outside observer, they were not without form or order. Hierarchical authority still mattered, and respondents did not seem confused. They still knew who was boss, but their relationships with that boss involved more exchange and mutual influence than in the more formal, bureaucratized districts.

In starting their new jobs, the twelve superintendents entered different organizational contexts with various degrees of formality. In some districts the search process led to a close match between the selected individual and the district organization. Those who preferred highly structured systems ended up heading districts where the people were accustomed to top-down control, while candidates who felt comfortable in looser arrangements found places in more flexible organizations. In several districts, selecting a new superintendent created a much-needed opportunity to change how the district was managed and its business conducted. Thus in some cases superintendents were selected because they promised to change a district's organizational structure, either to tighten it by bringing order and greater control or loosen it by releasing and dispersing authority and creating new channels of communication and opportunities for influence.

In the twelve districts studied, eight superintendents tried to transform managerial structures, policies, and practices. Two moved toward more formal, bureaucratic structures, while two others pursued more decentralized, informal arrangements. Structural change did not always line up on a continuum running from formal to informal management, however; in four other districts, the superintendent asserted greater authority and simultaneously sought to create a more open and flexible structure that would allow others to exercise leadership as well. In the four remaining districts superintendents made little apparent effort to change the way business was done. Three of these districts— Riverton, Ashmont, and Glendale—were headed by insiders elevated from other central office positions, and the fourth, Oakville, was administered by an outsider thought to be so like his predecessor that he would perpetuate the successful practices already in place.[2]

A close look at three districts—one in which order was imposed, one in which controls were loosened, and one in which both changes were initiated—illustrates what the different contexts presented, what superintendents had in mind, and how their constituents responded to changes in the management of their districts.

Returning Order to Westford

Before Thomas Wells became superintendent in Westford, many people thought the district operated too loosely. Westford was a small, working-class city where few school department employees challenged the legitimacy of formal authority or the wisdom of maintaining order. It was a socially, if not politically, conservative community.

The prior superintendent, John Fox, had been something of an anomaly for Westford—a "philosopher" some called him, who introduced many new practices but provided little direction on how to make them work. A central office administrator characterized Fox as a "progressive, open-minded type of guy," and a principal called him a "free and easy, off-the-wall decision maker" who generally disregarded the hierarchy of the system: "If he had to, he went right over the heads of his administrators to reach teachers who could deliver for him."

Those in the Westford central office found Fox's administration confusing and disruptive; it was never clear to them what to do or how educational progress was to be made. One assistant superintendent recalled, "He believed in decentralization. . . . We would meet individually, but never as a group. He knew all the parts but no one else did, and it was frustrating at times because you would get communications from somebody and say, 'Where did that come from?'" This confusion at district headquarters was apparent to those in the schools. A principal said, "His front office was in turmoil. Stuff down there didn't get done."

Some Westford teachers welcomed Fox's energetic administration, but one said that his ideas "went against the grain of the majority of teachers in the system." One who saw both sides said Fox just "liked an atmosphere of creativity." But he went on to note that such an atmosphere "can also be a little chaotic and a little messy, and not always comfortable for people."

Thomas Wells, known and hired for his managerial skill, introduced a series of structural changes, all intended to reestablish order and control in Westford so that children could be better served. First, he sought to clarify people's roles and align their responsibilities. Whereas the district's curriculum supervisors had previously reported directly to the superintendent, Wells required them to report to the assistant superintendents for curriculum, who then reported to him. Although Wells acknowledged that the curriculum supervisors felt their status had been diminished "as a result of reporting to someone lower in the hierarchy," he thought it logical to have them report to the people "whose exclusive responsibility [was] curriculum." Wells also decided that principals were not meeting their obligation to evaluate teachers and insisted that they fulfill these responsibilities. A central office administrator said that Wells's emphasis on supervision was part of an effort to introduce order "and straighten out what is in the system." One teacher said, "You just get a feeling that your immediate supervisor has got more control over the situation again than they did before. . . . You know where the authority is, where before you never knew who was going to have authority. . . . It's a big difference from the previous superintendent." A school board member concurred: "The lines are very clearly delineated. I think it's important for people to know . . . their responsibilities and who they're responsible to."

Wells also sought to reinstate the chain of command both in communication and in decision making; no longer would the superintendent deal directly with teachers or make decisions without consulting administrators. The principal who had characterized Fox as an "off-the-wall decision maker" said that with Wells, by contrast, "it would never happen that way. You know, somebody would come to me, sell me the idea, I would bring it to him, sell him the idea. We'd make sure the funding was there. None of this stuff of sitting here one day and finding out that there's a full-blown program in your building, and where did it come from, and who approved it?" Teachers, too, were aware of the reinstated order. One said that she had heard stories about "individuals who have jumped the chain of command and called the superintendent's office and the answer has been, 'You go back and you talk to your department head, or you talk to your principal, or you talk to your union official.'" Another described how decisions moved up and down the organization in an orderly way: "It's like whatever is discussed and required at the building principals' meetings then filters down to the vice principals' meetings and then eventually to the teachers."

In addition to defining roles and reinforcing the chain of command, Wells sought to increase accountability through all levels of the hierarchy. Teachers felt the effects of this change when district administrators published and compared schools' test scores. One teacher said, "In the seventeen years I've been in this building, teachers have never approached their work differently because of a superintendent. . . . But the emphasis on basic skills is one way in which teachers' behaviors change. . . . We publish the scores. The test person sent out the last round of basic skills tests and highlighted the schools that did less well than they ought to have done." This teacher, who regarded the decision to publish test scores as an act of "poor judgment," acknowledged that Wells had secured teachers' attention and compliance with the move. Another teacher discerned a shift toward accountability in the schools: "More questions are being asked by the superintendent, and more responses are being demanded. The superintendent expects greater accountability. He expects people to do things; he wants to know what they're doing; and he wants answers to his questions."

What effects did these moves to tighten hierarchical control have on the practices of the district's teachers and principals? There was, as the teacher above explained, greater attention to teaching basic skills so that test scores would rise, and there was, as several administrators reported, more attention to following routines and procedures. Life became more predictable, though one principal said that he was working "a lot harder, under a lot more pressure." Although respondents reported a new emphasis on compliance, there was little evidence of independent initiative or leadership among teachers and principals. One principal said that his goal of making "clustering" work at his school came from Fox: "That's what got me reading and involved in and now committed to it. But it was [Wells's] predecessor, not him. . . . I can't say that [Wells] has changed my style, or my goals, or my objectives yet." When we asked another principal, "Have you done anything differently since the new superintendent has been here?" he responded, "Not really." That response echoed throughout our interviews.

Westford respondents offered mixed assessments of the tighter, more defined organization. Many appreciated the calm that the changes imposed, though others missed the excitement of the prior administration. Some, like this teacher, saw both sides: "I think things have been very orderly, very methodical, very careful. We do things by the book. I'm not sure that we've been encouraged to be particularly creative, but that, I think, is because the cooling down was going to come."

Empowering and Experimenting in Clayton

Clayton, where schooling was a serious enterprise, had a history of administrative centralization. One prior superintendent of considerable stature built a large and highly skilled corps of subject matter specialists in the central office. One principal recalled, "He had built a strong curriculum structure right beneath him, consisting of an assistant superintendent for curriculum and instruction, a bunch of directors, and coordinators for all curriculum areas." This former superintendent had been the undisputed intellectual and administrative authority in the district, until school board members began to resent his power and pressured him to leave, replacing him with another man who was at once autocratic, indecisive, and, as one teacher said, ineffectual.

When Cronin became superintendent, he decided to move in different ways, talking with everyone and empowering those in the schools. As we saw in Chapter Seven, Cronin met with an array of constituents when he entered the district, and in doing so, he quickly built a strong base for political leadership. A central office administrator said, "He really got around and talked to everybody. But he played it much more spontaneously, so you didn't have this sense that you were being grilled and interviewed." He often dropped ideas "to see how people responded." She called it a "catch-you-by-surprise-and-see-how-you-react kind of style, and that's unusual in Clayton. But it had a kind of appeal because you saw him a lot; he seemed to be everywhere." She acknowledged that although some might have found this approach "disconcerting," it was also "delightful," because before Cronin arrived the district had addressed problems "in one-hour blocks, which is a funny way of thinking of doing business."

If people wanted to talk with Cronin they could. An administrator observed, "I feel like his door is always open. I don't have to work up through any hierarchy. I don't have to see my supervisor and be sure she knows. It isn't like that." Teachers also felt free to initiate conversations with the superintendent. When asked how she might convey her views to him, one teacher said, "I'd call and get an appointment and go and talk to him. Or if I saw him, I'd just grab him. . . . I wouldn't necessarily ignore [my principal]. . . . I wouldn't avoid her at all. But I'd feel pretty comfortable just saying, 'I want to talk to Andy.'"

Communication and influence were repeatedly said to be both top-down and bottom-up in this organization. As Cronin said, "I'm connecting. I'm meeting with them. I'm struggling with them. I'm developing their confidence. I'm working issues out." In soliciting people's views, he was very clear about his own. A teacher described the interaction: "Andy is interested in informing people. And his style seems to be, 'This is what we're talking about. And everybody has the information up to here. I'm still thinking about what I'm going to do. . . . I'm still thinking about this. But everybody has all this information. I've asked everybody their opinions.'"

Cronin quite deliberately shifted decision making down the system, moving more authority to teachers and administrators. He expanded his cabinet, once composed only of central office administrators, to include principals. He concluded, "It's changed the whole approach of the cabinet." A central office administrator admired Cronin's capacity to engage others in important work: "He's a good initiator. . . . He empowers a group to go off and come up with their own best ideas, and then he's very patient along the process in allowing people to sort of struggle through and stumble along. And he doesn't get flustered in the middle." A principal confirmed that Cronin was patient: "He leaves us alone, but he knows what's going on and he checks in, checks in a lot."

Respondents said that Cronin also encouraged open exchange by others across levels of the system. A central office administrator said that Cronin had helped him resolve a problem with a principal about space: "It was interesting the way that he worked. He really didn't get in the middle of it. He really sat back in a way and gave me things to think about. He has an interesting way of making suggestions but not proposing that it's something you ought to do, and giving you the leadership role, but clearly knowing you have his support and that you can go back to him."

There were two intriguing features of Cronin's approach to loosening the system. First, there was no doubt that he remained in charge. Despite widespread accounts of his efforts to delegate authority and engage others in taking the initiative and making decisions, respondents said Cronin could take a stand. A principal remarked, "He clearly is a boss in charge, you know. He's the superintendent, and he has to make a decision." A school board member agreed: "There is no doubt that there is someone at the helm, someone there who hears what people say . . . and then responds to them. . . . Somehow, everyone is made important. . . . I mean, everybody knows that there is someone in charge. And everyone is made to feel that they are contributing to the health of the system." She wondered how to label his approach: "He's very effective in promoting a sense of empowerment. I'm not sure that that is the same thing as leadership. . . . There is a sense that somebody is driving, but you never can put your finger on what it is that's doing it." This blend of certainty and ambiguity seemed to be exactly what Cronin was after.

Second, Cronin had confidence in his staff and therefore was willing to be held accountable for other people's actions. Where Wells's goal in Westford was to exact more accountability from those who worked below him, Cronin was intent on urging people to act independently, without fear of reprisal. A central office administrator said, "He gets a lot of things rolling, he checks in on them, he empowers, he blesses. He does all of that stuff, and then he gets out of the way and allows the people to do it for themselves." Most surprising, though, was that "he holds himself accountable for it. That's the beauty, because he protects. He says, 'If it comes through all of this process and gets to me, then it's going to be mine and I'm going to defend it, and you're not going to have to run around and worry that I won't be there.'"

A teacher praised Cronin for having taken "some very sensitive issues and found a gracious solution, even if it meant that he waited and sweated out while teachers or administrators pulled it together." This teacher recalled with admiration the school board meeting where a parent challenged Cronin with "Who will be accountable?" and he said, "I am accountable." His response, the teacher realized, demonstrated Cronin's trust in the staff, but it also underscored his ultimate authority: "And I thought, 'Oh lady, did you get what just happened here? This man just said, "It's my ball. It's my bat. And you're standing on my sneakers." ' He's there. He's there."

What effects did this new effort to empower others and open new lines of communication and influence have on the schools? Constituents throughout the system said that there was more trust, more exchange, and more initiative. Virtually no one spoke of compliance, caution, or hunkering down. A principal described new energy and optimism, saying it hadn't been since the departure of an earlier, revered superintendent "that teachers have felt as though the school was moving in a forward direction, that there was . . . enough energy, that there was leadership. And so what's happened is that there has been an energizing—that this job is worth it again, that you really are doing it under the leadership of somebody who is ready to make a difference." A teacher concluded that Cronin was "able to pull together lots of leaders. I don't think there's a lot of followership going on here."

Asserting Authority and Opening Channels in Union

While Thomas Wells moved to tighten the bureaucratic structures of Westford and Andrew Cronin sought to loosen them in Clayton, Clara Underwood, the newly appointed superintendent in Union, simultaneously moved in both directions, pointedly asserting her top-down authority while also opening channels for influence throughout the system.

Clara Underwood was appointed following a period of receivership, after district officials had been indicted for financial mismanagement and political corruption. Underwood's predecessor, an elementary school principal who held the position of acting superintendent for three years, was not implicated in the wrongdoing, but many believed her lack of expertise in budgeting and management had exacerbated the district's problems. According to a central office administrator, she was also distant and formal: "Even though she was just acting [superintendent], she tended to put herself up here and everyone else down here. She was kind of like this untouchable person. You had to call and make an appointment, days in advance . . . just to ask her the most simple, basic question." A school board member concluded that this acting superintendent "was not a leader, and she was not a superintendent, but for three years, she had the position."

When Clara Underwood arrived as the new superintendent, she encountered a system out of control. Respondents repeatedly described a state of chaos, negligence, and failure. A community activist said that Underwood "came into a district that was torn apart, was really torn apart, literally torn apart. There was no direction. The principals didn't listen to anybody; they went their merry way. The district office . . . was not professional." A principal's characterization was even more extreme: "She inherited a cesspool."

By all accounts, Underwood took charge and worked relentlessly to restore order and reassert the authority of the superintendency. First, she made it clear that she was boss, something that was not easy to do in a disorganized and permissive district where principals ran their schools with complete license. A school board member told of one principal "who used to get away with murder with other superintendents" who "came to a meeting and almost challenged Clara Underwood. And Clara said, 'Are you challenging my authority?'" Underwood reported that one time she called a meeting of principals, and one sent his assistant principal in his place. She confronted him, saying, "Listen. I expect to see *you* when I call a meeting. I don't call a meeting for your underling. I call a meeting for you, and I'd better see you there." A teacher praised Underwood for "letting people know that she is the superintendent. . . . Before she came here, I think that you had twenty-two fiefdoms. Every school did their own thing. Every principal did his or her own thing."

If each of those "fiefdoms" had been educating children, Underwood might have been less insistent that principals comply with her orders. But Union's schools were failing the children, and the children were what mattered to her. A teacher explained, "What she has accomplished during the seven months that I've been here is to let people know that there is leadership in this district and there will be initiatives from the district office with respect to the needs of the children, based on what the schools say they need. But no longer will we sit idly by and accept mediocrity when it's not being changed." Reclaiming authority and flexing administrative muscle were not acts that Underwood came to comfortably. As she said, "I'm not one to pull rank, but I have had to do it in this district."

Underwood assessed the schools' performance with confidence, recommended new practices, and disciplined individuals who failed to make an effort. First, she had central office administrators publish test scores so that those in the schools would understand how poorly students were performing. A parent activist recalled, "With the reading scores and the math scores, she had a comparison chart made for three years showing how we accelerated, how we dropped, or how we stayed the same. She pointed out the weaknesses of those schools that went up or that dropped or that stayed the same. She has asked the coordinators to get in those schools and work on it." Underwood did not rely on test scores alone, however. As one central office administrator explained, she moved into the schools, organizing "a task force of supervisors in the district office to visit every single school. We're looking into the curriculum, the performance of our principals, the tone, the climate, homework policy, suspensions, absenteeism—and finding out just why certain schools in our district are working well and others are not working well." The group "started with one school visit, and five of us went to the school, . . . and we visited forty-five teachers in one day. And by doing this we were able to get a real picture of the needs, of the problems, of the philosophy of the principals, whether or not they are implementing the goals and objectives of the superintendent." Although some in the schools complained that this was a top-down intervention, they could not dismiss it as superficial.

In response to poor math scores, Underwood assigned districtwide math coordinators to assist teachers in their classrooms. As she explained, "I formed a math committee. . . . [They're] coming in as, you know, technical assistants to the school. But the bottom line is 'You have to do what we say,' because it was *bad*." Many teachers welcomed the help. And those who didn't gradually recognized that Underwood's math committee would not give up and go away.

To address the anonymity of student life in junior high schools having as many as 1,800 students, Underwood mandated that each divide into several minischools. A central office administrator said that "this has worked in most cases, with the teachers working with students in small groups in a wing of the school. They get to know the children; the parents get to know them. And this has been very helpful." She wondered "why someone had not thought about this before, but evidently the district itself lacked the leadership that took the schools' needs seriously." She credited Underwood with having the insight and courage to institute the change.

Also, Underwood banned separate classrooms for bilingual students in the junior high schools because they segregated the students from their English-speaking peers and delayed their movement into mainstream classes. A teacher who praised this decision said, "This should have been addressed years ago," explaining that the schools had persisted with the old practice largely because it made scheduling easier.

Underwood's gentle but firm style was misleading to some. Principals who were more accustomed to wielding authority than respecting it underestimated her determination. One explained, "I call her Quiet Storm. . . . This district has been used to [superintendents] with the kind of personality I have—aggressive, abrasive. She came here with a different leadership style, quiet listening and all. . . . It just shows you don't have to be loud to be strong." A central office administrator described Underwood's unusual mix of gentleness and firmness: "She has no problem going into the schools and telling the principals off, in the privacy of their own office. She's not somebody to embarrass even the smallest child; that comes from her guidance experience. But she tries to make the principals responsible for what they have to get done." A community activist said Underwood was "very professional, and yet she's down-to-earth. She's a no-nonsense person. She doesn't mind speaking up. She doesn't mind writing up. She doesn't mind authorizing people to be terminated."

After two years, respondents said that they appreciated Underwood's decisive, authoritative style. A principal said, "I am happy to have some structure in this district—and structure comes from the superintendent. The superintendent can't be wishy-washy." Another school board member said that Underwood's most significant accomplishment was "bringing order, eliminating suspicion, monitoring and supervising a staff that she has made respect and admire her."

At the same time that Clara Underwood was capturing and asserting her authority as superintendent, she was also creating new pathways of influence and communication throughout the district, pathways that departed from the conventional top-down routes. Underwood maintained an open door and an open mind, listening carefully and responsively to everyone who wanted her attention— teachers, principals, parents, students, and school board members.

Respondents attested again and again to Underwood's accessibility. A principal said, "You can reach this superintendent by picking up the telephone and calling any time. If she is not available, she will get back to you. And that is something that we did not always have available to us as principals out here in the field. I found that to be a key to her success." Another principal concurred: "I feel that, really, I talk to her and I tell her what it is that we need and I ask her to consider my point of view. She doesn't close me off." A school board member said that people in all roles felt the same kind of openness: "I don't think that there's any principal or any assistant principal or any staff person who does not feel that they can go in there anytime they want—anytime—to talk to her. She's approachable. 'You came to see me? Okay, I'll give you five minutes.' She'll stop whatever she's doing. They love her. She has a rare kind of leadership." When we asked Underwood whether her open-door policy worked, she chuckled and sighed, "Yeah. It works. It overworks me, but it works."

Underwood wanted others in the district to follow suit. She knew that some principals refused to listen to others or to modify their practices, and she was convinced that creating opportunities for expression and exchange among parents, teachers, and building administrators was essential for school improvement: "There are some schools where the principals feel they know it all, and they know what's right. And parents aren't allowed in the schools. Children are still not learning. Teachers are not teaching. And they're busy saying, 'I run a good school. I run a tight ship.' But the kids aren't learning. It has no meaning for me. So, I think until there is more give-and-take in some schools, there will never be a change."

When Underwood concluded that the district's principals were not listening to parents, she moved the forum for discussion into the schools and presided as facilitator and mediator herself. In one school, where the parents were "very dissatisfied" with their principal and had "not been able to go in and talk to the principal the way they want," Underwood intervened. She realized that "in most cases a superintendent would say, 'That's a parent-principal matter. See if you can't settle it at this level.' However, if you have an unhappy principal and an unhappy parent group, the kids are the ones that will suffer." After listening to the parents and the principal separately, Underwood suggested a compromise, and the parties on both sides praised her intervention.

Underwood used this approach of convening concerned parties throughout the district. A teachers union leader praised her willingness to talk straight: "Everything is open, on the table." A parent activist applauded her for encouraging exchange and promoting respect among diverse groups: "Anything that pertains to education in this district, Mrs. Underwood calls everybody in who's a part of that organization. She calls in the professional organizations, the unions, and the parent organizations. And we sit down together. [The prior superintendent] didn't. She called us in one by one. And we never were on the same level of discussion. Clara Underwood does something else. All of us are equal. There's no 'little I, big You.'" Underwood was credited by one central office administrator with having been "able to bring the community at large and the school community together in a good working relationship, where before she came, it was in sort of a turmoil."

One of the most remarkable features of Underwood's approach was the ease with which she simultaneously asserted control and authorized others to express their concerns and contribute to finding solutions. A teacher explained how Underwood combined the leverage that comes from being superintendent with a desire to promote sharing: "You know, 'We're all in this together; we work together; we have similar goals; and I'm the facilitator.'" Initially, some administrators balked, resisting the expectation that they should be responsive to their subordinates. A teacher recalled: "She met with the supervisors. She got a lot of flak in the beginning from supervisors because she made teachers feel that they were a part of what was happening here, an important part. . . . And she has effectively made us understand that change is coming, and we must be moving in line with the change." After two and a half years, Underwood had successfully combined the authority of the superintendency with her open manner to deal directly with people throughout the organization.

Like Cronin, Underwood provided a safety net for those who took risks, granting them time to make things work and being patient when their initiatives went awry. But she maintained and exercised her right to hold others accountable for unprofessional practices. A teacher who was taking on staff development responsibilities asked Underwood if he could begin to try out some of his ideas. He had expected some delay for formal review, but her response was quick.

She told him to do it as quickly as he could. "So it gave me the impetus to work harder and work faster on trying to put together what I thought an overall plan should look like," he said, "because I immediately got the feeling that the support was there." Similarly, a teacher said that she and her colleagues "are more confident in their work, and I know they believe that they will be supported, where in the past they had doubts, with past superintendents."

There was wide agreement in Union that Underwood's manner of taking charge while reaching out had changed people's approach to their work and to working with one another. A teacher said that "principals are talking with principals and sharing their knowledge and their expertise, . . . and a lot of people have overcome a feeling that they need to keep their successes to themselves. . . . More people seem to see now that they can benefit from sharing what they have done. And I think that's directly from Clara Underwood's bringing people together and promoting dialogue."

Underwood had, according to one principal, stabilized the district and compelled people to focus on the curriculum, introducing a new kind of accountability that teachers and principals could respond to: "accountability in terms of resources—what are we doing with the resources that we are given?" Underwood served as a model for principals who had thought that high expectations and goodwill might be incompatible or that accountability and innovation were necessarily at odds.

Managing and Leading in Context

All three of these superintendents were regarded as effective managers, implementing school board policies, developing budgets, hiring staff, monitoring students' performance, and intervening in the affairs of schools when necessary. Constituents praised their managerial skills; they appreciated having someone in charge, and they valued the orderly environments these superintendents established.

Identifying competent management is relatively easy. Locating leadership, however, is a more complicated matter, for leadership goes well beyond creating order and ensuring compliance. Effective school leaders encourage independent initiative and creative solutions. They model and promote collaboration. Leadership is simultaneously top-down, bottom-up, and side-to-side. In two of these districts—Clayton and Union—there was abundant evidence of leadership in the schools, and respondents repeatedly credited their new superintendent with generating it. Cronin and Underwood were widely regarded as exceptional leaders, largely because their approaches empowered others; they were accessible, responsive, encouraging, and supportive. Respondents in these districts cited many instances in which teachers, principals, parents, and central office administrators confidently initiated changes. By contrast, respondents in Westford talked more of following and complying than of leading or innovating. They conformed to the chain of command, carried out the responsibilities of their jobs, and appreciated the order that Wells's administration had brought to the district. By many accounts, good management was what the district needed at the time; but it led to satisfaction rather than enthusiasm, accommodation rather than renewed commitment.

In no district did we find evidence of effective leadership without effective management. There were, however, stories of prior superintendents who had generated new ideas but lacked the managerial skills to implement them. Respondents described how their initial excitement and responsiveness to those former superintendents' proposals gave way to confusion and cynicism when resources failed to follow inspiration and the central office failed to provide systematic support.

It is not enough for superintendents who lead to ensure that bureaucratic routines work (though they must). What proved to be most interesting in these cases was how these effective leaders led *through* managing. They were deliberate in their use of authority, calculating in their delivery and receipt of information, and purposeful in their demands for accountability. None of them saw leadership as distinct from management; none believed that formal structures should be abandoned. Notably, however, they did not manage rigidly; rather, they used authority and structure strategically, to ensure good practices and to promote leadership in the schools.

Each individual's approach was, again, responsive to the context of the district. Cronin headed a prosperous school system where students did well on standardized tests and highly educated staff members were eager to contribute new ideas and enthusiasm. Underwood took on a district in crisis, where economically disadvantaged students performed poorly, principals acted irresponsibly, and staff members, lacking advanced training and teaching resources, were dispirited. Where Cronin could set aside concerns about accountability, Underwood had to raise attention to school performance. Where Cronin could move more authority to the schools, Underwood had to assert greater authority over teachers and principals. Each assessed the opportunities for engendering responsible initiatives in the schools and responded accordingly. Still, both were seen to be in charge, and no respondents complained that their new superintendent had failed as a manager.

Although Cronin had moved to relinquish and disperse authority and Underwood had aimed to reassert hers, both promoted open discussion and exchange at all levels of their systems. In both districts the chain of command was downplayed, as the superintendent encouraged everyone to raise concerns and offer suggestions. Such open exchange generated optimism, creativity, collaboration, and commitment. Teachers and principals did not feel confined to the boxes of their classrooms and schools; parents did not feel excluded.

These superintendents' approaches to leadership were shaped not only by the contexts in which they worked but also by their personal styles and predilections. Although Underwood explained that she was not entirely comfortable acting in an authoritarian way, she could do so if the circumstances required it—and they did. Cronin seemed totally at ease combining managerial decision-making responsibilities with the opportunity to solicit ideas and encourage entrepreneurs in the schools. Wells, who had likened his district to a computer and himself to a computer programmer, found his task of bringing order to the system consistent with his personal style. But he was not inclined to breach conventional boundaries or encourage violations of routine practices in order to promote more independent leadership in the schools.

Some might review these three cases and conclude that they describe two leaders and one manager, for respondents provided much evidence of leadership in Clayton and Union but talked primarily about compliance and control in Westford. It would be more accurate, though, to say that Cronin and Underwood led through managing, for constituents provided ample evidence that their districts were both well managed and well led—and that the second characteristic rested on the first. One school board member in Clayton who had considered the relationship between leadership and management reached a similar conclusion: "Somebody said that leaders do the right thing and managers do things right. Andy's done both. He's managing very well, but he's also doing the right thing, and he's saying the right things. So, it's difficult to separate out leadership and management. I'm not sure a good leader doesn't have to be a good manager." In Chapter Eight we examine more closely how the superintendents used their authority and the managerial structures of their districts in their efforts to lead. Each new superintendent faced decisions about how centralized and standardized the district should be, how best to organize the central office, and whether to participate in selecting and supervising principals. Each of these decisions was a lever that could be used to augment a superintendent's managerial leadership.

Notes

1. Joseph C. Rost (1991) agrees, arguing that leadership is not the same as good management. He regards leadership as an "influence relationship" and management as an "authority relationship." Rost

takes pains to note that this distinction is not meant to disparage managers: "Effective managers are a joy to behold and a pleasure to work with in any organization" (p. 142). Robert C. Tucker (1981) also places managers and leaders in distinct camps: "One might argue that even in ordinary, day-to-day group life, when no great uncertainties exist, groups are in need of being directed. But such routine direction might better be described as *management,* reserving the term *leadership* for the directing of a group at times of choice, change, and decision, times when deliberation and authoritative decision occur, followed by steps to implement decisions reached" (p. 16). It may well be that for schools the past decade has been a period of "choice, change, and decision," thus requiring both management and leadership.

2. Selection of superintendents in the twelve districts was consistent with the findings of Carlson (1972) and subsequent researchers who distinguish between career-bound superintendents (typically outsiders) and place-bound superintendents (typically insiders). Erwin Miklos (1988), who reviewed these studies, concluded that "outsiders, or career-bound administrators, tend to be appointed when conditions are considered to be unsatisfactory and when there is support for change. Whereas outsiders are expected to demonstrate creative performance and are given a mandate to carry out change, insiders, or place-bound administrators, are expected to demonstrate stabilizing performance and are less likely to receive a clear mandate for introducing change" (p. 64).

9

Managerial Levers

Schools across the United States are remarkably uniform: buildings, teaching, and books look much alike from site to site. March (1978) observes that "a student can go from almost any school in the country to almost any other school and find a curriculum that is understandable. Students transfer easily from one school to another, from schools in the East to schools in the West, from rural schools to urban schools, from progressive schools to conservative schools" (p. 220). Yet, superintendents surveying their local realms often see things differently; to them, schools seem resiliently independent, more likely to deviate than conform and to defy rather than comply. Superintendents' formal authority does not lead with any certainty to constructive change in their schools; leading through managing is a much more complex and indirect endeavor.

The new superintendents in the twelve districts studied expected varying degrees of compliance and standardization from their schools. Some desired faithful implementation of the district's plans and programs, others encouraged independent initiative by teachers and principals. Whatever variation they promoted, all regarded their schools as interdependent components of a larger system and sought to bring coherence to their varied efforts. One teacher in Union described Clara Underwood's work as an effort to coordinate the district "rather than leaving little factions going off in different directions." But the superintendent's capacity to compel this change was limited, as another Union teacher observed: "You know, as a superintendent, she can give her suggestions and she can say, 'This is what we need to do,' but it is up to us to take the baton and run with it." All of the new superintendents faced the challenge of building systemwide understanding and support for their visions, their values, their priorities, and their programs within organizations that, by virtue of their loosely coupled structure (Weick, 1976) and tradition of local control, encouraged independent practice.

Three related management questions proved to be salient for these superintendents as they tried to lead through the formal structure of their district. First, what is the right balance between centralization and decentralization, standardization and variation? That is, where should decision-making authority rest—in the central office or in the schools—and how much conformity among school practices is warranted and worthwhile? There were, of course, no simple or uniform answers to such questions, since so many kinds of decisions had to be made—about budgeting, curriculum, staffing, programs, and pedagogy. And no single site was appropriate for making all of them. The challenge was to sensibly distribute the decision-making authority that existed and reach agreement among those concerned about how much autonomy and variation made sense.

Second, new superintendents considered how best to organize their central office—both internally, as a support system for the superintendency, and externally, as a service provider and supervisory system for the schools. Some of these new superintendents had inherited hierarchical and hidebound central office organizations that were discounted by the public and disparaged by the teachers and principals. A number of them sought to revitalize these self-serving and controlling central offices, converting them into organizations that served and supported the schools.

Third, these superintendents, without exception, believed that the future of the schools in their district rested on the quality of their principals. The processes they used for selecting and supervising site administrators afforded them a unique opportunity for exercising influence. Yet, for many superintendents, administrative layers as well as geographical distance separated them from the principals. Their desire to create opportunities for influence and the challenge of bridging the gap between superintendent and principal affected how they recruited, interviewed, and hired principals and influenced how they went about overseeing the principals' work.

Although no superintendent had a deliberate, comprehensive plan for linking these three issues, many demonstrated an understanding of the relationships among them. It was easier, for example, for a superintendent to feel confident about administering a decentralized system that allowed for varied practices in the schools if the superintendent personally supervised principals and felt assured that central office administrators could support school-based initiatives. By considering how these new superintendents handled their management decisions, we can better understand how they sought to lead through the existing structure of their organizations.

Letting Go While Holding On

During the past decade, prominent school reformers have promoted decentralization for school districts and self-determination for schools, arguing that teachers, principals, and parents become committed to constructive change if they are allowed to set policies and practices for their schools themselves. Often champions of decentralization reduce the choice to an either/or decision: either a district decentralizes or it does not. As Jerome T. Murphy (1989) explains, however, neither alternative, in itself, produces a wise arrangement: "Decentralization needs to be accompanied by forceful central action, even though that sounds contradictory. The center plays a crucial role in promoting the good of the district as a whole—the vitality of the parts *and* the common good" (p. 809). No district is, should be, or can be completely centralized or decentralized. Some balance is always achieved between the decision-making authority of the central office and that of the schools. The wisdom of instituting such a balance hinges on a variety of local factors—the history of the district, the quality of the schools, the skills and judgment of the teachers and principals, and the differences among local neighborhoods.

Most of the superintendents in the districts studied tried to move in two seemingly different directions. They wanted to make their schools more publicly accountable and increase the coordination of activities across the district while at the same time granting schools powers and encouraging them to exercise more autonomy. Those who promoted greater school-based decision making often coupled that encouragement with more explicit expectations and reporting requirements. A central office administrator in Oakville said of Mike Ogden, "He's tried to shift the accountability and responsibility to the building." Schools were granted more discretion to develop district practices, but at the same time they were expected to make decisions that were consistent with predetermined, districtwide priorities.

These superintendents experimented with different ways of bringing order to their districts that were less obtrusive than the top-down regulation so discredited in the late 1980s. Still, despite considerable talk about decentralization, all twelve superintendents encouraged coordination and accountability more than variety and independence. Their preference for order was consistent with their roles and responsibilities—they were in charge of the school *system* rather than the schools. But the superintendents' response was also consonant with the times, a period when the public sought more certainty and predictability in schools and faculty expected a greater professional voice in matters of policy and practice. These superintendents searched for ways to provide both.

The superintendents employed several strategies to coordinate varied school-specific practices, including holding districtwide meetings for administrators, developing strategic plans and reporting processes, and systematically promoting core values and purposes. Each will be explored briefly.

Meeting Around the Table

Several superintendents tried to promote greater understanding of the challenges their districts faced by establishing new forums for exchange among principals and central office administrators. These superintendents believed that if administrators met to discuss their work within the context of district policies, shared understandings about goals as well as more consistent practices would result. Suburban superintendent Arthur Holzman decided that he could not personally supervise Highboro's fifteen principals; instead he included them in the weekly meetings of his administrative council, which had previously included only central office administrators. The meetings were somewhat unwieldy, with twenty to twenty-five participants, but convening principals and central office administrators around one table ensured an efficient flow of information, a focused dialogue that incorporated various perspectives, and a more integrated approach to site-level practices. Mike Ogden also instituted several types of meetings to encourage collaboration among Oakville administrators. A central office administrator there explained that instead of just having meetings with central office administrators, Ogden "had his monthly meetings with the administrative council, which is central office and principals. I have monthly meetings with the curriculum coordinators. I also have monthly meetings with the elementary principals. On many occasions, we've brought the directors' meetings and the administrative council together, and this just helps to make the administrative group more cohesive, in the sense of working together rather than working in competition with each other." Most superintendents once relied on midlevel managers to convey expectations, process complaints, and document compliance. However, at least half of the superintendents we studied convened such districtwide meetings instead, to encourage mutual understanding and calibrate practices as much as to provide forums for governance and laboratories for spawning new ideas.

Planning Ahead

Long-range planning also served to bring order and direction to varied site-specific practices. Both Anna Niles and Andrew Cronin launched extensive strategic planning processes, in which teachers, administrators, and citizens throughout their districts assessed the schools and drew up plans for their improvement. More common was school-based planning, which required teams or councils at the schools to meet to review their current practices and develop strategies for achieving greater success.

In some instances, school-based planning provided teachers, principals, and parents with the structure they needed for making important decisions about their work and the education of their children. In others, however, the process was more regulatory than empowering. A Highboro central administrator was assigned to "work with the principals in the establishment of school development plans . . . the road map that the building principal and the staff develop for meeting certain goals during the year." Those in the schools understood, he said, "that there must be something in the school development plans related to the district's goals." Although they could chart their own course toward achieving their goals, they could not head toward whatever goals they chose. Another central office colleague explained that principals in Highboro would be judged on their success in achieving the district's goals: "Principals are putting together data on what's occurred relative to the systemwide goals. I'll meet with the principals in January, and then I'll give each of them a written response with my assessment of how they're doing relative to trying to accomplish those goals." Although schools were charged with the responsibility of drawing up their own plans, the central office specified much about what issues those plans had to address.

Leading the Way with Values

In addition to holding districtwide meetings, Arthur Holzman relied on a set of core values—respect for diversity, the centrality of the classroom, and collegiality among teachers—to coordinate the practices of his district's schools, which had historically been very autonomous. He relied on statements of personal commitment as well as the formal structure of the district to transmit and inculcate these values, but he called upon principals and teachers to give them meaning in practice: "I see that as a building-based initiative, and I don't care if the specific activities that a staff engages in differ from building to building to building, just as long as they can explain what they're doing and have a rationale for it and are somewhat successful. . . . And I'm going to be asking this question at every meeting." When asked how he would nudge these values along, Holzman said that he would explain their importance and rely on his formal authority to ensure that they would get the attention they deserved "by continuing to talk about why it's important, by continuing to ask the building principals to define how they will address it, by continuing to feel comfortable commenting on how well I believe it's addressed, and by holding people accountable for results." Jerome T. Murphy (1989), who calls this approach the "institutionalization of precarious values," notes, "Saint Augustine put the notion nicely: 'Love God and do what you want'" (p. 811).

The new superintendents used various managerial strategies to promote coordinated practices across their districts. Generally their approaches invited participation more than they exacted compliance; they accommodated variation from school to school more than they required conformity. The strategies did not, however, offer unfettered opportunities for school-based change; independent action was increasingly welcomed, but it had to occur within boundaries. And differences among schools, though permitted, were not expected to be great.

Making "Downtown" Efficient and Responsive

School people often refer to the central office as "Downtown," a term connoting physical, intellectual, and psychological distance from the real work of teachers. During the 1970s, central administrations grew steadily in response to mandated programs such as Chapter 1 and PL 94–142, and administrators often flexed their bureaucratic muscle by requiring principals and teachers to document compliance with complicated regulations. Having to complete what they considered excessive and useless paperwork only increased teachers' and principals' contempt for central office administrators. As a result they rarely looked to Downtown for expertise, answers, or leadership.

The new superintendents encountered not only doubts about whether they could promote change but also deep skepticism about whether central office administrators had anything to offer the schools. Constituents often believed central office administrators were protecting their own position and authority while rigidly monitoring site practices. Though certainly there were many intelligent and diligent district administrators, respondents seldom mentioned them, pointing instead to ones they thought were bureaucratic functionaries. In assessing their central offices, a number of superintendents conceded that their staffs could, and should, be far more effective.

One superintendent, Mike Ogden in Oakville, reported being fully satisfied with his central office staff: "I am surrounded by a very, very strong staff. And when I say strong, I don't mean just in terms of their technical abilities and talents, but in the richness of what I think they bring to an understanding of education, and of people and of how to work with each other, and how to design structures." His view, widely shared by others in the district, is an important reminder that there are strong and able central office staffs; but this situation was by no means the norm. Other superintendents arrived to discover that their central office organizations had but few responsive and effective administrators.

In several districts, key administrative positions were vacant or had been eliminated. Large-scale turnover in Glendale left Ray Garcetti with little help. He said that he had been "doing seven jobs at once" and had to "replace the whole staff here. I had to replace the director of elementary education, a director of secondary education, and a director of special services," all of whom had been attracted by the state's new retirement incentives. The school board in Millsburg, according to one district administrator, had decided "that central office was oversubscribed and possibly inept and ineffectual," and it proceeded to cut key positions accordingly. One respondent said that in Union the central office had retained only those few people "who weren't indicted or fired . . . a skeleton staff of individuals that were afraid to take any initiative at all." Other superintendents coped with administrators who had been "kicked upstairs" during times of plenty, when slack in the personnel budget allowed for sinecures that concealed incompetence. Often the new superintendents confronted ineffectual administrators whose job security was ensured by legal guarantees or political favors. One school board member in Westford observed, "I think if we could clean house, we would. But we can't. We're not in a position to clean house. . . . Tom Wells realizes that he has to deal with what he has."

Therefore, the challenges for new superintendents included creating new positions or filling vacant ones, moving out unproductive or counterproductive staff members, and reshaping the attitudes and approaches of those who would likely hold their positions long after their new boss had moved on. Given that most superintendents hoped to rely on their central office administrators as agents of their leadership, this disarray seriously compromised many of their early efforts.

Most superintendents believed that, ideally, their central office staff should be their greatest support, and constituents thus often said it was legitimate for superintendents to hire "their own people." A Summit school board member said that superintendents deserve to "reorganize their central offices, and reorganize personnel and replace personnel, if they see fit. Because for them to be successful, I think they need to have a support team around them that allows that."

Superintendents saw great opportunity in the prospect of hiring an assistant, associate, or deputy superintendent. For example, Clara Underwood, whose central office had been decimated when Union was in receivership, appointed a deputy who said that she supported Underwood "1,000 percent" and reported that they had been "working as a team, unselfishly and completely dedicated to seeing that we turn the district around." Other Union respondents confirmed that this appointment greatly enhanced the superintendent's effectiveness. Few other superintendents had the chance to make such appointments upon entry, however.

Rearranging the Central Office Puzzle

When new appointments were out of the question, superintendents usually reorganized their central office instead, arranging people's assignments in ways that would feature the skills of able administrators and offset the incompetence of others. Frequently superintendents presented clear and convincing rationales for their reorganization strategies.

For example, Wayne Saunders described his plans this way: "The previous organization had an assistant superintendent for education. We then took the other assistant superintendent, who had previously been for elementary, and made him assistant superintendent for what we call operations. I changed the job of the assistant superintendent of education into the assistant superintendent for business. Then, in order to have line leadership to education, to the schools, to our educational programs, I created directors, one at elementary and one at secondary." Saunders explained that these changes "flattened the central office. Whereas last year I only had three people reporting to me in the central office, I now have seven." A member of this new team thought the central office was more effective as a result of this reorganization, which brought "people together on a flat playing field, rather than a hierarchical one." However, principals and teachers offered conflicting assessments of the change, ranging from those who thought that the central office had become more responsive to those who believed that reorganization was simply an expensive shell game.

Saunders acknowledged the criticisms of the naysayers: "Some people have said, 'Oh, he's just moving people around, and some of these people who ought to be fired are being maintained.'" A teacher complained that having more people report directly to the superintendent had made Saunders less accessible to teachers and principals: "He has surrounded himself with a lot of people at central office, but in a way it almost feels like he's sort of walling himself in." A principal complained that the larger group of district administrators who met with the superintendent were excluding him and his colleagues from important discussions: "A lot of decisions are being made, but they are not being made involving the building-level principals. . . . We're accustomed to being involved all the way through the process. . . . But maybe on the positive side, I've been spared a lot of agony that goes along with the budget process." From this principal's perspective, a reorganization designed to flatten the administrative structure had, ironically, distanced him from decisions that affected his school.

In Newbridge, Anna Niles sought to fill the recently vacated position of personnel director. Some members of the school board argued that the responsibilities of the position were more clerical than professional and opposed filling it with a new administrator. Anna Niles recognized the importance of the position, however, and saw possibilities for expanding it, to include responsibility for professional development—a priority of her administration. She convinced the board to create an expanded position with greater influence. The administrator who was subsequently appointed explained that when Niles redefined the job, "she not only changed the position, she also changed the kind of person who would be

interested in having that position, I think. In other words, my interest is very much toward teachers and curriculum and general management of the schools." Teachers and principals praised both the
new position and the individual who assumed it.

Therefore, while most superintendents inherited problematic
administrative staffs, some had the chance to hire new people, rede-
fine responsibilities, or rearrange roles. Superintendents who could
make new appointments were intent on selecting individuals who
would be loyal supporters and advocates of their program. Frequently, changed titles, reassigned offices, and rewritten job descrip-
tions had no consequence for teachers and principals, except to
alter information circuits or reporting relationships. Teachers and
principals expected such changes to occur, but they seldom imagined that they would improve education. When a new superintendent's appointments signaled changes in priorities or values, though,
such as when the district hired an outsider after a purposeful search,
teachers and principals noted and even welcomed them.

Connecting the Central Office to the Schools

Well over half of the superintendents believed that their central
office could and should serve the schools better. In part they were
convinced that the schools needed the additional expertise that
skilled administrators or curriculum specialists might offer; but they
also thought that they could have greater influence on school and
classroom practices if their staff observed classes, offered advice, and
provided training. Respondents made it clear that the success of such
ventures depended on central office administrators being true
experts—authorities by virtue of their knowledge, skill, and experience rather than their title. If the central office administrators were
to be influential emissaries, they had to respectfully and collegially
approach those teachers and principals whose practices they hoped
to affect. Introductions that sounded like "We're from the central
office and we're here to help you" evoked predictable skepticism.

Several superintendents successfully redirected their staff to serve the schools. Ben Moreno, whose central office staff was thought by many to be entrenched and unresponsive, assigned several curriculum specialists to work directly in the schools. A Millsburg teacher praised the effort: "He got them to come out of Central Office and into the schools, to see what's going on and to help out—not to come as a threatening type of thing, but to take a look and see what needs to be done, how they can help us do it, how they can help the people in the classroom do their job efficiently and effectively. I really like that a lot."

In Union, where Clara Underwood also assigned central office specialists to the schools, principals saw the importance of the change. One said he was grateful to have curriculum coordinators clarify the new superintendent's priorities and assist teachers and principals in achieving her goals: "She's set down some guidelines . . . about the way the district coordinators come into the schools. She set down some guidelines that evidently were very clear to her people in district office, because they're constantly in and out, checking on this, doing that. And it seems like things are running a little more efficiently. She's given us some goals. She's set down some goals and objectives." A Union teacher was pleased that central office administrators were "out in the field more, rather than just sitting back and doing the paperwork for the reading tests and math tests." Another teacher agreed that Union's curriculum coordinators had valuable expertise to offer: "She has allowed the people that she has working with her, the coordinators and supervisors, to bring in innovative ideas and to present them to the staff, because we have ongoing staff development taking place, and they go out to the schools."

Such changes were not simple to achieve, since they required teachers and administrators to alter their attitudes as well as their practices. Central office administrators had to become collaborators, and teachers had to entertain the possibility that someone from Downtown might have good advice to offer. One newly appointed administrator in Highboro described Holzman's expectations of him: "My job, specifically, is to get stuff out of the way for principals so that they can turn around and work more closely with their teachers and get stuff out of their way, so that the teachers can teach and work with kids." This interpretation of responsibilities differs notably from that of conventional central office bureaucrats, who not only fail to clear the way for teachers and principals but often are said to obstruct them from moving forward by requiring excessive paperwork or justifications for novel practices.

In each of the districts where the superintendent was striving to create a more productive relationship between the district office and the schools, teachers and principals watched to see whether the new arrangement would be reciprocal. Occasionally central office administrators, like the one from Highboro quoted above, facilitated rather than regulated reform. More often, though, these agents of central administration carried with them more obligations than help, requiring the schools to step into line in support of the superintendent's priorities. When the schools' need for support was great, teachers and principals accepted what assistance was offered. But when central administrators moved into the schools with a mission—without tailoring their assistance to local needs—teachers and principals resented their presence and spurned their offers of help.

Clearly, new superintendents can enhance their leadership by having skilled central office administrators who simultaneously support their boss and serve the schools. However, the new superintendents we studied seldom had the opportunity to appoint new people, and the challenge of retraining weak staff was daunting. Reorganizing the central office consumed a great deal of their time, often carried a high political price, and seldom convinced those in the schools that anything was different.

Choosing and Guiding School Principals

One repeated finding of research on school reform is that principals are central agents of effective change. Seymour Sarason wrote in

1982 that "more than any other single position in the American school hierarchy, the principal represents the pivotal exchange point, the most important point of connection between teachers, students, and parents on the one hand and the educational policy-making structure—superintendent, school board, and taxpayer—on the other" (p. 180). Strategies for reform have changed radically since Sarason wrote, but principals continue to be key in the process of school improvement. Although no one would contend that a principal can single-handedly reform a school, few would argue that a school could change in meaningful and lasting ways without the principal being actively engaged in the process, respected by teachers, and resourceful in organizing support from a variety of sources. The new superintendents shared this view of the principal, recognizing that they could never achieve their goals for the schools without having effective site leaders whose purposes were compatible with their own.

Selecting Principals

Early in their terms, the new superintendents had to decide what role to play in appointing principals. Ray Garcetti, facing the nine principals' vacancies created by the state's incentive for early retirement, chose not to be involved in the process. By contrast, other superintendents, who had many fewer opportunities, considered their choices with care. Maureen Reilly, who had four vacancies to fill in Riverton, reasoned, "These appointments are one of my greatest legacies to the school system. When I leave, they'll be here." A veteran principal agreed, saying, "People will talk about her administration as an administration that created a new generation within the Riverton public schools—a new generation of principals, a new generation of teachers, and, likely, a new generation of programs." In Clayton, where teachers and parents in one school had been very dissatisfied with the prior principal, much attention focused on Cronin's choice of a successor. A central office administrator believed that Cronin's reputation rested on the success of this appointment: "This is his first principal appointment really, so it'll be very important for him to be able to make some significant changes there. I consider this a real test of his courage, because the school needs some radical reorganizing, and some people really ought to leave. . . . It will be the end of the honeymoon if he doesn't fix it."

Districts had various procedures for selecting principals, many of them developed during two decades of activism by citizens and teachers. Where once superintendents could appoint principals after a few phone calls, now they spent several months steering a comprehensive search process. In Riverton, for example, a desegregation agreement required that parents participate at several stages in the selection process. In other districts past practice called for multiple levels of interviews, beginning with a school-based team of parents and teachers and moving to a midlevel review by district administrators, personal interviews with the superintendent, and, finally, the school board's public interview of the superintendent's recommended candidate.

Several of the new superintendents sought to improve the selection process in their districts so that these important appointments would be sound ones and the chosen principals would be positioned to lead in their schools. In some cases that meant opening the process for broader participation, while in others it meant streamlining it for more efficient action.

In Newbridge, where the school board usually promoted people from inside the district, Anna Niles asked teachers and parents to participate in the search and worked hard to attract candidates from outside. A teacher endorsed this new open and orderly approach: "She has a process, whether it be for posting positions or for selecting new personnel. . . . And I think by having this process it makes it much more equitable, much fairer. It's just totally different than what we've had before, so that's an improvement." Members of the Newbridge search committee visited the candidates' current school and spoke with parents and teachers. Local parent groups interviewed the candidates. One teacher said, "I see that as all very positive. In the past it would simply be a search committee, on which teachers or administrators might sit, but parents wouldn't have been as involved as they were this time. I see that as her initiative."

Niles was intent on finding the best person for the job, but she knew that a principal's prospects for leadership depended on many people sharing the view that this was, indeed, the best person. A Newbridge teacher who lost her bid for the principal's position recalled "a very long, involved process. We were interviewed by the entire parent body of the school, by the entire teaching staff of the school, by a screening committee of eleven people. There were two one-hour interviews with the superintendent and then a school board meeting with sixty people in attendance, and then we were interviewed by the entire school board in public session, with TV cameras, the whole bit. It was nerve-racking for four weeks." The successful candidate, who called it "an incredibly inclusive, grueling process," said that Niles "really looks to get a lot of people to buy into the outcome by virtue of having been part of the process."

By contrast, on arriving in Highboro, Arthur Holzman found an extensive and open selection process. Judging it to be confusing and somewhat redundant, he moved to simplify it. Before, the Highboro superintendent had not participated in the search until the school-based committee had conducted its interviews and sent along its short list of candidates to the superintendent; the superintendent then presented the school board with the names of several finalists, whom the board interviewed publicly. In the end the superintendent made the choice by presenting one name to the school board. The board could accept or reject it, but members could not substitute another candidate.

Holzman regarded this elaborate process as cumbersome and misleading. He explained, "You'd have a group of parents over here, and a group of staff over here, and a group of Central Office over here, and they would all do independent reviews of the candidates." Instead Holzman decided to have only one search committee, composed of a variety of stakeholders: "It's one committee. On the committee you have several teachers, several parents, several central office people, including your curriculum person and myself. . . . It's one group, and we're all in the same room at the same time. So, we all start out together. Everybody sees every application that comes in. Everybody has a say in whom we should identify. Everybody has a say in the questions we're going to ask. Everybody has a say in checking references. This is a shared responsibility . . . and most, if not all, people are happy." Holzman also clarified his role in making the final decision: "I make it clear at the beginning that they are an advisory group to me—that hopefully the decision will be made through a consensus, but if push comes to shove, I'll select the person I want." Holzman also ended the practice of school board interviews with the finalists, asking what right he had to ask candidates to participate in these sessions when he already knew who he was going to recommend. Holzman acknowledged that the school board was "a little uncomfortable about the fact that they only see one person," but he believed that the revised process matched reality, since only the superintendent held the legal right to recommend candidates—a right Holzman was not about to relinquish.

Niles and Holzman believed that by selecting new principals, superintendents could shape the future of their districts, bettering the chance that their own leadership initiatives would reach into the schools and classrooms. They thought that the choice should be informed by an array of interested parties, since principals must be responsive to many groups. But they also upheld the superintendent's right and responsibility to make the final choice. Because the existing procedures of the two districts differed—one was simple and closed, the other was complex and open—these two superintendents moved in different directions to improve them. Niles engaged more participants in reviewing the candidates, while Holzman reduced the number of subgroups participating and highlighted his own authority in making the final choice. Each improved the process, advancing the district's educational agenda.

Most superintendents agreed that the selection process should be broad-based and orderly, but they differed about whether to participate personally, and those that did participate differed on whether to enter early or late in the process. Garcetti, who faced nine vacancies within two months of taking office, said that he "stayed out of that whole process," leaving it to the director of elementary education, who "is going to have to work with these people." He did not see this as an opportunity to select principals who would support his values and programs and owe him allegiance. The other superintendents, on the other hand, believed that principal appointments represented one of their few certain levers of influence in the schools and thus chose to lead the process.

Controversy sometimes arose when candidates who were popular with parents and teachers did not meet the superintendent's expectations about what the district needed. An insider might be very popular locally but also hold narrow educational views. Several superintendents preferred "new blood"—principals who came in with fresh ideas and no political entanglements. In Riverton, where the superintendent entered the process late, community groups sometimes complained that Reilly ignored their recommendations. One committee member said, "Three people who came out high at the local end—the school level—didn't come out very high at the superintendent's level, which clearly indicates that there are different expectations or that there's something very wrong." But Reilly stuck by her decision.

Clara Underwood chose to participate early in the process, meeting with the first-level review group and sharing, as one central office administrator explained, "what her goals are for that particular school and the type of person that she feels would be right for that setting." But as Underwood found out, being involved early does not ensure that everyone will agree on the outcome. Underwood, who decided what names to submit to the school board, sometimes refused to send forth the names of highly ranked candidates. Like Reilly, she trusted her own judgement about who would best serve the school and the district. An administrator recalled, "She submitted names of individuals that she felt were the best, and the school board voted based upon her top selection. . . . She was honest with her selection, and she didn't lower herself to parent pressure, peer pressure. She said, 'These are the people that I want.'" This respondent emphasized, however, that Underwood listened carefully to the search committee's discussions: "She's not easily swayed, but if something tells her that this would be the wrong decision, she's not going to make it."

New superintendents often face difficult choices about the structure of the search process and their role in it. Broad participation by constituents enhances decisions, both politically and substantively. It would make little sense for a superintendent to appoint a new principal who had no support within the school, since that principal would almost certainly encounter dogged resistance in trying to lead. A school-based committee can bring to the superintendent's attention features and needs of the school that otherwise might be overlooked. Creating an array of forums and review groups can be confusing to participants, however, leading them to believe that they will have the final say when in fact they will not. Several of these superintendents sought to make their views known early on in meetings with the local search groups, either by serving on or meeting with the committee. Initial evidence suggested that this approach worked well, though there were sometimes lingering complaints from respondents about the superintendent's unwarranted power to make the final choice.

Supervising Principals

The principal, because he or she is in regular contact with teachers, students, and classrooms, has a direct and profound influence on individual schools' practices. Yet, in some districts, principals report to their superintendent through two or three administrative layers. Requests and recommendations move up the organization, responses and requirements move back down. Such bureaucratic arrangements fail to forge the personal connections between super-intendents and principals that are necessary for collaborative leadership. Alternatively, a superintendent can supervise principals directly, providing them with complete and accurate information about the superintendent's priorities and expectations while learning firsthand about the schools' needs and the principals' ideas. Although this approach might be expected to work only in small districts, it has succeeded in larger ones as well. For example, the 144 principals in Kentucky's Jefferson County Public Schools report directly to their superintendent, relying on a variety of intermediate collegial structures for support. Mary Brown Daniels (1995), who studied this "flattened pyramid," concludes that it enables the superintendent to convey his views clearly while empowering the principals to act independently.

Andrew Cronin decided to supervise Clayton's ten principals directly. One principal said, "We asked for it. . . . The principals had asked [the prior superintendent] for it, but he wouldn't do it. . . . We thought it would be great fun and good for us—and good for the system—to be supervised by the superintendent. So we're very supportive about it, and we said this would be a good idea, we would like it. And I think people are generally happy with it."

Another principal said that, as a result of this change, principals felt "much more incorporated and aligned." A third said that the arrangement made the principals "feel that the superintendent is much more accessible, and it makes us feel that we're more important than if supervision of us is delegated to an assistant." A fourth explained why the arrangement is mutually beneficial: "One of the best decisions Andy Cronin made was to supervise the principals, because it is a real fast way to make connections if you want to build a power base within the schools. It makes it real clear when he is able to do something for you. We know exactly where it's coming from, and that's a pretty powerful message. If you ask him to make your life easier and he then does something that creates a better situation for you, then you're more ready to put out and more willing to make accommodations for him." The interdependence that resulted from these structural arrangements provided both superintendents and principals with a substantial portion of the political capital they needed in order to lead.

In Union, with its twenty-four principals, Clara Underwood also chose to supervise them directly, less because she was dissatisfied with a bureaucratic approach to oversight than because no one had been doing the job at all. She explained: "When I came to this district, the principals had not been properly supervised. . . . I sat with each principal, and I know what their goals are for the year. I know how they plan to attain their goals. And I ask them to measure those goals. And I give them suggestions, as to ways that I think they can accomplish those goals. And then I do the review to see if they are accomplishing those goals." Underwood also visited the schools unannounced: "I explained this, you know, in the very beginning, that I come unannounced, because I don't want you putting on a show. I really want to see what's happening. And then I'd like to make suggestions as to how other things can happen."

The principals interviewed in Union confirmed Underwood's account of the arrangement. One said, "She does attempt to meet with each principal or to send a representative from the office to identify the goals and objectives. . . . Then she will call to find out, 'Are you working towards this? and how well? and what are your needs?'" This principal said that he had heard exchanges in which his colleagues had said, "'These are my needs.' And Underwood said, 'Okay, if this is what you say your needs are, I'm going to give you this. Will this satisfy you so that you can move toward your goals and your objectives for the next year?'" The exchange of support and obligation was explicit, and it seemed to work.

In addition to one-to-one meetings, Underwood used group sessions, called "principal conferences," for supervision. A central office administrator reported that these sessions both revealed and dealt with ineffectual administrators. When principals meet and discuss topics about which they are uninformed, their ignorance becomes apparent to all. "Everybody has seen you like you're naked out there. You're no longer holed up inside your little offices, with a secretary who is screening everything out from you. You know, they're being forced to produce . . . and they're not used to it." Predictably, while some Union principals welcomed this unprecedented supervision, others loathed it. Concerned about the administrative incompetence she found in the district, Underwood did not shield the principals from realistic assessment and reasonable expectations.

Arthur Holzman, who had moved from a small suburban district, where he had supervised principals directly, to Highboro, where he thought direct supervision would be unworkable, wondered aloud, "How much influence can you have when you don't directly supervise?" A former principal himself, he knew that a superintendent "couldn't bring about any change at the building level unless he had some understanding of who was the principal and what the principal was doing." Holzman resolved this dilemma by assigning direct supervisory responsibility to his assistant superintendents, while continuing to visit the schools and meet weekly with principals in the administrative council. Highboro principals appreciated having regular access to Holzman, and he felt satisfied relying on his assistants for routine oversight: "The saving grace of the whole thing is that I am comfortable accepting the perceptions of the two people who do supervise and evaluate the principals." Nevertheless, Holzman believed that his influence with principals was less far-reaching than it might be: "I don't have as much effect on their thinking, and they don't have as much understanding of my thinking."

A number of new superintendents, therefore, introduced approaches to supervising principals that would provide more frequent exchange of information and expectations. In some ways it was a more centralized process, with the superintendents giving more explicit directions about what could and should be done. But superintendents also learned from the principals, and the benefits were reciprocal. Frequent interaction freed the principals to exercise independent leadership in their schools. Steeped in discussions about the district's priorities, principals felt authorized to move ahead on their own. Direct supervision allowed superintendents to provide varying degrees of freedom to their principals, closely monitoring the work of some and releasing others to act autonomously.

Finally, it is important to note that although superintendents could exercise great influence on school practices by supervising principals well, the practices of tenured principals were sometimes beyond superintendents' reach no matter how much direct attention they received. Dick Fitzgerald struggled for two years with Fernwood's middle school principal, whose faculty, with Fitzgerald's encouragement, were prepared to restructure their school. The assistant superintendent said that the teachers had "no confidence in the principal to be supportive and to open up a climate where teachers have input." In the end, both the assistant superintendent and Fitzgerald concluded there was nothing they could do, because "that person will be here forever."

Managing to Support Educational Change

There are levers of leadership to be found both in the formal authority of the superintendency and in the formal structure of school districts. The hierarchical structure of the system, the supervisory and support roles of those in the central office, the district's procedures for selecting principals, and the reporting relationships of site administrators all afford superintendents means of securing influence in the organization. Sometimes superintendents use these managerial levers to wield control for its own sake; in such cases, teachers and principals are no more than subordinates following orders. In other cases, however, districts achieve a sensible balance between decisions that are controlled centrally and those that can be best made by teachers, principals, and parents. Principals, having better information about what matters to the superintendent and what matters to other principals, can often make the best choices for their schools.

Several of the superintendents we studied changed little more than the configuration of their central office and continued to run their district with conventional bureaucratic approaches, delegating responsibility through the chain of command, maintaining the central office as a regulatory organization, entering search processes during the final stages, and supervising principals from a distance. But this approach distanced those superintendents from life in the schools and diminished their opportunities for leadership. Principals, in turn, felt little incentive to work on behalf of their boss. Information about the superintendent's hopes and intentions was vague, scarce, or inaccurate. Mutual influence was rare.

Other superintendents chose to use their administrative authority to establish close connections with the schools, to draw the system together while also granting teachers and principals the freedom to explore and experiment. These superintendents, who expected the central office to serve the schools as well as oversee them, participated early and actively in selecting principals and played a direct role in their supervision. In such cases, principals and teachers were more likely to report that the central office understood their needs and that they knew what the superintendent wanted. They expressed confidence that they had the support and the authority they needed to work together for change in their schools.

The final chapter in this book explains why collaborative approaches to leadership are currently needed in schools. It explores how the teaching mission of the superintendency pervades the educational, political, and managerial aspects of leadership. And it considers how districts can expand their capacity to change while prospective superintendents enhance their ability to lead.

Part Five

Leading to Change

10

Toward a New Superintendency

Frank E. Spaulding, heroic school leader of the early 1900s, was a man of his time, a champion of efficiency with ready answers to challenging questions. Spaulding was not, however, a man for all times. As the accounts of these twelve districts illustrate, the demands on public education have changed greatly over the course of this century, and the schools of Spaulding's day no longer meet the needs of today's students.

The so-called factory model of schooling, developed by Spaulding and his colleagues, featured large classes, rigid schedules, and uniform approaches to instruction; it responded to industry's need for the mass production of skilled workers (Callahan, 1962). Today's school reformers reject the factory model because it fails to respond to the diverse expectations of communities and the varied needs of students. Its large schools and classes make teaching and learning an impersonal experience. Its rigid pedagogy promotes competition and rewards rote memorization, while discouraging creative problem solving, critical thinking, and teamwork. Therefore, reformers search intensely for alternative approaches—so-called break-the-mold schools—that are flexible, challenging, and responsive to students' needs.

Schools and Their Environment

Hierarchical, centralized structures are effective in organizations like armies or factories which have clear goals, strive for uniformity, seek adherence to widely accepted standards, and provide members with explicit roles and exact procedures for meeting their responsibilities. Orders can be issued at the top of such organizations, producing compliance and standardized results at the bottom. This certainty is possible because these organizations exist in stable environments where day-to-day life remains much the same.[1] In fact, when the environment suddenly changes—when the enemy substitutes guerilla tactics for conventional combat or advertising disrupts once stable markets, for example—the highly structured organization is not capable of rapid adjustment to new needs.

This is the case in public education, where the organizational environment is no longer stable or predictable. First, the purposes of public education are hotly contested throughout the country and from school to school. Some contend that public education should serve the interests of business and industry. Others argue that schooling should develop the many talents of an increasingly diverse group of students, preparing them for independent and productive lives in a democratic society. Still others contend that schools should reject secular, individualistic values (like those embodied in programs such as outcomes-based education) and endorse conservative social and religious values. Such divergent views are not easily accommodated by standardized organizations.

Second, educators now acknowledge that students are not uniform raw materials ready to be processed in an education factory. Children arrive at school with varying degrees of preparedness resulting from differences in wealth, family support, health and nutrition, language background, and prior schooling (Howe, 1993). We also now know that cognitive differences among children call for varied instructional approaches that tap and develop the abilities of all students rather than just a select few (Gardner, 1983). Students' social needs vary as well. Some children require extensive social support; some perform better in small groups; some drop out when they see no connection between school and work. As a result, schools cannot institute standardized instructional approaches and expect them to succeed with all students.

Meanwhile, the social and political environment in which schools operate is dynamic, even turbulent, with factors like immigration, fiscal cuts, and youth violence changing the work of teachers and principals. Threatened teacher layoffs, unexpected bus strikes, fights between opposing gang members, and transience caused by homelessness disrupt whatever orderly plans for schooling educators might have. Teachers and principals hoping to meet students' needs cannot count on continuity or calm in their schools. Expectations once commonly held by teachers—that students would attend school regularly, that the corridors would be safe, that parents would supervise homework—no longer hold. Changes in the schools' environment make the use of sequential curricula, long-term assignments, and in-class lectures less feasible. The steady conditions that once supported public education no longer exist, and therefore school districts must develop new, more flexible organizational structures that can adapt to uncertain conditions.

Leadership for the Twenty-First Century

Reforming districts requires a new kind of leadership, to support innovative approaches to schooling. Although "follow-me" leaders are effective in hierarchies, they falter in less formal organizations where roles, responsibilities, and procedures must change to serve the needs of particular programs, schools, and student groups.

Furthermore, superintendents cannot hope to lead districts without acknowledging their relationship to municipal and state interests and directives. As we have seen, school districts are not freestanding, self-sufficient organizations. The interests and practices of public education are entwined with those of government, business, community groups, and social agencies. This interdependence, unprecedented in U.S. education, demands superintendents' attention and response, for it brings both obligations and opportunities. Superintendents must now pay attention to the fiscal worries of mayors and the political interests of governors; however, they can also now build partnerships with social service agencies to support children and families. While interdependence surely limits the utility of top-down authority, making it virtually impossible for superintendents to lead in conventional ways, it also expands the chance for collaboration and shared leadership between educators and their communities.

Similarly, as educators begin to break down traditional boundaries between programs, roles, and classrooms, greater interdependence develops among teachers as well as between teachers and administrators. This means that formal authority, once situated in a single office and systematically distributed by a superior to subordinates, must move more freely throughout the district, as increased numbers of participants engage in defining problems, devising solutions, and mobilizing support for new initiatives. Positional authority is but a starting point for leading in a district characterized by such participation, because the superintendent can lead only if endorsed to do so by others. When consent to act is reciprocated between the superintendent and his or her constituents, collaborative leadership can emerge.

Superintendents who want principals and teachers to assume responsibility for change can disperse authority from the top of the organizational chart to the bottom. In fact, "top" and "bottom" will come to have little meaning as communication begins to move in many directions and patterns of communication resemble dense webs rather than simple chains. Participants in groups as varied as school councils, teaching teams, administrative cabinets, and student boards will find sufficient power to act constructively in their various arenas. Drawing upon districtwide visions and plans, individuals will reassess needs, reinterpret goals, and redesign strategies for use in their own classrooms and schools. Influence, emanating from all parts of the organization, will fuel newly formed alliances and generate additional energy. Collaborative leadership of this sort builds shared purpose, deepens commitment to improvement, and helps coordinate strategies for action. It permits variation and encourages adaptation, making reform possible.

Paradoxically, while the formal authority of the superintendency is far more limited than it was fifty years ago, the possibilities for educational, political, and managerial leadership in the position have actually expanded. The superintendent no longer acts as the sole educational authority but rather has the potential to be an influential educational leader whose authority is grounded in expertise and reaffirmed by constituents' respect and trust. In the complicated environment of public education today, there are increasing demands for the superintendent to build coalitions and negotiate agreements that will strengthen the standing of the schools in the community. Similarly, as school systems become more differentiated and diverse, there is a greater need for managerial leadership that will ensure that the district's structures promote sustained improvement while identifying how people can best coordinate their efforts. Running through all three leadership roles—educational, managerial, and political—is the superintendent's teaching mission.

The Teaching Mission of the Superintendency

Whether the superintendents studied for this book acted as educational, political, or managerial leaders, they were usually teaching those whom they sought to influence. This teaching role of the superintendency was apparent in the work of those superintendents regarded as effective leaders by their constituents. As teachers these superintendents were not pedantic or patronizing; they were illuminating, cooperative, and energizing. Sometimes they taught specific skills, such as how to read a budget or develop a strategic plan. Sometimes they advised on politics or procedures, such as how to convince the school board or where to get a waiver. They were as eager to learn as they were to instruct, and they adapted their lessons so that others could find meaning in them for future action. Effective superintendents modeled the kind of leadership that they hoped to inspire in others—listening attentively, asking good questions, and explaining their commitment to important principles. Their teaching was an investment in the future, for if superintendents educate their constituents well, those constituents will in turn educate others, augmenting the district's capacity for improvement.

Educational Leadership

New superintendents are expected to diagnose local educational needs and recommend strategies for improvement. Dick Fitzgerald saw the need for educators and citizens in Fernwood to enlarge students' aspirations. Anna Niles recognized the possibility for teacher development to flourish in Newbridge. Mike Ogden believed that Oakville schools would be more effective if teachers eliminated tracking from their elementary school classes. Each of these superintendents drew upon educational knowledge and beliefs to influence local practices. But teachers and principals did not immediately endorse these superintendents' ideas; rather, support grew over time. These superintendents' educational visions and plans reflected the collective perspective of many in the district, and they won acceptance for their initiatives only after considerable discussion, review, and refinement with others.

Effective superintendents demonstrated their respect for the real work of teaching by making meaningful, regular visits to classrooms. These superintendents learned about local practice and demonstrated their grasp of important instructional issues. When teachers became convinced that their new superintendents respected them as professionals and could offer worthwhile insights and advice about their teaching, they ventured to entertain those superintendents' ideas for change.

Managerial Leadership

In managing, too, superintendents educated others, helping them understand how the formal and informal structures of their district could be used to enhance progress. These superintendents treated their district's structures—its hierarchy, roles, meetings, and communication networks—as sources of connection and leverage to be used in integrating the ideas and efforts of individuals who otherwise might have been isolated and might have acted without regard to others. Some superintendents devised forums, such as Holzman's administrative council in Highboro, where participants could discuss their programs, compare expectations, exchange ideas, and adjust practices to accommodate one another. Clara Underwood opened her door to teachers and parents, thus creating new pathways for communication and influence that promoted further dialogue.

Some superintendents' managerial lessons were more didactic than others'. Clara Underwood decided that site administrators in Union needed close direction as they learned new skills and responsibilities; thus she took charge of the principals' conferences she instituted. By contrast, Anna Niles and Andrew Cronin judged that participants in their districts were ready to assume responsibility for examining local practices and proposing future actions. Therefore they guided, rather than directed, strategic planning in Newbridge and Clayton. All three of these superintendents adapted their managerial approaches to meet the readiness of their learners.

Political Leadership

As newcomers to their communities, the superintendents we studied usually arrived with only partial information about local politics. If they were to win public support for their initiatives, they had to quickly master the details of the political scene, learning from their own observations and the counsel of key informants what kind of politics prevailed, who the key political figures were, who made up the important coalitions, and who might become their allies and adversaries. They could then proceed to convince political players about their district's educational needs and build support for promising initiatives. Andrew Cronin educated the community of Clayton about the ethical and economic importance of building a new Kennedy

School. Dick Fitzgerald explained to Fernwood's finance committee what the impact of budget cuts would be. Not only did these superintendents achieve their specific objectives—approval of the Kennedy building, restoration of budget cuts—they also increased their community's understanding of the district and its needs.

The superintendents also faced political challenges within their districts. School board members, who could endorse or obstruct the superintendents' initiatives, had their own coalitions and personal agendas. In reminding school boards about their responsibility as representatives of the community's children, superintendents like Wayne Saunders helped members learn how to work together despite different, often conflicting and partisan interests. Discord among faculty members or within the community, as in the dispute over AP European History at Clayton High School, called upon superintendents' skills as mediators of seemingly unresolvable conflicts. When constituents collaborated as members of individual school councils, teaching teams, strategic planning groups, or labor-management panels, superintendents often taught them new ways of interpreting others' actions, considering alternative perspectives, and ultimately reaching agreement. Participants were empowered when they solved problems that mattered to them, and they could then take further action on their own.

The skills of educational, political, and managerial leadership require ongoing explanation and example. Thus, it was through their roles as teachers that these superintendents convinced others to lead with them—to participate in shaping a vision for change, to take principled stands about important issues, to accept responsibility for defining and solving problems, and to engage colleagues in finding better approaches to schooling. When these superintendents assumed this teaching role, as many did, they augmented the opportunities for leadership throughout their districts.

Developing the Capacity for Change

It was through these teaching and learning experiences that change occurred in the school districts studied for this book. Michael Fullan and Suzanne Stiegelbauer (1991) wisely observe that "the capacity to bring about change and the capacity to bring about improvement are two different matters" (p. 345). Some activities that superintendents initiated in the name of reform, such as the kickoff celebration for Glendale 2000, were no more than one-time events, promising little in the way of long-term improvement. They disheartened teachers and principals, making them skeptical about the prospects for real change.

But there were many instances when superintendents embarked on initiatives of real import. By the accounts of one group of faculty, Clara Underwood helped them rescue and redirect their elementary school. Anna Niles enhanced the professional standing of Newbridge teachers and won support for new approaches to staff development. Arthur Holzman directed attention to the diversity of Highboro's student body and charged teachers and principals with finding ways to address all students' needs.

More importantly, these superintendents developed their district's capacity for change during their first two years. Upon beginning their new jobs, superintendents found these districts in different states of readiness for reform, some more prepared to accept change than others. Some faculties were stimulated by the prospect of change, while others were cynical about all new ideas. Some teachers were decades behind in their fields, knew nothing of new instructional approaches, or feared technology. There were others who were well-informed and eager to share their ideas with others. Thus, these superintendents had to help constituents move through stages of resistance, acceptance, involvement, and investment.

Developing the capacity for change also meant redistributing power and influence among constituents. Ben Moreno and Clara Underwood created councils at their schools in an attempt to empower parents as well as teachers, increasing the possibility that all would assume responsibility for leadership. When members of site-based councils felt truly authorized to solve important problems, they started to see further possibilities for action and improvement.

Most of all, change required superintendents to reeducate themselves and others about the effects of their district's current practices and the possibilities for alternative ones. The superintendents who generated the greatest hopes for educational improvement listened carefully to local educators, seeking new understandings of educational challenges. Their approach was, as one teacher suggested, that of "cooperative learning" and "cooperative leading." A superintendent can best prepare a district for serious change not by providing answers as the educational expert but by participating as an educator among educators. Such individuals ask good questions in order to clarify purposes, help others understand when progress is being made or learning has become stalled, and draw upon others' insights for new perspectives on the work to be done.

It is through transformational leadership, inspired by the superintendent and exercised collaboratively by teachers, administrators, and parents over time, that districts develop the capacity to change. In so doing, schools learn to address the needs of their students and communities while holding fast to high standards. After two years, none of the districts surveyed had been "transformed." Becoming a "learning organization"—one that "is continually expanding its capacity to create its future" (Senge, 1990, p. 13)—is a much longer process (Fullan, 1993). But several districts were certainly in the process of transforming, for they had developed the capacity to assess and revise their practices, thus expanding both the opportunity and the responsibility for leadership. Superintendents in these districts were active participants in the change process—raising concerns, voicing expectations, asking questions, offering encouragement, making suggestions, and insisting that change occur.

Lessons for Collaborative Leadership

There are lessons that emerged from this study about how superintendents and their constituents can promote collaborative leadership for better schools. These lessons highlight the importance of individual values and action, the need to understand the local context, the power of shared purposes, the role of organizational structures and politics, and the difficulties of effecting meaningful change.

Collaborative Leadership Takes Purpose and Commitment

Fullan's aphorism, "Scratch a good teacher and you will find a moral purpose" (1993, p. 10), holds as well for a good superintendent. Because the central office is removed from the classroom, it is possible for any superintendent to feel distant from the core task of teaching and learning. School funding initiatives, asbestos crises, political campaigns, teacher strikes, and state mandates cause many a superintendent to lose touch with what matters most in education. This study suggests, though, that superintendents' capacity to lead rests in part on their own moral purpose, their commitment to education, and their courage to stand up for what they believe. When Maureen Reilly insisted on hiring an outstanding candidate despite angry opposition from school board and community members, she won support from constituents and increased the integrity of the entire district. Similarly, Mike Ogden urged complacent educators in Oakville to review their tracking practices and, in so doing, awakened them to issues of fairness that they had not considered; the district was stronger as a result.

When teachers and principals suspect that their superintendent took the job in order to boost his or her personal reputation or build a political empire, they doubt that constructive, collaborative leadership can emanate from the central office. But when they believe their superintendent is truly committed to children and dedicated to making schools work, when they see that their superintendent's political activities are always pursued on behalf of better teaching and learning, they are more likely to invest in school improvement.

Context Matters

School districts differ sharply as contexts for leadership. Some have histories of growth, others of stagnancy or decline. There are communities that support experimental curricula and teaching methods, while others demand traditional pedagogy. The unique features of local politics, district collective bargaining agreements, and city-school relations affect the possibility and pace of change. Ben Moreno and Anna Niles found districts eager for change but uncertain about what that change should be and unprepared for what it would entail. Mike Ogden discovered in Oakville a community satisfied with the status quo, while Clara Underwood entered a district that was in crisis and confusion. Each context was unique and presented these leaders with different challenges.

Superintendents must understand the unique features of their community's context and find approaches to change that will work there. Wise superintendents interview constituents widely when they begin their job, seeking to learn about recent history, current conventions, local politics, and community expectations. Wise constituents carefully educate their new superintendents about their district and community so that those superintendents can engage in leadership more responsively and successfully.

Leadership Is a Personal Interaction

Unlike the impersonal interactions that typify life in bureaucratic organizations, collaborative leadership requires a person-to-person approach. As Andrew Cronin said during the search process, leadership is about "people first, people second, and people third." It is clear from the twelve districts studied that effective leadership depends far less on roles than on the individuals who hold them. Superintendents like Thomas Wells and Clara Underwood made progress with their school boards less because they gained respect as formal authorities than because they responded to members' individual needs for information and assistance. Teachers in Highboro and Newbridge gave serious attention to their superintendent's initiatives because they believed that Arthur Holzman and Anna Niles knew them and respected their work. Principals in Clayton appreciated having Andrew Cronin supervise them directly and share with them his energy, insights, and strategies. Such personal encounters fueled the process of change.

Notably, constituents' interest in the personal side of leadership was apparent not only in small districts, where one-to-one encounters with superintendents were likely, but also in large districts, where such interactions rarely occurred. What mattered to teachers and principals was that they came to know their superintendent as an individual and as an educator. They might obtain that personal knowledge by meeting their superintendent one-to-one, seeing him or her in the media, or listening to stories about the superintendent that circulated through the schools. Respondents knew, for example, that Clara Underwood had run to the scene of a teenage shooting, that Maureen Reilly had been a superb classroom teacher, and that Wayne Saunders took the time to lead a counseling group in a junior high school. On the basis of such information, constituents drew conclusions about their superintendent's values, skills, and knowledge. Before personally investing in a superintendent's initiatives, constituents wanted to know about the person behind the initiatives. Does she care about children? Does he act with integrity? Does she respect others? If the answers to such questions were yes, those in the schools were more likely to commit their time and spirit to making change work.

Turnover, or even the rumor of turnover, seriously compromises the personal side of collaborative leadership. Teachers and principals who fear being left behind by ambitious leaders will wait warily before entertaining their superintendent's ideas for change. Rumors that Ben Moreno never planned to stay in Millsburg stalled change efforts there. Dick Fitzgerald's sudden departure from Fernwood disappointed those who had been drawn in by his collegial approach. Superintendents who think they can install programs and leave a district without harming it, and school board members who believe that firing a superintendent will open the way for better leadership, may be mistaken. When school leaders depart suddenly or there is repeated turnover, teachers close their classroom doors.

Shared Vision Provides Shared Purpose

If constituents are to embrace a new superintendent's ideas for school improvement, they must participate in the development of those ideas. This is not simply a matter of "signing on" to a superior's plans; rather, it means being involved in defining problems, debating alternative responses, and fashioning solutions. There were notable differences among the new superintendents in their approaches to developing vision and plans for change. Some, like Ben Moreno and Clara Underwood, arrived with diagnoses and answers in hand, while others, like Anna Niles and Mike Ogden, introduced processes for working with constituents as they defined problems and discovered good solutions.

From most constituents' perspective, what matters most is not that they participate every step of the way but that they are included in the process. When constituents listen to proposals, contribute their ideas, and suggest how change might be undertaken, the resulting vision is clearer and plans for action more realistic. But just as a superintendent's unilateral action can discourage constituents from participating, so too can excessive process. It is unreasonable to assign work to an array of task forces and expect a well-crafted vision or plan for improvement to emerge. Rather, superintendents like Cronin and Niles, who wanted districtwide planning, guide the process along the way, interpreting constituents' insights so that others can comprehend them, providing information when needed, contributing suggestions about what might be done, and then framing the emerging solutions so that others will see them as attractive, achievable, and deserving of support. The time and effort that new superintendents commit to such endeavors pays off in that their work not only produces coherent plans with cohesive support but also prepares the organization for the challenges that implementing those plans present.

Structure Can Expedite or Impede Change

School districts are bureaucratic organizations with many levels of authority and specified roles, rules, and procedures. The districts studied for this book make it clear, however, that structures can both enable and inhibit change. For example, superintendents can call meetings, organize forums, select and supervise principals, authorize expenditures, and review programs in an effort to focus attention, mobilize energy, and concentrate action. Those superintendents from the sample, such as Andrew Cronin, who used the formal authority of their position and the structures of their organization to encourage initiative, exchange, and the free flow of ideas and information were more successful in promoting shared leadership than those, such as Thomas Wells, who restricted access and centralized control. This was not, however, an either-or proposition, for Clara Underwood simultaneously exercised her authority to halt damaging practices while encouraging feedback and delegating responsibility. Such strategic use of structure in support of school improvement is the hallmark of managerial leadership.

Politics Can Promote or Impede Change

None of the twelve districts studied were free of politics, though the demands of political leadership varied greatly from place to place. At its best, participatory politics opens forums for debate and offers a means for reconciling differences and reaching workable compromises. For example, democratic participation in Newbridge, Clayton, and Oakville expanded under the leadership of Anna Niles, Andrew Cronin, and Mike Ogden. At its worst, patronage politics perverts educators' best efforts, as when Ashmont school officials decided about jobs or budget allocations on the basis of personal connections rather than merit.

As political leaders, superintendents need to work with the politics they find in their districts, whatever those politics might be. With care and over time, they might modify the political context by encouraging certain activities and discouraging others. A superintendent who sponsors public forums on controversial educational issues delivers a message about the importance of public deliberation and may shift some constituent behaviors as well. But progress here is inevitably slow, because constituents must drop past patterns of interaction and practice new ways of understanding their responsibilities and doing business together.

Implications for the Preparation of Superintendents

Much has been written about the wasteland of administrative training. Joseph Murphy (1992) notes that reviewers "have chronicled a system of preparing school leaders that is seriously flawed and that has been found wanting in nearly every aspect" (p. 79). Academic content and pedagogical approaches in administrative training programs are regularly reported to be narrow and unimaginative. The curriculum, Murphy observes, "is neither intellectually challenging nor useful to practitioners" (p. 103). Lecture and discussion dominate, with little opportunity for active, experiential learning. Given the current state of administrative training, what does this research suggest about how to prepare aspiring superintendents for the leadership challenges of their work?

First, as educational leaders, prospective superintendents must have thought deeply about the purposes of schooling, be informed about the history of public education, and understand current issues of pedagogy and school organization. Without such grounding, no superintendent can hope to become a credible educational leader. Some new superintendents come to their jobs with extensive teaching experience that has prepared them for the responsibilities of educational leadership. Others should undertake structured internships in which they observe and assist in classrooms and schools. For if a superintendent hopes to lead rather than simply oversee educational practice, such direct experience is essential.

Those who are not yet clear about their own educational values should become so; without such personal anchors, superintendents risk being swept away by professional fads or political currents. Jerome T. Murphy (1991) contends that "students should spend time reflecting on their own values and beliefs, their strengths, their shortcomings, and their blind spots" (p. 508). Joseph Murphy (1992) echoes this sentiment: "The first goal of preparation programs should be to help students articulate an explicit set of values and beliefs to guide their actions" (p. 141). The research described here supports that contention.

Second, aspiring superintendents must develop managerial skills. This involves more than gaining technical expertise in budgets, school law, and personnel management, though such competence is vitally important. Based on the accounts of superintendents' work, this study suggests that superintendents must be able to use positional authority skillfully in support of change, finding the right balance between centralization and decentralization and between expectations of uniformity and encouragement of variation. Thus, prospective superintendents need to develop strong analytical skills to support their understanding of how their organization works. They must think systematically and creatively about such issues as communication patterns, the role of incentives, and the limits of positional authority. In some instances, the new superintendents we studied assumed that the straightforward exercise of formal authority would substitute for managerial leadership; it did not.

Third, prospective superintendents must come to understand the political dimensions of education and develop skills that are often ignored by educators who eschew politics. Extensive experience in classrooms or principals' offices will be only moderately useful here, for the political domain of the superintendent is larger and more complex than that of anyone else in the district. Aspiring superintendents must learn about how schools are financed and how school boards work; they must practice alternative approaches to negotiation and mediation. Most who prepare for the job—particularly those without central office backgrounds—have little experience in the realm of politics. But if they ignore politics, children will certainly pay the price when the schools close early because of bankruptcy or the city eliminates valuable social programs because of rifts between agency heads and the central office.

This study was never meant to conclude with a plan for administrative preparation. In fact, we know only the barest outlines of our respondents' training and can say little about how they learned to do their jobs. However, we have discovered some important things about the superintendency that have implications for administrative preparation. First, successful leadership depends on superintendents having the ability to quickly diagnose a situation and take action. It is hard to learn this skill in conventional classroom settings. Therefore, programs that produce thoughtful, confident and responsive leaders are likely to be coherent rather than piecemeal and rely on various pedagogical approaches such as case discussion, simulation, field-based research and internships—all of which engage students actively in diagnosing organizational problems, collaboratively devising solutions, and planning for implementation and change.

Preparing prospective superintendents means providing for their intellectual, social, and emotional development, three strands of experience that entwine to strengthen the whole process of learning. Students may have to reach a new personal understanding before they can act in new ways. Past administrative training has centered primarily on educational theory and thus has been disconnected from the real problems of the superintendency and split off from the actual administrator who might use such theory as the basis for action (Murphy, 1992). Preparation programs should include (though few do) opportunities for aspiring superintendents to explore their own beliefs, prejudices, strengths, and deficiencies; to make judgments about ethical dilemmas of practice and consider what it takes to act in wise and just ways; and to develop a repertoire of personally tailored strategies with which to act more effectively and lead more successfully. Given that the school districts of the future will be far more diverse than those of the past, it makes sense for prospective superintendents to move through their preparation programs in diverse cohorts that reflect the demographic complexity of school populations. Coming to understand the experiences, expectations, and responses of people of varied backgrounds will strengthen prospective superintendents' personal insight and enable them to approach complex administrative challenges with greater sensitivity and skill.

Leading to Change

In their search for new leadership, school districts often ignore the leaders they already have—those teachers, administrators, and parents whose knowledge and investment in the district span the tenures of several superintendents. Similarly, new superintendents often arrive believing that good ideas and formal authority are all they need to change the schools. Both beliefs are mistaken, for the promise of school leadership lies not in the individual agency of one but in the collaborative efforts of many. Therefore, those who select new superintendents must recognize that the candidates most resembling heroic leaders may in fact be those least able to promote lasting change. Such superintendents will likely not convey that they want constituents' help or that they can learn from constituents' experience. Rather, their self-assured manner, confident answers, and superior stance may actually generate resistance and quiet defiance, setting back the cause of reform.

By contrast, those superintendents who promote collaborative leadership arrive with fresh perspectives, good questions, and useful knowledge about what works in education. These superintendents' plans are but rough sketches, designed to promote reflection and provoke review; they are subject to others' revision. What is fixed is the superintendent's conviction about the value of public education and his or her determination to serve children.

Some districts these days expressly seek noneducators to head their schools, believing that the challenges of public education can best be addressed with sound management or skillful politics. This study confirms that political and managerial expertise are essential for today's superintendent. However, being a proficient manager or effective politician is not enough to carry a school district through sustained and meaningful change. For while managers and politicians may successfully address the immediate problems of unbalanced budgets, ineffective control systems, or lagging public confidence, they are not likely to engage teachers and principals in the responsibilities of collaborative leadership. They must also impress their constituents as educational leaders who demonstrate an understanding of what happens in classrooms, who share a commitment to the cause of public education, who relish the teaching mission of the superintendency, and who are teachers of the first order—advising school boards, persuading mayors, coaching administrators, informing the public, and convincing those in the schools to join them in leading to change.

Note

1. For further discussions of the relationship between organization and environment, see Galbraith (1973) and Kanter (1983).

Appendix: Methodology

* *

This study of new superintendents was designed to explore superintendents' approaches to leadership, constituents' responses to their superintendent's initiatives, and the changes in practice that resulted from superintendents' and constituents' mutual influence. Twelve superintendents from four states in the Northeast were studied for approximately eighteen months each, over the course of three years. (We began work in four new districts in each of the first three years of the study.) Data collection for the study took place between February 1989 and April 1992.

The sample of superintendents and districts was selected to achieve as much variety as possible on a range of variables: district size; urban/suburban character of the community; racial, ethnic, and class makeup of the community; prior rate of turnover in the superintendency; prior experience of the new superintendent; and gender and race of the superintendent. Although I had planned to include one or two very large districts in the sample in order to better understand the role of district size in leadership, this was not possible since no such districts that were within our geographical range hired new superintendents during the period when we were selecting districts. All superintendents in the final sample were new to their jobs, although some had been superintendents elsewhere.

The twelve districts (five urban centers, five inner-ring suburbs, and two working-class towns) are diverse socioeconomically and ethnically; nine are diverse racially as well. They range in size from 2,600 to 27,000 students and in per-pupil expenditures from $3,400 to $8,000. Of the twelve superintendents, five were experienced superintendents and seven were new to the role. There are nine men and three women. Two are members of minority groups. Eight were appointed from outside their district, four from inside.

Data collection involved conducting two long interviews with each superintendent, one occurring approximately six months into his or her term and the second taking place a year later. These interviews were designed to explore the respondents' views about leadership, their assessments of their district, their view of the search and hiring process, their reflections on the early days of their administration, and their plans for leading and initiating change. Questions ranged from "How would you describe your approach to leadership?" to "With whom do you feel that you have had influence during the past year?"

In addition to the superintendent, approximately twenty-five constituents (central administrators, principals, teachers, school board members, and community members) were interviewed in each district. These individuals were carefully chosen after discussions with the superintendents and other respondents and reviews of newspaper coverage of the district. We sought to identify knowledgeable respondents who held various views about the past superintendent, the new superintendent, local politics, school programs, and pending issues. In each district we interviewed most central office administrators, selected school board members, and principals representing elementary, middle, and high schools. We also interviewed mayors, journalists, and parent activists who were actively involved in school governance or politics. In an effort to discern whether their views on the new superintendents changed over the course of the study, we interviewed thirty-eight key respondents twice, both early and late in the study. Interviews with constituents included such questions as "Why do you think this superintendent was hired?" and "How do you go about influencing the superintendent?"

By the time we entered the districts, the superintendents were known well by central office administrators, school board members, union leaders, local officials, and principals, all of whom had followed the search and selection processes carefully and watched the early months of their superintendent's tenure closely. Classroom teachers, however, were far less likely to have more than sketchy information about the superintendent within the first year. Therefore we chose to interview teachers during the final months of the study. In selecting this sample, we asked the principals whom we had already interviewed to identify a small, diverse group of respected teachers in each school who were either (1) active districtwide, (2) active schoolwide, or (3) focused solely on classroom instruction. Our goal was to learn whether, after almost two school years, teachers in all three groups were knowledgeable about and influenced by the new superintendent. We interviewed approximately ten teachers in each district, asking such questions as "Do you see your principal acting differently since the new superintendent came?" and "What advice might you offer him/her about what to do?"

Overall, 312 interviews were conducted (24 with superintendents, 56 with central office administrators, 6 with municipal officials, 27 with school board members, 74 with principals and assistant principals, 111 with teachers, 10 with parents, and 4 with others). A set of interview protocols is included below.

We also followed the events of the districts by subscribing to local newspapers and attending important school board meetings. Information gathered here served as the basis for additional interview questions about current issues.

All interviews were tape-recorded and transcribed. We indexed the transcriptions using seventy-three different codes, such as "interaction with principals," "search process," and "administrative style," and then organized the data for analysis using *Ethnograph*, a data management system designed for use with qualitative data. The codes were drawn from the literature on leadership as well as from initial analysis of the data. Because *Ethnograph* makes it possible to assign multiple codes to any segment of data, we could systematically review printouts of all respondents' comments about a single topic, considering the range and distribution of responses by district and role, and repeatedly test emerging findings against the data.

Data analysis was a complicated, iterative process guided by the following kinds of questions:

- How do superintendents and constituents conceive of leadership? Do superintendents want constituents to follow or lead? Do constituents want to follow or lead? What do superintendents and constituents do in an effort to influence each other?

- What do constituents expect from a superintendent? How are these expectations shaped by differences in local community and school district contexts?

- How do superintendents use their formal authority to manage the school district, and how do their actions relate to leadership?

- What evidence, if any, is there that constituents do their work differently as a result of the new superintendent's presence?

- What does the superintendent do in initiating or responding to key issues or events? How do constituents interpret and assess the superintendent's actions?

- Are there notable changes in policy and practice as a result of the superintendent's leadership?

In an effort to provide confidentiality, the names of districts and individuals have been changed. When individuals expressed concern that either they or their districts would be negatively affected by the reports of specific incidents, identifying details were changed.

This qualitative approach to data collection and analysis made it possible to explore in depth and in context the interactive character of leadership among superintendents and constituents. It led to informative findings as well as promising possibilities for further research. The size and geographical restrictions of the sample limit generalizations that might emerge from this study, although the rich data and complex accounts will enable those involved in education to better understand their own experiences and expectations. Those readers with experiences and interests in different types of organizations will necessarily interpret and adjust the findings for their particular contexts.

Sample Interview Protocols

The questions listed below formed the core of the interviews, with researchers asking the respondents to elaborate on their answers and provide examples. All interviews were adapted to the particular districts and superintendents, exploring current issues and local circumstances.

Superintendents

Initial Interview

- Tell me about your background in education.

- Why were you selected for this position?

- Can you tell me about some things that you did in your last job that you would regard as examples of leadership?

- What do you think are the strengths and weaknesses of this school district?

- How would you describe your approach to leadership?

- What do you think that others expect of you as superintendent?

- What do you need to do in order to keep your job?

- What are three or four areas or programs in which you hope to exercise leadership as superintendent of this district? What are your strategies for each? How will you judge whether or not you are making progress on each of these? How soon do you expect to see results?

- What challenges do you see ahead of you as superintendent?

- With which individuals do you hope to have influence during these first two years?

Second Interview

- What are the expectations of you as a leader in this district? Are these expectations consistent with who you are and how you prefer to lead?

- In the initial interview, you said that your approach to leadership was _____. Have you changed that in any way? Are you finding that your approach is effective?

- Have you found yourself adapting your approach as others have responded to your efforts?

- With whom (individuals or groups) do you feel that you have had influence during the past year? In what ways?

- With whom (individuals or groups) do you feel that you've had less influence than you had hoped or expected?

- After one and a half years as superintendent, what evidence of your leadership would you hope or expect to find among teachers?

- On what issues or initiatives have you made the most progress? the least? How do you explain the differences?

- There is much talk about vision—the expectation that a leader should have a clear idea about where to take the organization and a plan to get it there. Would you say that you have such a vision for _____? If so, when and how did you develop it? Was it shaped by others?

- What issue or incident tested you most as a leader? How did you respond? Who are your critics?

- What do you see to be the challenges ahead for you as a leader? Where are your greatest opportunities?

District Administrators, School Board Members, Principals, Union Leaders

- Tell me about your background in education.

- What do you expect of a superintendent?

- Why do you think this superintendent was hired? Was he/she the right choice at the right time for this district?

- I'm interested in knowing how much contact or interaction you have with the new superintendent. In what circumstances do you meet him/her? How often?

- How has your job and how you approach it changed since _____ has been superintendent?

- From your perspective, what does the superintendent stand for?

- What does he/she hope to accomplish? How do you know about his/her goals?

- Specifically, what has the superintendent done so far? What initiatives has she/he taken? Are these actions consistent with what you think he/she should be doing as superintendent? Has he/she had setbacks?

- How would you describe the superintendent's approach to dealing with the school board? How does that compare with the prior superintendent's approach?

- From what you can see, do teachers approach their work differently since _____ has been superintendent?

- There's a lot of talk about vision today. Would you say that _____ has a vision for the _____ schools? If so, what is it? What are his/her goals?

- How do you go about influencing the superintendent?

- What are the challenges he/she faces? Who are his/her critics?

- What advice might you offer him/her about what to do?

Teachers

- Background information: How long have you worked in the district? How long have you taught at this school? Are you involved outside the school in districtwide initiatives?

- What do you expect of a superintendent?

- Why do you think this superintendent was hired? Was he/she the right choice at the right time?

- I'm interested in knowing how much contact or interaction you have had with the new superintendent.
  Have you met him/her? Have you met *with* him/her?
  Have you read anything he/she's written? Have you
  heard him/her speak?

- From your perspective as a teacher, what, if anything, is
  different since _____ has been superintendent? Have
  you done anything differently? Do you anticipate that
  you will be doing anything differently?

- Do you see your principal acting differently since the
  superintendent arrived?

- How would you go about influencing the superintendent?

- What does this superintendent stand for?

- What do you think this superintendent wants to
  accomplish? What are his/her goals? How has he/she
  made these known?

- What specific actions or initiatives has the superintendent taken? How have they been received by teachers?
  Do you think that the superintendent's goals and initiatives match the needs of the system at this time?

- From your perspective, what are the challenges that
  the superintendent faces in carrying out these initiatives or meeting these goals?

- What advice might you offer him/her about what to do?

References

Barnes, L. B. & and Kriger, M. P. (1986). The hidden side of organizational leadership. *Sloan Management Review, 27,* 15–25.

Barth, R. B. (1990). *Improving schools from within.* San Francisco: Jossey-Bass.

Bennis, W. (1990). *Why leaders can't lead: The unconscious conspiracy continues.* San Francisco: Jossey-Bass.

Bennis, W. & Nanus, B. (1985). *Leaders: The strategies for taking charge.* New York: Harper & Row.

Berger, P. L. & Luckmann, T. (1966). *The social construction of reality.* New York: Doubleday.

Berman, P. & McLaughlin, M. W. (1977). *Federal programs supporting educational change: Vol. 7. Factors affecting implementation and continuation.* Santa Monica, CA: RAND Corporation.

Birnbaum, R. (1988). Presidential searches and the discovery of organizational goals. *Journal of Higher Education, 59*(5), 489–509.

Blumberg, A. (1985). *The school superintendent: Living with conflict.* New York: Teachers College Press.

Bolman, L. G. & Deal, T. E. (1991). *Reframing organizations: Artistry, choice and leadership.* San Francisco: Jossey-Bass.

Bolman, L. G. & Deal, T. E. (1994). Looking for leadership: Another search party's report. *Educational Administration Quarterly, 30*(1), 77–96.

Bolman L. G., Johnson, S. M., Murphy, J. T., & Weiss, C. H. (1991). Rethinking school leadership: An agenda for research and reform. In P. W. Thurston & P. P. Zodhiates (Eds.), *Advances in educational administration: Volume 2* (pp. 21–50). Greenwich, CT: JAI Press.

Bossert, S. T., Dwyer, D. C., Rowan B., & Lee, G. V. (1982). The instructional management role of the principal. *Educational Administration Quarterly, 18,* 34–64.

Boyan, N. J. (Ed.). (1988). *Handbook of research on educational administration.* New York: Longman.

Bridges, E. M. (1982). Research on the school administrator: The state of the art, 1967–1980. *Educational Administration Quarterly, 18*(3), 12–33.

Bridges, E. W. (1977). The nature of leadership. In L. L. Cunningham, W. G. Hack, & R. O. Nystrand (Eds.), *Educational administration: The developing decades* (pp. 202–230). Berkeley, CA: McCutchan.

Burns, J. M. (1978). *Leadership.* New York: Harper & Row.

Callahan, R. E. (1962). *Education and the cult of efficiency.* Chicago: University of Chicago Press.

Carlson, R. O. (1972). *School superintendents: Careers and performance.* Columbus, OH: Merrill.

Chait, R. (1993). Colleges should not be blinded by vision. *The Chronicle of Higher Education, 27*(3), B-1.

Chemers, M. M. (1969). Cultural training as a means for improving situational favorableness. *Human Relations, 22,* 531–546.

Cohen, D. K. (1990). A revolution in one classroom: The case of Mrs. Oublier. *Educational Evaluation and Policy Analysis, 12*(3), 311–329.

Cohen, M. D. & March, J. G. (1989). *Leadership and ambiguity: The American college president.* Boston: Harvard Business School Press.

Conger, J. A., Kanungo, R. N., & Associates. (1988). *Charismatic leadership: The elusive factor in organizational effectiveness.* San Francisco: Jossey-Bass.

Crowson, R. & Morris, V. C. (1991). The superintendency and school leadership. In P. W. Thurston & P. P. Zodhiates (Eds.), *Advances in educational administration: Vol. 2* (pp. 191–215). Greenwich, CT: JAI Press.

Cuban, L. (1976). *Urban school chiefs under fire.* Chicago: University of Chicago Press.

Cuban L. (1988). *The managerial imperative and the practice of leadership in schools.* Albany: State University of New York Press.

Cunningham, L. L., Hack, W. G., & Nystrand, R. O. (1977). *Educational administration: The developing decades.* Berkeley, CA: McCutchan.

Daniels, M. B. (1995). *Flattening the administrative pyramid: A case study of the Jefferson County Public Schools.* Unpublished doctoral dissertation, Harvard University, Cambridge, MA.

David, J. L., Purkey, S., & White, P. (1989). *Restructuring in progress: Lessons from pioneering districts.* Washington, DC: National Governors Association.

Deal, T. E. & Kennedy, A. A. (1982). *Corporate cultures: The rites and rituals of corporate life.* Reading, MA: Addison-Wesley.

Deal, T. E. & Peterson, K. D. (1994). *The Leadership paradox: Balancing logic and artistry in schools.* San Francisco: Jossey-Bass.

Drath, W. H. & Palus, C. J. (1994). *Making common sense: Leadership as meaning-making in a community of practice.* Greensboro, NC: Center for Creative Leadership.

Elmore, R. & Associates. (1990). *Restructuring schools: The next generation of educational reform*. San Francisco: Jossey-Bass.

Enochs, J. C. (1981). Up from management. *Phi Delta Kappan, 177–178*.

Fullan, M. G. (1992). Visions that blind. *Educational Leadership, 49, 19–20*.

Fullan, M. G. (1993). *Change Forces*. London, England: Falmer Press.

Fullan, M. G. & Stiegelbauer, S. (1991). *The new meaning of educational change*. New York: Teachers College Press.

Galbraith, J. (1973). *Designing complex organizations*. Reading, MA: Addison-Wesley.

Gardner, H. (1983). *Frames of mind: The theory of multiple intelligences*. New York: Basic Books.

Gardner, H. (1995). *Leading minds: An anatomy of leadership*. New York: Basic Books.

Gardner, J. W. (1986a). *The tasks of leadership*. Washington DC: Independent Sector.

Gardner, J. W. (1986b). *The heart of the matter: Leader-constituent interaction*. Washington, DC: Independent Sector.

Gardner, J. W. (1990). *On leadership*. New York: Free Press.

Glass, T. E. (1992). *The 1992 study of the American school superintendency*. Arlington, VA: American Association of School Administrators.

Gouldner, A. W. (Ed.). (1965). *Studies in leadership: Leadership and democratic action*. New York: Russell & Russell.

Hallinger, P. & Murphy, J. (1987). Instructional leadership in the school context. In W. Greenfield (Ed.), *Instructional leadership: Concepts, issues, and controversies* (pp. 179–203). Boston: Allyn & Bacon.

Hart, A. W. (1991). Leader succession and socialization: A synthesis. *Review of Educational Research, 61*(4), 451–474.

Heifitz, R. A. (1994). *Leadership without easy answers*. Cambridge, MA: Harvard University Press.

Heifitz, R. A. & Sinder, R. M. (1988). Political leadership: Managing the public's problem solving. In R. B. Reich (Ed.), *The power of public ideas* (pp. 179–203). Cambridge, MA: Harvard University Press.

Hersey, P. (1984). *The situational leader*. New York: Warner Books.

Hill, C. M. (1936). *Educational progress and school administration: A tribute to Frank Ellsworth Spaulding*. New Haven, CT: Yale University Press.

Hill, M. A. (1984). *The law of the father: Leadership and symbolic authority in psychoanalysis*. In B. Kellerman (Ed.), *Leadership: Multidisciplinary perspectives* (pp. 23–38). Englewood Cliffs, NJ: Prentice-Hall.

Howe, H. I. (1993). *Thinking about our kids: An agenda for American education*. New York: Free Press.

Hunt, S. M. (1984). *The role of leadership in the construction of reality*. In B. Kellerman (Ed.), *Leadership: Multidisciplinary perspectives* (pp. 157–178). Englewood Cliffs, NJ: Prentice-Hall.

Immegart, G. L. (1988). Leadership and leader behavior. In N. J. Boyan (Ed.), *Handbook of research on educational administration* (pp. 259–277). New York: Longman.

Johnson, S. M. (1990). *Teachers at work: Achieving success in our schools*. New York: Basic Books.

Kanter, R. M. (1983). *The changemasters: Innovation for productivity in the American corporation*. New York: Simon & Schuster.

Kegan, R. & Lahey, L. L. (1984). *Adult leadership and adult development: A constructionist view*. In B. Kellerman (Ed.), *Leadership: Multidisciplinary perspectives* (pp. 199–230). Englewood Cliffs, NJ: Prentice-Hall.

Kellerman, B. (Ed.). (1984a). *Leadership: Multidisciplinary perspectives*. Englewood Cliffs, NJ: Prentice-Hall.

Kellerman, B. (1984b). Leadership as a political act. In B. Kellerman (Ed.), *Leadership: Multidisciplinary perspectives* (pp. 63–89). Englewood Cliffs, NJ: Prentice-Hall.

Kotter, J. P. (1985). *Power and influence: Beyond formal authority*. New York: Free Press.

Kotter, J. P. (1988). *The leadership factor*. New York: Free Press.

Kotter, J. P. (1992). What leaders really do. In M. Syrett & C. Hogg (Eds.), *Frontiers of leadership: An essential reader* (pp. 16–24). Oxford, England: Blackwell.

Leithwood, K. A. (1992). The move toward transformational leadership. *Educational Leadership, 49*, 8–11.

Leithwood, K., Begley, P. T., & Cousins, J. B. (1992). *Developing expert leadership for future schools*. Washington, DC: Falmer Press.

Louis, K. S. & Miles, M. (1990). *Improving the urban high school: What works and why*. New York: Teachers College Press.

McCall, M. W., Jr., & Lombardo, M. M. (1978). *Leadership: Where else can we go?* Durham, NC: Duke University Press.

Maccoby, M. (1981). *The leader*. New York: Ballantine.

McNeil, L. M. (1986). *Contradictions of control: School structure and school knowledge*. New York: Routledge & Kegan Paul.

March, J. G. (1978). American public school administration: A short analysis. *School Review, 86*, 217–250.

Mazlish, B. (1984). History, psychology, and leadership. In B. Kellerman (Ed.), *Leadership: Multidisciplinary perspectives* (pp. 1–21). Englewood Cliffs, NJ: Prentice-Hall.

Miklos, E. (1988). Administrator selection, career patterns, succession and socialization. In N. J. Boyan (Ed.), *Handbook of research on educational administration* (pp. 53–76). New York: Longman.

Mintzberg, H. (1973). *The nature of managerial work*. New York: HarperCollins.

Murphy, J. (1992). *The landscape of leadership preparation.* Newbury Park, CA: Corwin Press.

Murphy, J. T. (1988). The unheroic side of leadership: Notes from the swamp. *Phi Delta Kappan, 69*(9), 654–659.

Murphy, J. T. (1989). The paradox of decentralizing schools: Lessons from business, government, and the Catholic Church. *Phi Delta Kappan, 70,* 808–812.

Murphy, J. T. (1991). Superintendents as saviors: From the Terminator to Pogo. *Phi Delta Kappan, 72,* 507–513.

Nahm, M. C. (1964). *Selections from early Greek philosophy.* New York: Appleton-Century-Crofts.

Neustadt, R. E. (1990). *Presidential power and the modern presidents.* New York: Free Press.

Ogawa, R. T. & Bossert, S. T. (1995). Leadership as an organizational quality. *Educational Administration Quarterly, 31*(2), 224–243.

Pfeffer, J. (1978). The ambiguity of leadership. In M. M. Lombardo & M. W. McCall, Jr. (Eds.), *Leadership: Where can we go from here?* (pp. 3–34). Durham, NC: Duke University Press.

Pfeffer, J. (1981). *Power in organizations.* Marshfield, MA: Pitman Publishing.

Pitner, N. J. & Ogawa, R. T. (1981). Organizational leadership: The case of the school superintendent. *Educational Administration Quarterly, 17*(2), 45–65.

Rosen, D. M. (1984). Leadership in world cultures. In B. Kellerman (Ed.), *Leadership: Multidisciplinary perspectives* (pp. 39–62). Englewood Cliffs, NJ: Prentice-Hall.

Rost, J. C. (1991). *Leadership for the twenty-first century.* New York: Praeger.

Sarason, S. B. (1982). *The culture of the school and the problem of change* (2nd ed.). Boston, MA: Allyn & Bacon.

Sarason, S. B. (1990). *The predictable failure of educational reform: Can we change course before it's too late?* San Francisco: Jossey-Bass.

Schein, E. H. (1992). *Organizational culture and leadership* (2nd ed.). San Francisco: Jossey-Bass.

Schön, D. A. (1987). *Educating the reflective practitioner.* San Francisco: Jossey-Bass.

Selznick, P. (1957). *Leadership in administration: A sociological interpretation.* Evanston, IL: Row, Peterson and Company.

Senge, P. (1990). *The Fifth Discipline.* New York: Doubleday.

Sennett, R. (1980). *Authority.* New York: Knopf.

Sergiovanni, T. J. (1990). *Value-added leadership.* San Francisco: Jossey-Bass.

Sergiovanni, T. J. (1992a). *Moral leadership: Getting to the heart of school improvement.* San Francisco: Jossey-Bass.

Sergiovanni, T. J. (1992b). Why we should seek substitutes for leadership. *Educational Leadership, 41,* 41–49.

Sizer, T. R. (1992). *Horace's school: Redesigning the American high school*. Boston: Houghton Mifflin.

Smith, K. K. & Berg, D. N. (1987). *Paradoxes of Group Life*. San Francisco: Jossey-Bass.

Spaulding, F. E. (1955). *School superintendents in action in five cities*. Rindge, NH: Richard R. Smith.

Stogdill, R. M. (1948). Personal factors associated with leadership: A survey of the literature. *Journal of Psychology, 25*, 35–71.

Thurston, P. W. & Zodhiates, P. P. (Eds.). (1991). *Advances in educational administration*. Greenwich, CT: JAI Press.

Tucker, R. C. (1981). *Politics as leadership*. Columbia: University of Missouri Press.

Tyack, D. B. (1976). *The one best system: A history of American urban education*. New York: Basic Books.

Tyack, D. B. & Cummings, R. (1977). Leadership in American public schools before 1954: Historical configurations and conjectures. In L. L. Cunningham, W. G. Hack., & R. O. Nystrand (Eds.), *Educational administration: The developing decades* (pp. 46–66). Berkeley, CA: McCutchan.

Tyack, D. & Hansot, E. (1982). *Managers of virtue: Public school leadership in America, 1820–1980*. New York: Basic Books.

Vroom, V. H. & Jago, A. G. (1988). *The new leadership: Managing participation in organizations*. Englewood Cliffs, NJ: Prentice-Hall.

Weber, M. (1947). *The theory of social and economic organizations*. New York: Free Press.

Weick, K. E. (1976). Educational organizations as loosely coupled systems. *Administrative Science Quarterly, 21*(1), 1–19.

Weick, K. E. (1978). The spines of leaders. In M. W. McCall, Jr. & M. M. Lombardo (Eds.), *Leadership: Where else can we go?* (pp. 37–61). Durham, NC: Duke University Press.

Weiss, C. H. & Cambone, J. (1991). *Trouble in Paradise: Teacher conflicts in shared decision making* (Occasional Paper No. 15). Cambridge, MA: National Center for Educational Leadership, Harvard University.

Willner, A. R. (1984). *The spellbinders: Charismatic political leadership*. New Haven, CT: Yale University Press.

Wills, G. (1994a, April). What makes a good leader? *The Atlantic Monthly*, pp. 53–80.

Wills, G. (1994b). *Certain trumpets: The call of leaders*. New York: Simon & Schuster.

Wirt, F. M. (1991). The missing link in instructional leadership: The superintendent, conflict, and maintenance. In P. G. Thurston & P. P. Zodhiates (Eds.), *Advances in educational administration: Volume 2* (pp. 159–189). Greenwich, CT: JAI Press.

Zaleznik, A. (1992, March-April). Managers and leaders: Are they different? *Harvard Business Review*, pp. 126–135.

Index

The Author

Susan Moore Johnson is professor of education and academic dean at the Harvard Graduate School of Education. A former high school teacher and administrator in Brookline, Massachusetts, Johnson studies school organization, educational policy, and change in school systems. She has conducted research on collective bargaining, performance-based layoffs, merit pay, school-based management, and the school as a workplace. She pursues her current interest in leadership not only through research but also through teaching current and aspiring administrators and in her role as academic dean.

Johnson received her A.B. degree (1967) in English literature from Mount Holyoke College and her M.A.T. degree (1969) in English and her Ed.D. degree (1982) in administration and policy from the Harvard Graduate School of Education.

Johnson is the author of *Teacher Unions in Schools* (1984), a qualitative study of the day-to-day impact of collective bargaining in schools, and *Teachers at Work* (1990), an analysis of exemplary teachers' views of their schools as workplaces.

Acknowledgments

When I began this project with the newly formed National Center for Educational Leadership in 1988, I never imagined that it would be seven years before I would formally acknowledge all the people who have helped me. Had I known what was ahead, I might have devised something simpler; but, ever naive, I lunged forward, stumbling often along the way. Fortunately, colleagues, friends, and family were there in support, and they surely deserve my thanks.

The superintendents and constituents from the twelve districts studied were exceedingly generous with their time and candid in their observations. It is unnerving to have outsiders poke and probe during the early days of one's tenure, and I am deeply indebted to these superintendents for having the courage and patience to participate. They agreed because they believed that this study might help others; I sincerely hope that it will.

The Office of Educational Research and Improvement of the U.S. Department of Education funded this research. Project monitors Ron Anson and David Stevenson were exceedingly patient throughout, offering sound suggestions and steady encouragement. I am particularly indebted to Lee Bolman and Terry Deal, codirectors of the National Center for Educational Leadership and experts in leadership, who provided valuable advice and enthusiastic support from the beginning to the end of this study, never expressing doubts that I would eventually finish. They and my other NCEL colleagues, Jerry Murphy, Carol Weiss, Dan Lortie, Phil Hallinger, and Joe Murphy, improved this study with their suggestions; my work was enriched by reading and discussing their own studies of leadership. Linda Corey, administrative assistant for NCEL, was a constant source of assistance and cheer throughout this period, carefully overseeing the progress of transcription and data coding.

During the course of the study, a number of extraordinary graduate students assisted me, many of them experienced administrators with deep insights about issues of school leadership. Research assistants Donna Jones and John Verre, who assumed major responsibilities for data collection and analysis, contributed greatly to the design of the project and interpretation of the data. Richard Fossey, Tom Hehir, Leslie Hergert, Isabel Londono, Manny Rivera, Steve Seleznow, and Toby Tettenbaum were exceptional interviewers, probing for clarity and searching for meaning.

Wendy Angus, Sydney Owens, and Sharon Singleton transcribed interviews with amazing speed and accuracy. Along with Linda Corey, Caroline Johnson provided valuable technical assistance in organizing the data for Ethnograph, while Arlene Ackerman, Elois Brooks, Linda Carrigan, Kate Crozier Laguarda, Karen Cardoza Kane, Doreen Kelly-Carney, Douglass Ann Kinkade, Melanie Morey, Peggy Mueller, Jean Murray, and Stephanie Rogen coded the data for analysis with painstaking care.

During the final, painful weeks and days of completing the manuscript, Beth Bernstein, Susan Eaton, Erika Johnson, and Belinda Tucker worked intensely, reading and rereading drafts, discovering flaws, offering wise judgments and making valuable suggestions. The staff in the dean's office, particularly Maribel Blanco Ryan, encouraged and protected me so that I could finish. I am deeply grateful to all of them.

Good friends have been there for me all along the way. I am particularly indebted to my running partner of ten years, Lori Berry, for her early-morning insights about leadership, her frank advice about life, and her sharp wit.

My children, Krister and Erika, moved through adolescence to adulthood during the course of this project. They entertained me and sustained me with their stories and insights during this period of wondrous growth in their lives. They encouraged me all along the way, fully confident that "Dr. Mama" would come through. Glenn, my husband and longtime companion, enriched and steadied my life during this period, regularly reminding me what matters most. He provided help when I asked for it and distractions when I didn't; both were immensely valuable. I look forward to our adventures together, calmer perhaps than the final, harrowing drive to the FedEx office at Logan Airport, dramatically punctuating the end of this project.